For Clinton J. Ancker III
with all best wishes

Roy Benning

A SPY'S LONDON

A SPY'S LONDON

by
ROY BERKELEY

FOREWORD
by
NIGEL WEST

Maps by Ellen Perry Berkeley

Photographs by Roy Berkeley

LEO COOPER
LONDON

First published in 1994 by
LEO COOPER
190 Shaftesbury Avenue London WC2H 8JL
an imprint of
Pen & Sword Books Ltd
47 Church Street, Barnsley, South Yorkshire S70 2AS

A CIP record for this book is available from
the British Library

ISBN 0 85052 113 0

Typeset by Yorkshire Web,
Church Street, Barnsley.

Printed by Redwood Books,
Trowbridge, Wiltshire

CONTENTS

Foreword   iv

Introduction   vii

Acknowledgments   xi

The Walks

    A.   Westminster Walk (Sites 1-10)   1

    B.   Pimlico Walk (Sites 11-12)   20

    C.   Belgravia Walk (Sites 13-25)   28

    D.   Sloane Square Walk (Sites 26-31)   56

    E.   Chelsea Walk (Sites 32-38)   68

    F.   South Kensington Walk (Sites 39-46)   86

    G.   Knightsbridge Walk (Sites 47-49)   106

    H.   Earl's Court Walk (Site 50)   113

    I.   Holland Walk (Sites 51-54)   119

    J.   Notting Hill Walk (Sites 55-57)   134

    K.   Maida Vale Walk (Site 58)   142

    L.   Marylebone Walk (Sites 59-66)   148

    M.   Baker Street Walk (Sites 67-74)   164

    N.   Edgware Walk (Sites 75-82)   184

    O.   Regent's Park Walk (Sites 83-88)   212

    P.   Euston Walk (Sites 89-90)   232

    Q.   City Walk (Sites 91-93)   240

    R.   Strand Walk (Sites 94-97)   249

    S.   Charing Cross Walk (Sites 98-106)   268

    T.   Piccadilly Walk (Sites 107-122)   286

    U.   Mayfair Walk (Sites 123-136)   319

Glossary   349

Index   357

FOREWORD

by

NIGEL WEST

It is only by visiting the locations of so many famous episodes in Britain's colourful espionage history that the *aficionado* can really flavour the full drama of the events that shaped postwar Europe. Most of the sites remain just as they were. The imposing façade of 21 Queen Anne's Gate, for more than four decades the headquarters of the Secret Intelligence Service, is exactly as it was before the war when its chief, Sir Hugh Sinclair, struggled to persuade Prime Minister Chamberlain that the strength of Hitler's *Luftwaffe* had been underestimated and that it presented a serious strategic threat. Only those indoctrinated into SIS's secrets were allowed to know that the rear of the elegant town house was connected to a large anonymous office block in Broadway where the cream of the nation's debutantes acted as secretaries to the academics and other wartime volunteers who managed SIS's operations across the globe.

These were not the inconsequential pinpricks that marked so many futile clandestine operations, but rather the episodes that changed the course of the world. Imagine the tension as a group of senior intelligence professionals huddled around the teleprinter in Broadway Buildings awaiting news of the battleship *Deutschland* immediately after the Munich crisis in 1938. After its goodwill visit to Vigo the warship was supposed to continue its voyage into the Atlantic and make further courtesy calls to foreign ports. But SIS had calculated that if Hitler intended to renege on his agreement with Chamberlain it was likely to return home to Germany to prepare for war. Suddenly the machine chattered a report from the wireless direction-finding equipment which monitored the ship's every radio transmission. From the interception of its signals, the traffic analysts had determined that the *Deutschland* had taken a southerly course; peace had been assured, at least temporarily. And throughout, the public at large gained no clue to the drama, or had any reason to suppose Europe had been on the brink of war. Only in recent years have the war's murkiest secrets emerged, and the locations of these events been revealed.

Are there still traces of the corpses of French traitors that were rumoured to have been buried in the basement of 10 Duke Street by General de Gaulle's ruthless henchmen? Do the ghosts of betrayed SOE agents haunt the safe-houses and flats in the Baker Street area where so many ill-fated missions were planned?

Looking up at the window of the office on the corner of South Audley Street which Sir Roger Hollis inhabited for nine years, the view quite unchanged from the long dark days of the MI5 molehunts when Peter Wright accused his director-general of treachery, one can imagine the scene. At the height of the Cold War, with the Security Service wracked by the fear of hostile penetration, Hollis is confronted by his aide. Exasperated by Wright's paranoia, he gazes out across the street and turns to deny the charges against him. In not dissimilar circumstances, in his flat in the Courtauld Institute, overlooking Portman Square, Anthony Blunt had poured himself a stiff gin and tonic and, taking a deep breath, had confessed to his interrogator that he had indeed been a KGB spy for more than 25 years.

Some of the premises described in this remarkable book are still in use, and the eager but unsuspecting spy-spotter may unwittingly witness occasions of great moment. Was there an innocent spectator present outside George Blake's old office at 3 Carlton Gardens when a chauffeur-driven limousine swung up to the front door in 1989 and deposited Paul Henderson and his case-officer? Henderson was a director of Matrix Churchill, and SIS's most trusted source inside the Iraqi arms industry, attending one of a series of debriefings routinely conducted upon his return from Baghdad. Had Saddam Hussein acquired the necessary technology for the successful construction of a nuclear weapon? What progress had been achieved in building the supergun? One can only guess at the conversation that must have passed between the two men as they stepped out of the car and into the colonnaded building which, to this day, has no exterior sign of its secret purpose and is listed simply as a branch of the Foreign and Commonwealth Office.

Tracing these buildings where history was made, and in some examples continues to be made, has required assiduous research and plenty of patient legwork. This book is the fruit of a painstaking project that has taken the author from one end of London to the other, and across the more than one hundred years between the start of a modern British intelligence capability and our own day. Each site is accompanied by accurate and often humorous pen-portraits of the practitioners of the arcane arts who inhabited each carefully documented site. As one turns the page or crosses the road one encounters another authentic episode of the astonishing events that shaped the unavowed conflicts that continued beyond 1945 and into the decades of nuclear and political stalemate.

These are the authentic locations for many of Britain's most notorious cases of espionage, the scenes of arrests, betrayals and raids; of surreptitious break-ins, suicides and mysterious disappearances, sophisticated eavesdropping schemes and deniable surveillance operations. The era of superpower confrontation and the search for Nazi parachutists is long gone, but as you stand outside the Cabinet War Rooms in Great George Street you can almost hear Churchill's voice booming from deep below; you can almost spot the MI5 Watcher teams scurrying from their observation posts and camera positions as their quarry emerges from Kensington Palace Gardens. Is he a trusted agent whose loyalty is under test, or the source of a leakage of classified information, or perhaps a professional intelligence officer masquerading as a diplomat? As you follow the recommended routes, keep your eyes peeled, for London remains the espionage capital of the world.

Nigel West

INTRODUCTION

London is my favourite city, and if this book is in your hands perhaps you share my view — and my reasons. My own fondness for London comes from two special circumstances in addition to the more usual ones. First, I have every historian's attachment to London, shaped further by the toughest course I took at college: in British constitutional history. Second, my special interest in the history of intelligence and unconventional warfare has made me keenly aware of London's rich presence in this narrow area of historical enquiry. Other places (Paris, Vienna, virtually any city in Switzerland) have certainly seen their share of spookery, but I am unswerving in my loyalty to London as pre-eminent in these matters. It will be my pleasure to urge you to a similar conclusion.

This project began on a whim. Before the recent explosion of books on intelligence and unconventional warfare, I had read most of the available accounts about SOE and had noted with interest their disclosure of a number of once-secret locations. On a subsequent trip to London I went to Baker Street with a list of these locations in hand. To my delight, I found that all buildings on my list had survived the best efforts of both the *Luftwaffe* and the real-estate developers. Except for the little building in Dorset Square, though, none was marked in any way to tell the passer-by just what he or she was passing by. I stood across from one of these buildings (Norgeby House, as I recall) thinking of all that had happened there: things I knew about and things I didn't. In this seemingly ordinary building, operations of great moment had been conceived and planned and worried about and exulted over. I was struck by the vibrancy of history made real.

Several years (and some 100 buildings) later, this book is itself a reality. The book isn't about these relatively ordinary buildings, of course, but about the extraordinary activities inside them. Mundane buildings, however, are a useful reminder that the history of intelligence is the record of achievements and failures of real people, many of them wearing an air of purposeful anonymity, to be sure, but all of them involved, like the rest of us, in thoughts about the weather and traffic and what to have for dinner. Even the most flamboyant of these actors on the stage of history has had traits, ideas and pastimes of the most excruciating banality and has lived and worked among us in surroundings of the most exquisite ordinariness.

This book is for the general reader as well as the 'intelligencer' (amateur or professional) with an already established interest in these matters. And the book is for the armchair traveller as well as the sensibly shod tourist. If you're on the ground you might want to follow the walks in order; the end of one walk usually delivers you to the start of the next. (Beginning at Westminster, the route spirals outward through Belgravia and Chelsea, up to South Kensington and Holland Park, east to Marylebone and Baker Street, farther east to the City, then back to the centre through the Strand, Piccadilly, and Mayfair.) The 21 walks are of varied length. Their only similarity is that (with few exceptions) all begin and end at tube stations.

All walks are within central London and therefore exclude many compelling sites in the larger metropolitan area, these three among them: the only residence of a 'secret agent' that is marked with one of London's Blue Plaques (it is the home of Violette Szabo who lived in SW9 and died with SOE); the final resting place of Karl Marx in Highgate Cemetery; and the Ealing villa of an MI6 officer who was assumed to have been abducted and assassinated in 1971 but whose skeleton was found three years later in his locked study (the body having been overlooked during all that time by his family, a lodger, and three dogs).

To visit any of the 136 sites in this book, no prior arrangements are necessary. A number of the buildings can be entered, but don't be surprised if the current proprietors or occupants know less than you do.

You might want to have a good overall map of London with you; the A-Z at super scale in atlas format is my favourite. It is best to be armed, too, with a sense of the irrationality of London's street-names: Watergate Walk is a pathway, for instance, while Birdcage Walk is a roadway; Whitehall Court is also a roadway, while Grove Court is a building. And York Buildings is a street. Let the little minds worry about consistency. Sometimes the same name will continue for numerous turns (as in any of the Gardens), and sometimes a street will be renamed every few blocks even when it makes no turns at all.

The attentive reader will discover that definitive truth is often inaccessible in this area of history. I give my own views on some of the great unanswerables and I stay out of the way on others. I suspect that readers will have similar reactions, sometimes being virtually certain (with me) about the rightness of a particular interpretation, and sometimes being ready to argue interminably or being just as eager to turn the page and let others argue.

I make no apology for my own views, which are mostly quite apparent. My bias as an Anglophile, not always apparent, should never be doubted. I am a lifelong admirer of British institutions and the British people. If I occasionally say harsh things about either, I speak as a friend: the British deserve the best from their secret services and I hope they are now getting it.

The scrupulously attentive reader will note occasional departures from some of the accepted wisdom as published elsewhere. I have been startled by the discrepancies, the errors, the molehills of misinformation appearing in the work of some of the most acclaimed writers in this field. Misinformed sources have relied on other misinformed sources, as perhaps I have done myself, until an error is virtually carved in stone. Even so generally accepted a legend as Smith-Cumming's wooden leg may not be true; it has been refuted in print by a highly regarded intelligence historian who tells me, however, that he is unable to recall his source and is unfortunately an ocean removed from his notes. (At his suggestion, I'm staying with the original story.) Perhaps, on a more serious level, any written history in this field must be imperfect, marred both by misinformation and disinformation. Insiders could probably supply another 136 sites for this book − or supply the 'real' story on any of my sites. I will welcome corrections and additions that readers can bring to my attention.

Soon, I suspect, we will all know more as new revelations come from Moscow. 'The KGB has gone into the history business,' writes one journalist. But quite apart from the certainty that not all archives have survived and not all materials have entered an archive 'unsanitized', we have the real problem that the people now running Russia's Foreign Intelligence Service are the same people who ran the KGB; they have past secrets to protect and future recruits to reassure. (And they are probably not above doing mischief to the Western alliance, stirring up discord and mistrust out of habit and on general principle.)

Many secrets will remain secret. Will we ever learn whether Sir Percy Sillitoe, head of MI5, was correct in doubting the loyalty of the unnamed lesbian wife of a postwar prime minister? Will we ever learn whether Andrew Boyle (who uncovered Blunt's treachery) was correct in suspecting an additional 25 traitors in British Intelligence? Will we ever learn the full details even about the people whose names we already have?

Those in the West who see no need for intelligence services or subversion operations, now that the Soviet empire has disintegrated, are almost certainly indulging in fantasy − as some of the same people did when they saw no danger from the Soviets. My own view is that we have seen only the end of a round, in the ongoing contest between totalitarian barbarism and the humane democracies. Because I am on the side of the latter in this struggle, I see intelligence-gathering, subversion, sabotage, even assassination, as essential weapons. To lay aside these weapons is to accept a needless handicap. (I cannot help but think that the Soviet collapse might have happened far sooner, at a tremendous saving in human death and misery, had the West been committed to subverting the communist dictatorships with the same fervour that they were dedicating to subverting us.)

Not knowing the full outline of the enemy poses a difficulty, of course, in this time after the Cold War, but this difficulty would seem to argue for more and not less attention to the gathering of intelligence, and for more and not less willingness to act according to the best analysis of that intelligence. The 136 sites in this book, then, aren't so much history: acts of folly or bravery or treachery or commitment, all long past. They are a sampling of the activities that will continue as long as human beings find themselves in an imperfect world − that is to say, for ever. We will forget this at our peril.

ACKNOWLEDGMENTS

I am indebted to many people for their assistance on this project: to Vera Atkins, DeWitt S. Copp, Arnaud de Borchgrave, P. William Filby, Professor M. R. D. Foot, Sally Garland, Jack Hewit, Bob Iveson-Watt, Caroline Levy (Walberry Productions), Kathy Manners (the BBC Late Show), H. Keith Melton, Vern Andreas Mills MD, Barrie Penrose, Arch Puddington, Ronald Radosh, Anthony Read, Joseph S. Schick, Denise Scott Brown, Michael F. Speers, Michael Strohbach, John C. Thackray (The Natural History Museum), Diana and Romer Topham, Thomas F. Troy, Professor Robin W. Winks, and David H. Winton. In addition, I owe thanks to staff of the Guildhall Library, to staff of the Imperial War Museum, to fellow members of the Association of Former Intelligence Officers, to members of the Veterans of OSS, and to the many historians and other writers mentioned in these pages whose works I have read with great interest and (usually) with high regard.

Several individuals deserve special thanks. For giving my idea his early encouragement and for gracing my product with his knowledgeable Foreword, I am exceedingly grateful to intelligence historian Nigel West (Rupert Allason, MP). I couldn't have wished for a better publisher than Leo Cooper. His initial enthusiasm and unflagging patience have been important to me; his many excellent books have been a standard that has guided my own work. And almost beyond words, I am ever thankful to my wife, Ellen Perry Berkeley, who put aside her own writing to help me in my efforts; it is she who, among other things, created the splendid maps and she who, with her scrupulous editing, kept this book to a size we could all consider portable.

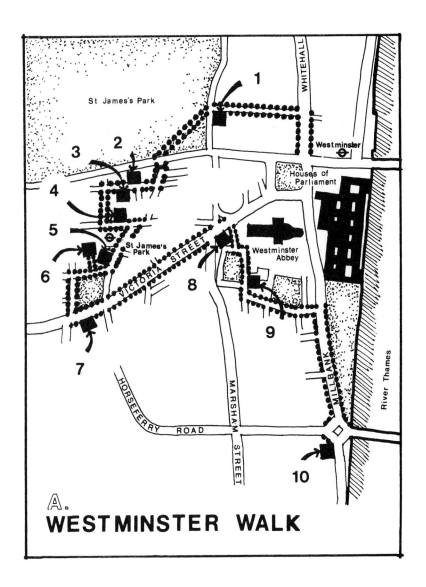

A.
WESTMINSTER WALK

A. WESTMINSTER WALK

Begin at Parliament Square, at the very centre of England's spiritual and political life. With the Abbey behind you and Big Ben to your R, walk N one block into the quiet neoclassical grandeur of King Charles Street. At the end of the block, on the L, you'll see

Site 1: **the Cabinet War Rooms.** The Kaiser's small air force inflicted impressive damage on Britain during WWI. With another war likely, it was obvious that the Cabinet and the vital military and intelligence staffs would be primary targets of Hitler's more powerful air arm. The Home Office hastily prepared a bunker in the basement of the massive government offices in Great George Street. (From the park you can see the structure's fortification at ground level.)

Open to the public today, the Cabinet War Rooms appear virtually as they were then; 21 underground rooms have been painstakingly restored by the Imperial War Museum. You can feel the purposefulness and tension in this bunker where Churchill and his Cabinet and military staff worked and often slept. The place is submarine-like: windowless, cramped, militarily squared-away. You are in close touch with the pin-pricked maps, the scrambler-equipped telephones, even the special telephone (hidden in a closet) on which Churchill and Roosevelt spoke over direct radio link. Did the Germans listen in? I've heard arguments both ways. I wouldn't be surprised if the enemy *had* managed to eavesdrop on FDR and the Former Naval Person; the German intelligence people were often quite good and the technology didn't permit a fully secure link until 1943.

Shortly after Churchill became prime minister he entered these subterranean quarters and said, 'This is the room from which I'll direct the war.' And when William Donovan, later to head America's OSS, visited Churchill in 1940, this is where the British convinced Donovan (and therefore Roosevelt) that Britain would fight and win despite the defeatist reports of Ambassador Kennedy. Since Britain really *couldn't* have repulsed a German invasion at the time, Donovan's visit marked the first of many deception operations to be mounted here.

Here too, in April, 1941, Churchill established the London Controlling Section to plan the stratagems of British (and later American) 'special means.' This 'vaguely sinister term,' writes Anthony Cave Brown in *Bodyguard of Lies*, 'included a wide variety of surreptitious, sometimes murderous, always intricate operations of covert warfare designed to cloak overt military operations in secrecy and to mystify Hitler about the real intentions of the Allies.' The major use of special means during WWII and the creation of a central agency to co-ordinate them, writes Brown, was 'probably [Churchill's] greatest single contribution to military theory and practice'. Every British (and later American) war planning staff was linked to the LCS in an extraordinary effort to utilize the most comprehensive deceptions alongside the more normal military methods of war. Trying to trick the enemy is as old as war itself, writes Brown, but 'Churchill undertook to institutionalise deception both in military affairs and statehood; and that was startlingly new'.

Churchill routinely offered advice to the workmen as they

reinforced the ceiling of the Cabinet War Rooms. Once he jumped off a girder into a pool of not-yet-dry concrete. Are his footprints still in that three-foot-thick slab? No matter; the entire place is imprinted with his *persona*. This was a major planning centre for a complex modern war. But because those days preceded the high-tech handling of information, we can see the men behind the decisions — and perhaps the war itself — more vividly.

Cross the street into the oldest of London's royal parks. Cut through the near-L corner to reach Birdcage Walk at the Cockpit Steps. Climb these 12 gentle steps. Opposite the venerable Two Chairmen pub, turn R into Queen Anne's Gate. On the R is

Site 2: **16-18 Queen Anne's Gate.** The Intelligence Branch of the British Army worked from this small house between 1884 and 1901. During those years of dominion over palm and pine, Britain sent military officers all over the world to gather information on friendly

and neutral nations as well as likely enemies. Then, as now, today's ally may be tomorrow's enemy – or may be occupied by the enemy.

Much of this work was done by regular officers posing as tourists or by patriotic amateurs who *were* tourists. In the latter category, almost every history of British intelligence mentions Lord Baden-Powell's work in Dalmatia. Posing as an entymologist he sketched the fortress of Cattara, working its guns and fortifications into his drawings of butterfly wings. Local counter-intelligence types dismissed him as a harmless British eccentric. They were only partially right.

Walk farther down this charming block. Blue Plaques honour many former residents, among them the foreign secretary (Sir Edward Grey) who said at the start of WWI, 'The lamps are going out all over Europe; we shall not see them lit again in our lifetime.' On the L, dating from 1704, is

Site 3: **21 Queen Anne's Gate.** For 47 years this house was the office and official residence of the first chief of MI6. Here the legendary Mansfield Smith-Cumming launched the more pretentious traditions of the service: the chief is called 'C' whatever his real name; he is unknown to the public, even if fully known to adversarial intelligence services; he alone may use green ink for written communication. (Reinhard Heydrich was so impressed with SIS, I understand, that when he headed Hitler's *Sicherheitsdienst* he too insisted on being called 'C' and he too established a green-ink monopoly.)

The first 'C', born Mansfield Smith in 1859, changed his name to flatter his wife's wealthy grandfather. Severe seasickness threatened his naval career until he obtained shore assignments and did well at them. When he became chief of SIS he was still a very junior officer, his service outranked and outbudgeted by the intelligence sections of the army and navy; only in the 1920s did MI6 begin to attain its currently pre-eminent position.

Any novelist inventing a Captain Mansfield Smith-Cumming would be hooted out of town by the reviewers. The man fancied disguises and swordsticks. He built a secret passageway between this building and 54 Broadway. And after an automobile accident in 1914, it was probably he who initiated the tale that he had freed himself from the

Site 3: **21 Queen Anne's Gate.**

wreckage by hacking off his own leg. (The limb was surgically amputated the next day.) Smith-Cumming even used his wooden leg to promote his bizarre image, often stabbing the prosthesis with his letter-opener during conversation.

Smith-Cumming's successors here eschewed his calculatedly

6

colourful ways. And in 1966 SIS moved to modern Century House, south of the Thames, two miles away geographically but light-years away in the style of operation within.

At the end of this block, turn L (still Queen Anne's Gate). At Broadway, cross the street to see the magnificent mansard roof of

Site 4: **the Broadway Buildings, 54 Broadway.** The home of SIS from 1924 until 1966, this handsome building saw successive chiefs of service topple governments (or prop them up) and use burglary, pickpocketing, forgery, blackmail, and occasionally murder to implement Britain's interests.

The James Bond films encourage us to imagine Secret Service headquarters as glossy, glamorous, sophisticated. The reality here was otherwise. Kim Philby, who had no reason to dissemble in *this* matter, described 54 Broadway as 'a dingy building, a warren of wooden partitions and frosted glass windows' served by an 'ancient lift'. The building itself is quite solid. Its steel frame probably prevented its collapse in 1944 when a V-1 flying bomb demolished a nearby chapel. Only by accident was the bomb deflected from slamming a ton of high explosives into the fourth-floor executive offices of MI6.

Imagine with me how the building looked in, say, 1942. The windows are taped (or boarded over) to protect against flying glass. A discreet brass plaque at the sandbagged entrance identifies the building as the home of the Minimax Fire Extinguisher Company. In the lobby is a commissionaire, one of the legions of retired soldiers and sailors working as doormen and messengers all over London. Passers-by often take shelter here from air-raids or weather; the commissionaire only interferes when anyone tries to go beyond the lobby. Few try. The roof has a thicket of radio antennae: odd, for a fire-extinguisher company. The roof also has a pigeon loft. Sir Stewart Menzies, who was 'C' from 1939 to 1952, mistrusted radio communications for his operatives in France; he may have headed the intelligence service of a nuclear power but he had been a horse-cavalry officer in WWI and he remained, in many ways, a 19th-century man.

And, like his predecessors and successors, Menzies was a secretive man. A well-known story, possibly even true, has George VI and Menzies conversing over dinner.

> The King: Menzies, who is our man in Berlin?
> Menzies: Sire, if my service has a man in Berlin, I may not divulge his identity.
> The King: Menzies, what would you say if I said, 'Give me the name of our man in Berlin or "Off with your head"'?
> Menzies: Sire, were you to give such an order, and were that order carried out, my head would roll with my lips still sealed.

The undisclosing mindset, which for years denied the very existence of MI6, persisted even after Radio Berlin announced 54 Broadway as MI6 headquarters! (The *Sicherheitsdienst* had obtained this information from two SIS officers kidnapped in the Netherlands.) Why, even then, did The Firm still masquerade as the Minimax Fire Extinguisher Company? Malcolm Muggeridge, who worked in MI6 during WWII, explains: 'Secrecy is as essential to Intelligence as vestments and incense to a Mass or darkness to a spiritualist seance and must at all costs be maintained, quite irrespective of whether or not it serves any purpose.' Of course. A secret service *should* be secret.

Follow the perimeter of the London Transport offices as Broadway turns S. In Tothill Street, during WW11, the inventor-farmer-evangelist Charles Fraser-Smith worked for the Ministry of Supply (actually for MI6, MI9, and SOE) fitting ordinary items with hidden gadgetry. His hairbrushes contained saws, his buttons contained compasses, his playing cards were lined with maps. The noted historian M. R. D. Foot carried several of Fraser-Smith's famous compasses long ago, one of which, Foot reports, 'survived two searches of my clothes when I was only wearing a blanket.' In Broadway, opposite New Scotland Yard, is

Site 5: **2 Caxton Street.** In 1938 MI6 created Section D to explore the possibility of sabotage and subversion behind enemy lines in event of war. Section D (for Destruction, it was said) merged with the new Special Operations Executive when war came; the two original staffs worked here.

The newly-formed SOE operated quite casually, as Bickham Sweet-Escott reports in his *Baker Street Irregular*. Assigned to send £200 to agents in Budapest, this former banker expected to cable the money through a Hungarian bank. He was told instead to mail the sum in five-pound notes! Even more startling to Sweet-Escott, the

SOE cashier apparently kept no record of disbursements. These people all knew each other – or felt that they did. They came from the same backgrounds and schools; they trusted each other. Nevertheless, Sweet-Escott began to record the expenditures of the Balkans Section in a two-shilling account book. In time, SOE's procedures undoubtedly became more crisp. But a clubby atmosphere of trust marked those years throughout the secret services, even though not all club members proved worthy of that trust.

Next door, stop for tea or coffee in the attractive foyer of

Site 6: **St Ermin's Hotel, Caxton Street.** The lounge is bright and cheerful today. But early in WWII, Malcolm Muggeridge (a new recruit to MI6) found it 'dim and quiet, suggestive of conferences to promote world governments, family planning or the practice of eurhythmics'. How much does this description owe to the legendary Muggeridge waspishness, I wonder, and how much to the blackout?

With 54 Broadway nearby (*see Site 4*), MI6 often interviewed potential recruits here over lunch or dinner. Philby was interviewed twice at St Ermin's. But MI6 used more than the restaurant – by 1939, the fifth and sixth floors were solidly MI6. The lifts showed stops at four floors only. New recruits like Noel Coward were astonished to be escorted to the secret MI6 outpost above.

Nor were outsiders encouraged to disembark at the fourth floor; SOE's Operations Section (the old Section D, now called SO2) had moved here to what M. R. D. Foot describes as 'three gloomy rooms'. During its tenure at St Ermin's, SO2 planned such operations as the destruction of Romania's oil fields, the removal of Amsterdam's industrial diamonds, the evacuation of Belgium's gold reserves, and the rescue of Madame de Gaulle – some of which happened and some of which didn't. SO2 stored explosives here. Did colleagues on the upper floors know they were literally sitting on a powder keg?

Proceed farther on Caxton Street to Palmer Street. To the R and across the street, No. 8-9 served for many years as GCHQ's chief listening post for radio traffic from London's many embassies. In the other direction on Palmer Street, walk into the modern walkway that nicely resembles an old alleyway. Turn L at Victoria Street, itself a fairly modern path: it was cut through the slums surrounding the Abbey in the mid-19th century. Across the street you'll see the large letters identifying

Site 7: **Artillery Mansions, Victoria Street.** These flats weren't just 'another piece of Victorian speculation,' notes a little guidebook; they were unusual in having a two-storey marble archway leading into a handsomely-paved fountain courtyard. Unusual too were some of the visitors. SIS located its Production Research Department here, recruiting British businessmen whose work often took them abroad. Here, among others, George Blake worked (*see Site 84*) and Greville Wynne reported (*see Site 34*).

Businessmen have often been used as part-time agents – as case-officers, contacts or couriers. A businessman can be taught the rudiments of spy tradecraft far more readily than a spy can be taught the tradecraft of commerce. And only the rudiments are necessary; the businessman will not be photographing documents, for instance, but will merely be transporting what the defector-in-place has already gathered. A businessman also has the perfect cover; he is *supposed* to be where he is. In the 1930s Vernon Kell of MI5 noted the

Site 7: **Artillery Mansions, Victoria Street.**

difficulties of recruiting such people: 'It is not easy to find good excuses for frequent travelling unless you have real business, and those who have real business are probably making too much money to risk their necks as spies.' But by the 1960s, as Phillip Knightley writes in *The Second Oldest Profession*, 'SIS was constantly inundated with offers from British businessmen going abroad who wanted to do a little espionage work on the side.' In a sense, of course, all foreign businessmen visiting the Soviet bloc were spies, able to report first-hand on the biggest state secret of all: the failure of the entire communist system.

Continue E on Victoria Street, past tedious blocks of government offices. Ahead of you as you approach Westminster Abbey is the yellow stone of

Site 8: **1 Sanctuary Buildings.** In this building, on a site where the Abbey had long sheltered outcasts, the British Union of Fascists maintained its headquarters. Its members considered themselves not outcasts but the vanguard of a new society. They enjoyed a brief vision of power − not even a taste of it − before their movement was itself cast out, a casualty of the war and of the eminent good sense of the British people.

The BUF was founded in 1932 by Sir Oswald Mosley, a rich baronet who believed (on very thin evidence) that he was one of the century's great thinkers. An MP first with the Conservatives and then with Labour, Mosley deserted Marxist socialism (as had Mussolini before him) for the new and appealing fascism.

Fascism, we must remember, was not a conservative ideology but a radical and revolutionary creed, opposed by the conservative sector everywhere. Mosley's fascism (like the others) was statist, socialist, and based heavily in the same fears and resentments within the working class and lower-middle class as was communism. Mosley himself was of the same class and social set as Britain's leading leftist figures and might easily have led a Marxist party. He was basically a Leninist. He believed in a charismatic leader presiding over a nationalist, one-party state committed to various forms of social engineering – nothing conservative about any of that. (He believed too in 'corporatism', Mussolini's idea for a third way between capitalism and communism. Central planning. No competition. Cartels of industry, of labour, of agriculture, controlled by state technocrats. To the extent that corporatism was implemented, it didn't work any better in Italy than communism did in Russia – or anywhere else.)

The 1920s and 1930s saw an impatience with democracy among many privileged individuals. They considered democracy and capitalism too tame, too middle class, too disorganized, too free, too unpredictable, too old and familiar – too *democratic*. And many considered Italy, even more than Russia, the exciting Wave of the Future. A popular song, 'You're the Top' celebrated the modernity of cellophane and Mussolini with equal admiration.

To be sure, Mosley liked the idea and image of Mussolini's fascism, with its anthem 'Giovanezza' (youth) epitomizing the reinvigorated Italy. But Mosley also saw in totalitarianism a vehicle for his own intense ambition. In the scattered fascist grouplets of Britain he saw a movement he could consolidate.

As war approached, MI5 thoroughly infiltrated the BUF and thought Special Branch didn't take either the CPGB or the BUF seriously enough. Both organizations used 'illegal and violent methods', MI5 noted. Mosley used some proven fascist tactics, such as provocative marches in snappy uniforms, but borrowed more tactics from the communists – appearing at an eviction to return the furniture to the flat, occupying a farm threatened by foreclosure, and engaging in street battles.

The BUF's Judeophobia was probably only a tactic on Mosley's part, adding what he perceived as lower-middle-class and working-class hostility towards Jews to what he perceived as the hostility of these groups towards capitalists. Some serious violence occurred, particularly in London's East End, which was then a working-class neighbourhood of Cockneys and recent Jewish immigrants; shop windows were broken and individuals of Jewish appearance were beaten. Judeophobia, however, was not inherent in fascism; Mussolini and Franco had nothing against Jews. Mosley undoubtedly knew the 19th-century aphorism, 'Anti-Semitism is the socialism of fools.' And perhaps this tells us something about his assessment of his followers.

With other suspected traitors, Mosley was interned on the Isle of Man in 1940 upon Tyler Kent's arrest (*see Site 81*). The government had no evidence of espionage by BUF members, but remembered Mosley's effective street riots and was worried that he might co-ordinate a *coup d'état* with a German invasion. Nobody worried about the BUF winning an election; Mosley's BUF did even worse with voters than his failed New Party had done.

What killed the BUF? Paul Cohen, writing in the journal *Intelligence and National Security*, points to the withdrawal of funding by the Italian government on the one hand and, on the other, to the use by police of the Public Order Act, neutralizing demonstrations and riots by the CPGB and BUF alike. I like to think, too, that the BUF died because of the inherent good judgment of those it hoped to attract.

Immediately past the Sanctuary, enter the large courtyard that is Dean's Yard. Two-thirds up the L side is Little Dean's Yard, around which is

Site 9: **Westminster School.** Founded in 1560 by Elizabeth I as successor to a 14th-century Benedictine school, Westminster School counts among its alumni the justly honoured John Dryden, Christopher Wren, John Locke, Edward Gibbon and Jeremy Bentham. Another alumnus is the traitor Harold Adrian Russell Philby, who infiltrated MI6 for the Soviets during WWII and seemed.

Site 9: **Westminster School.**

likely to become chief of MI6 until he was suspected (by everyone but MI6) of being a Soviet mole.

Kim Philby entered Westminster School in 1924, aged 12, following in the footsteps of his father, the noted Arabist and (later) Nazi sympathizer Harry St John Bridger Philby. For all that Philby *père* may have been anti-Establishment, he sent his son to undeniably Establishment institutions. Westminster students are entitled to seats next door at important Abbey ceremonies; at coronations they may cry *'Vivat!'* after the Sovereign is crowned. Like his father, Kim Philby was a King's Scholar at Westminster, and thus entitled to attend debates at the House of Commons across the road. Unlike his father, the young Philby was not a brilliant student at Westminster (or at Cambridge, where his father also studied). But he was diligent, persistent and steadfast − as he was, too, in his work for the Soviet empire.

In his autobiography, Philby proudly describes his constancy to Leninism: his 'confident faith that the principles of the Revolution would outlive the aberrations of individuals, however enormous.' Philby paints himself as an idealist, loyal to communism despite the death camps, the murders, the torture chambers, the lies, the

16

state-sponsored terror. I think, though, that he was an élitist, loyal to communism *because of* the death camps, the murders, the torture chambers, the lies, the state-sponsored terror. He was an upper-class totalitarian who rejected modern British democracy because it didn't suit his notion that Those Who Know Best should rule (without any nonsense from the governed). I am appalled that Britain bred, nourished, cultivated this viper at her bosom, at her very heart, in the shadow of the two buildings embodying her spiritual and temporal heartbeat.

Leave Dean's Yard by the S and walk towards the river on Great College Street. Ponder the fact that Parliament can never be wholly surrounded by angry crowds; on the advice of the Duke of Wellington, it was placed at the very edge of the Thames. Enter Victoria Tower Gardens, south of Parliament, and watch the river traffic from the Silver Jubilee Walkway (1977); not everything in London is centuries old. At the end of the gardens, glance to the R down Horseferry Road where a joint headquarters for MI5 and MI6 was envisioned after the war at Marsham Street; the proposal foundered on the lack of amity between the two agencies. Beyond the heavy traffic lumbering in over Lambeth Bridge is

Site 10: **Thames House, Millbank.** In 1937 Britain's domestic security organization moved from Cromwell Road (*see Site 44*) to two floors of Thames House, subsequently spilling over into offices in Horseferry Road. The move was uncomplicated; the entire staff numbered only 28! All of MI5 could, and did, gather for tea in one room here.

The atmosphere must have been quite collegial at the office (or The Office, as some initiates say). Sir Vernon Kell still headed the organization he had founded 28 years earlier. His hiring policies stressed family background and military record, and his recruits fitted in well with each other — they *were* each other. They were never investigated for subversive leanings; someone from the proper background *couldn't* be traitorous. (The women hired as clerks and typists came from similar families but were required, in addition, to have good legs.)

Site 10: **Thames House, Millbank.**

With the increasing threat of Axis subversion and sabotage, Kell moved all of MI5's files (and his staff of 92) to Wormwood Scrubs. Personnel commuted from Central London, solemnly warned not to reveal their employment even when conductors on the No. 72 bus were heard to announce cheerily, 'Wormwood Scrubs, all change for MI5.' A beguiling amateurism marked British intelligence efforts in those days. As a precaution against air-raid damage, Kell ordered MI5's files photographed for storage elsewhere; only after the war were the negatives found to be overexposed and useless.

Today an enlarged and refurbished Thames House is once again MI5 headquarters. But these days women are valued for more than their legs. MI5's first female chief, Stella Whitehouse Rimington, has been described by the press as 'a formidable intellect and administrator' and 'one of a group of female high-flyers within MI5.' She heads a force of approximately 2,300 − just over half of them women − and is said to have annual expenditures of 'between £300 million and £500 million'. (Until the new openness promised by John Major takes place, we must be content with such estimates.) The focus of MI5 has also shifted from its early days; with the threat of subversion reduced, a very large percentage of MI5's resources now goes into fighting terrorism and some may soon go into fighting organized crime. But Kell would be utterly astounded by the new complaints mechanism for the citizenry, and by talk of a press office (!), a telephone number for public access (!), and an all-party parliamentary committee to which the service would be accountable (!).

This concludes Westminster Walk. The nearest tube station is at Parliament Square. You may want, instead, to go several blocks S on Millbank to the Tate Gallery. If you take tea here before continuing with the next walk, pay homage to Sir Henry Tate, inventor of the sugar cube. Or you may want to cross Lambeth Bridge and go several blocks E to the always-interesting Imperial War Museum. Near the museum, just behind Lambeth North tube station, is Century House, former headquarters of MI6. It isn't much of a building, except in height, and a burglar who walked in off the street later complained that there was 'nothing worth nicking' inside.

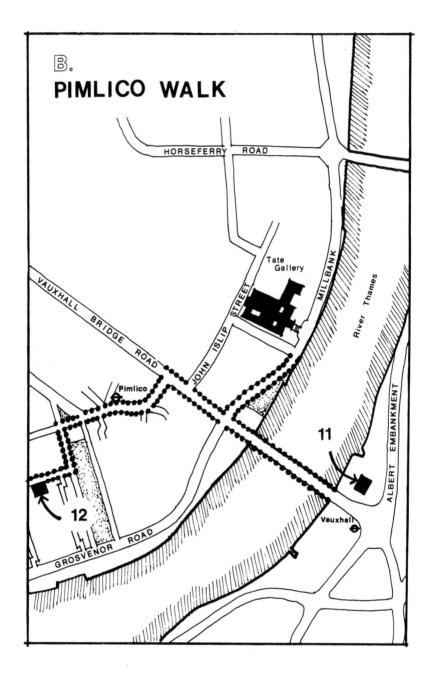

B.

PIMLICO WALK

HORSEFERRY ROAD

Tate Gallery

VAUXHALL BRIDGE ROAD

JOHN ISLIP STREET

MILLBANK

River Thames

ALBERT EMBANKMENT

Pimlico

11

12

GROSVENOR ROAD

Vauxhall

B. PIMLICO WALK

Across from the Tate Gallery, S of the Thames, is

Site 11: **the new MI6 headquarters, Vauxhall Cross.** Like any other major world capital, London has its share of showy new buildings. But like no other serious world power, Britain has made available one of its showiest new architectural landmarks to its Secret Intelligence Service, an organization still technically non-existent at the start of construction. Rumoured to cost £240 million, the building has between nine and twelve visible storeys (no one seems able to make a definitive count) and reportedly five more levels of 'computer citadel' below. Portions of the exterior are deep green in colour, which probably offends the purists no less than does the presence

altogether of this blatantly strange – and strangely blatant – edifice. The building was actually a speculative project built for the government's Property Services Agency and was not therefore purpose-built for SIS. But the government offered it to SIS and SIS took it, creating what is now generally considered a public relations disaster (compounded, no doubt, by the additional £85 million spent to adapt the building for its first occupant).

As MI6 prepared to leave nearby Century House (the anonymous-looking tower at Lambeth North station), many secrets began to be left behind. The chief of SIS was routinely identified in the press. A high-level retired officer spoke on television about the future of the service. Various media mentioned that the staff of SIS was 'about 2,000 full-time officers' and that 'a third of its resources' had been directed to the Soviet bloc. By 1992 the Prime Minister had publicly acknowledged the existence of SIS and promised to 'sweep away some of the cobwebs of secrecy.'

With the high visibility of the new headquarters came unabashed speculation about the organization within. One observer opined on BBC that 'MI6 has perhaps got nothing to do now [the Soviet Union having self-destructed], so it might as well come out of the closet'. I doubt that MI6's job is over. The Soviet Union is history, to be sure. But while we are told that the 'new KGB' has been reduced, we are also told that it continues to expand. The GRU has certainly not been reduced, and the GRU has traditionally been the vehicle for the industrial and economic espionage that will increasingly occupy the former Soviet Union. (In fact, the successor to the KGB – Russia's Foreign Intelligence Service – has indicated that its own emphasis will now be on industrial espionage.) A portion of MI6's attention must remain with this major power, even while the job of MI6 in the new polycentric world has increased geometrically; MI6 must now keep tabs on many countries and blocs. Every schoolchild knows the problems: nuclear proliferation, chemical and biological capabilities, international terrorism and drug trafficking, newly unleashed nationalisms, aggressive Islamic fundamentalism. And it is not unreasonable to fear a resurgent Russian empire: nationalistic, authoritarian, religious, expansionist, and unhampered by the dead hand of Marxism. So while one observer likens this new building, with some delight, to an Aztec or Mayan temple, I doubt that SIS will soon go the way of those dead civilizations.

Interestingly, MI6 has responded to a changed world by increasing its recruitment of old-fashioned on-the-ground intelligence agents. Will the new headquarters cause these agents to become more 'ostentatious' or 'extravagant' or 'flamboyant' as one commentator imagines? I think not. It takes more than a building to shape an institution. Despite the new showiness of MI6 (with this building) and despite the new openness altogether, I doubt that secrecy will soon pass from the scene. I doubt that casual visitors will be admitted here, for instance – even to the new two-room museum that a Whitehall source has likened to the KGB museum in the Lubyanka.

N of the Thames, leave the river along Bessborough Gardens. Turn L at Drummond Gate and continue past Pimlico tube station to Lupus Street. Turn L at the far edge of St George's Square. (At No. 33 lived Major Walter Clopton Winfield, father of lawn tennis.) Just beyond the school, enter Chichester Street. On your L are the prewar luxury flats called

Site 12: **Dolphin Square.** For at least three people living here, life was full of unexpected turns, all for the worse.

Christine Keeler, protégée of society osteopath Stephen Ward (*see*

Site 86), took a flat here in 1961. Her West Indian lover, Lucky Gordon, hounded her jealously and slept on her fire escape here in the summer of 1962. Here too she entertained her most prominent lover – John Profumo, Secretary of State for War. Profumo resigned in 1963 when it was alleged that he was pillow-talking Keeler while she was simultaneously pillow-talking a GRU officer from the London embassy.

To what extent may Profumo have been manipulated by the Soviets because of all this? For two years, he was 'highly vulnerable to pressure from anyone with knowledge of his affair with Keeler,' write Anthony Summers and Stephen Dorril in their 1987 book *Honeytrap*. The GRU officer, Yevgeny Ivanov, surfaced in 1992 to say that a Soviet blackmail attempt had been considered but was foiled by Keeler's going public. (Predictably she wasn't hailed as a national heroine upon this news.)

Two of Keeler's subsequent residences were Holloway Prison, where she did nine months for perjury on a different matter entirely, and World's End council flats, where she enjoyed amenities more reminiscent of Holloway than of Dolphin Square.

Another resident of Dolphin Square who made headlines in a spy scandal was William John Christopher Vassall, son of a prominent clergyman. Vassall went to Moscow as a clerk in the British Embassy in 1954 and within a year was spying for the Soviets. A year later he was back in London giving classified documents to the Soviets, while serving variously in the Admiralty's Naval Intelligence Division, the office of the Civil Lord of the Admiralty, and the Admiralty's Military Branch. Security was so poor in London that Vassall simply slipped the documents inside his *Times* and walked out with them.

Security had been no better in Moscow. An interpreter named Mikhailsky was procuring all manner of goods and services for embassy personnel. He was a Pole, he said, and hated the Russians. But he worked closely enough with them to escort Vassall to a homosexual party organized by the KGB. At this party Vassall got drunk, got involved in what he later called 'a complicated array of sexual activities with a number of different men' and (should we be surprised?) got photographed doing so.

Dame Rebecca West, in *The New Meaning of Treason*, doesn't believe Vassall's story that he was forced into spying. The drunken party, she writes, was 'probably engineered so that Vassall might refer to it, should his treachery ever be discovered'. Pointing to his resourcefulness during seven years of spying, she believes he was not the 'weak and silly little man, poor in intellect and indecisive in character' implied by the blackmail story. Her theory is intriguing, responding as it does to the usual protestation that if homosexuality hadn't been against the law (as it was then) and if the nation hadn't had so many secrets, the Soviets would have had fewer Vassalls working for them.

Like Rebecca West, I prefer to blame Vassall's acts on the man himself and on those who hired him. One cannot overlook Vassall's pleasure in his Savile Row suits (19 of them!), his foreign travel, his antiques, his expensive flat. One cannot assume that Vassall regretted what he did − or that he did it against his will and better judgment.

According to Rebecca West, 'someone in the embassy' must have been 'extremely anxious that the activities of Mikhailsky and Vassall should go unchecked'. I'm not so sure. Security in those times was altogether appalling; when Vassall returned to London, he was vetted almost a year *after* he began working for the Admiralty − and so superficially that nobody noticed he was spending £10 a week on the flat in Dolphin Square while earning £14 a week in Whitehall. Under surveillance finally, he 'proved a difficult subject' even with a listening post in the adjacent flat here in Hood House, writes Nigel West in *The Circus*.

Vassall had been named by two Soviet defectors, one of whom was later discredited as a plant, and Nigel West mentions 'the suspicion [in MI5] that Vassall had been a discard' − a decoy to protect a more important Admiralty spy. The capture of Vassall has been touted as one of Hollis's great 'successes' as director-general of MI5. Was Vassall given away to make Hollis look good?

Vassall went to prison in 1962 and vanished into a Sussex monastery ten years later. He broke his long silence to express bitterness only towards Anthony Blunt, who had done what he had done, and worse, without spending a day in custody.

Quite a different person going in and out of these anonymous flats at Dolphin Square was Maxwell Knight. But like Keeler and Vassall, he saw his life dramatically changed when he left here.

Knight had been a Latin teacher in 1925 when he met Vernon Kell at a dinner party. He joined MI5 the next day and by 1930 was in charge of placing agents inside the CPGB. The Woolwich Arsenal case in 1938 (*see Site 51*) was a personal triumph: henceforth all counter-subversion ops in MI5 would be under Knight.

He worked apart from the rest of MI5 using two flats at Dolphin Square: 308 Hood House as office and safe-house, 10 Collingwood House as operational headquarters. 'Knight's office was unique within MI5,' writes Nigel West in *MI5*, 'and was held in some awe because of its mystery and the amount of autonomy granted to it.' His recruits were an élite: bright young things who called themselves Knight's Black Agents after 'night's black agents' in *Macbeth*. Knight conducted interviews here in various uniforms, under various pseudonyms, and with his wife's name on one of the doorbells. But the Germans knew what went on here anyway, Nigel West tells me, from one of several double agents.

Knight was a resourceful foe of fascism *and* communism. Nobody else in MI5 shared his view of a double threat; during the war years, fascism was the only concern. Knight's downfall probably began in 1940 with the sacking of Vernon Kell. In 1941 the handwriting was clearly on the wall in the response to Knight's report, 'The Comintern Is Not Dead'. Many believe that Roger Hollis (*see Sites 52 and 54*) rejected the report, finding it 'over-theoretical' as one agent recalls. But one historian, Richard Deacon, holds that Guy Liddell (*see Site 32*) was 'foremost' in securing its rejection. Rejected it was, however, and its author along with it, his anti-communist section increasingly subject to criticism and ridicule.

Knight's star declined precipitously after the war. Sir Percy Sillitoe, who became director-general of MI5 in 1946, considered him a relic of the past and moved him into a reorganized counter-subversion department in Leconfield House. Sir Dick White, who succeeded Sillitoe in 1953, reduced Knight's role further. Knight soon retired, after 32 years in MI5, going on to enormous success as a popular naturalist. Had his credibility remained high within MI5, that organization might have caught Anthony Blunt at the very least. (When an agent of Knight's in the CPGB was exposed in 1941, Knight couldn't convince anyone in MI5 that the tip-off to the CPGB must have come from someone inside MI5. In fact, it came from

Blunt.) Once deemed MI5's 'most brilliant case officer', Knight had made too many enemies, too many errors (*see Site 49*). His unusual tenure at Dolphin Square — unusual both for him and for MI5 — was a thing of the past.

You can sit in the sheltered gardens of Dolphin Square or dine in the 1930s-style restaurant. You can even rent a furnished flat here, by day or by week. To go on with your day, retrace your steps to Pimlico tube station. To start the next walk, hail a taxi. (Sorry, it's the only time I'll suggest a taxi, but I do insist.)

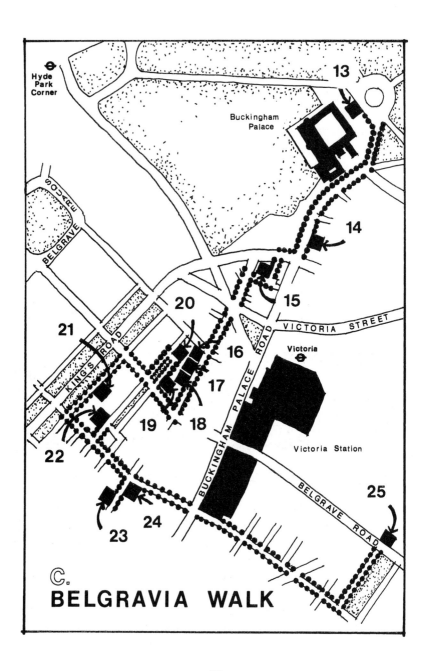

Hyde
Park
Corner

13

Buckingham
Palace

14

15

20

21

16

Victoria

17

19   18

VICTORIA STREET

Victoria Station

22

BELGRAVE ROAD

25

23   24

KING'S ROAD

BELGRAVE

BUCKINGHAM PALACE ROAD

© .
BELGRAVIA WALK

C. BELGRAVIA WALK

The first site on this walk is nowhere near the underground. Best to find a taxi. Tell the driver in your most regal manner to take you immediately, please, to

Site 13: **Buckingham Palace.** Although this palace must have witnessed intrigues of every personal and political kind during its 160-odd years as the London residence of the Sovereign, no story can be as intriguing as that linking the Duke of Windsor, friend of Hitler's Germany, with Anthony Blunt, agent of Stalin's Russia. The story includes acts bordering on treason by a man who was King of England, and acts of loyal service to the Crown by a man who was one of England's greatest traitors.

These matters are so closely guarded that the Queen's private secretary in 1965 gave spycatcher Peter Wright a single *caveat* concerning his interrogation of Blunt. 'From time to time,' Wright recalls being told, 'you may find Blunt referring to an assignment he undertook on behalf of the Palace – a visit to Germany at the end of the war. Please do not pursue this matter. Strictly speaking, it is not relevant to considerations of national security.' Wright never learnt Blunt's secret in six years of interrogation. But others have pieced it together.

At war's end, probably at the request of George VI, Blunt and the royal archivist went into occupied Germany to retrieve certain documents. The papers they brought back to England were very likely those of Prince Philip of Hesse, formerly a general in Hitler's Brownshirts and, not incidentally, a cousin of the Duke of Windsor. These papers would have disclosed the role of Philip of Hesse as intermediary between Hitler and the Duke and, of course, would have disclosed the nature of the contact between the two. 'Was the Duke really unwavering in his loyalty to the British cause?' asks historian John Costello in *Mask of Treachery*. 'An objective reading leaves an uncomfortably wide margin for suspicion.'

Well before the war, the sympathies of this member of the royal family were apparent. During his brief year as King, he argued against his government's policies toward Mussolini and Hitler, siding with Italy in its invasion of Ethiopia and opposing any response to Germany's militarization of the Rhineland. While still on the Throne, he was 'in the process,' Costello states, 'of setting out the basis of a deal with Hitler.'

His ambitious paramour was an eager partner in all of this. The Germans had courted Wallis Simpson from the start; Joachim von Ribbentrop claimed to have been appointed ambassador to London primarily because of his friendship with her. By 1936 Wallis's domination of the King was 'overwhelming and inexorable', according to Edward's private secretary – 'every decision, big or small, was subordinated to her will.' By the middle of 1936, reports John Parker in *King of Fools*, American intelligence concluded that (in Parker's words) 'Ribbentrop was clearly passing on state secrets that emanated from Edward, through Mrs Simpson.' When Whitehall learnt that secret documents lay strewn about Edward's weekend retreat for all of Wallis's friends to see – some documents having been used as coasters! – Edward was relieved of the burden of seeing additional sensitive material. He became the only British whose access to government documents was screened by his own security services.

Further indiscretions followed Edward's abdication. In 1937 the newly married Windsors accepted Hitler's invitation to tour Germany, and the Duke met Hitler at Berchtesgaden. Notes of their meeting, known to exist, never turned up after the war. 'The probability,' writes Parker, is that these notes are 'somewhere in the Royal archives, along with many other sensitive reports concerning the activities of the Duke and Duchess of Windsor.'

In 1938 the Windsors wanted to visit England. Their request was denied, Parker writes, because of the belief 'that Windsor's mere presence in the country constituted a danger' — a danger 'linked quite positively' with the British Union of Fascists. Mosley of the BUF 'was still aligning his speeches toward the former King,' Parker observes, and although the fascists proclaimed their loyalty to the Crown, 'that did not necessarily mean to George VI.'

Then came the Duke's activities during the war. Assigned to the British Military Mission in France, he was privy to all Allied military plans. 'By comparing Allied and German records,' writes Costello, 'it is now possible to develop a convincing case that an intelligence leak leading back to the Duke of Windsor may well have played a significant part in prompting Hitler to order his generals to change their battle plan.' The result was the Nazi drive through the Ardennes, cutting off the British at Dunkirk.

But perhaps nothing can compare with the events during the summer of 1940, after the Duke fled France for Madrid. Churchill ordered him home, only to have the Duke demand suitable employment for himself and proper recognition for the Duchess. London refused. Churchill had to threaten a court-martial before the Windsors left for Lisbon and, they thought, for London. But once in Lisbon the Duke was offered the governorship of the Bahamas (no lesser position being available), and Churchill made clear that no alternative was possible. German officials and intermediaries were wooing the Duke meanwhile, suggesting that he 'hold himself in readiness for further developments ... especially with a view to the assumption of the English Throne by the Duke and Duchess.' Berlin in turn was told by the German Minister in Lisbon that the Duke was 'a firm supporter of a peaceful compromise with Germany' and 'definitely believes that continued severe bombing would make England ready for peace.' MI6 and German operatives hovered round the Duke night and day. Berlin made plans to kidnap him. Invasion of Britain seemed imminent. Incredibly, two days after Hitler demanded England's surrender, the Duke urged George VI to dismiss Churchill and negotiate for peace. Nothing could have been less likely. The Windsors soon left Lisbon, the Duke promising Germany that he could still take action from the Bahamas – or so it was reported to Berlin.

Controversy continues over these matters. The Duke denied that he ever contemplated regaining the Throne, and he disputed other damaging assertions. But his inclination towards Germany and his advocacy of appeasement were well known. Like many of his class he thought England could use some of the 'stiffening up' that impressed admirers of Italian and German fascism. Like many of his class, too, he recalled the horrors of WWI and the loss of an entire generation of upper-class Englishmen. Moreover, he said, 'every drop of blood in my veins is German'; 14 of his 16 great-great-grandparents were Teutonic.

Churchill seems to have had a persistent sympathy for the Duke as well as a patriot's desire to keep the Duke's transgressions from becoming public. After the war Churchill tried valiantly to halt publication of some of the materials captured from the German Foreign Ministry. The file on the Duke of Windsor was published only in 1957. It was damaging enough even without the missing record of the meeting with Hitler.

Anthony Blunt, we can be sure, didn't protect the Duke out of sympathy for him; the Duke's well-known taste for fascism came partially from his well-known distaste for communism. The motive, then? Blunt bought for himself what Costello calls a 'gold-plated insurance policy.' The Queen was aware, for years, of his spying for the Soviets. But Blunt was aware of one of the darkest royal secrets, and although he didn't keep it to himself (he told the Soviets) he apparently kept it from the multitudes.

Surely we are not at the end of the revelations about the Duke and Duchess. Costello tells us that the FBI has an 'even more substantial file on the Windsors' not yet declassified. Nor are we at the end of the speculations about Blunt. In their 1991 book *Elizabeth and*

Philip: The Untold Story of the Queen of England and Her Prince, Charles Higham and Roy Moseley say that Blunt had 'several royal flushes up his sleeve.' He not only retrieved the Duke's correspondence with Hitler and Ribbentrop, he probably knew other royal secrets: that during WWII certain members of the royal family 'were in breach of the Trading with the Enemy Act by corresponding with their relatives, enemy nationals' or that 'the Queen and her family held a major shareholding in Courtaulds, a fact not supposed to be made public.' Was it all of this — or even more — that assured Blunt his long-term position as director of the Courtauld Institute of Art, his long-term position as Surveyor of the King's (and then the Queen's) Pictures, and his long-term protection from exposure as a Soviet agent?

Leaving the Palace environs via Buckingham Gate (the gate), bear R into Buckingham Gate (the road) for two small blocks. Opposite the Royal Mews is

Site 14: **the Rubens Hotel, Buckingham Palace Road.** General Wladislaw Sikorski, Polish Prime Minister and Commander-in-Chief of Polish forces in WWII, had his headquarters here from 1940 until

his death in 1943. This much we know from the plaque outside the hotel. There is more to the story.

The first consequence of the Hitler-Stalin Pact of 1939 was the invasion and annexation of Poland jointly by Germany and the USSR. (Popular history often omits Soviet participation in this event that began WWII.) Half a million Poles fled to France. When France fell, Sikorski fled to London, angrily defying the French promise to surrender all Polish forces with their own. Some 250,000 Poles ultimately reached Britain and the Commonwealth. From these headquarters in the Rubens Hotel, the Poles operated more independently than almost any other resistance group or government-in-exile, even using their own cyphers and radios. (Two intelligence coups of inestimable value were the work of the Poles: before the war they obtained two copies of the German government's Enigma code machine and during the war they supplied key parts of Germany's V-2 rocket.)

Sikorski's was not the only Polish government-in-exile, but was the only one working to liberate Poland from German *and* Soviet imperialism. Moscow's puppet was the Lublin government-in-exile (Polish communists who would return to Warsaw in 1944 virtually in the knapsacks of the Red Army). Naturally the Soviet Union could more easily maintain this puppet régime after the war if the charismatic and brilliant Sikorski were out of the way. And the Soviets must have hated Sikorski for defeating the Bolsheviks outside Warsaw in 1920 and ending for two decades afterward the Soviet threat to Poland.

But was the Soviet Union responsible for Sikorski's death? He died in July, 1943, after an inspection trip of Free Polish Forces fighting alongside the British in North Africa and the Middle East; his Liberator crashed on take-off at Gibraltar. Sikorski's biographer claims that the NKVD had obtained Sikorski's itinerary from Soviet mole Kim Philby, head of MI6 counter-intelligence for the Iberian peninsula.

Supporting the theory that the USSR had rid itself of a troublesome Sikorski was the Katyn Massacre. Some 15,000 Polish military officers had been murdered in 1940, their mass graves near Katyn discovered by the Germans early in 1943. The Germans immediately accused the Soviets, who immediately denied responsibility. In April, 1943, Sikorski showed Churchill persuasive evidence that the Soviets had committed the atrocity. (Churchill didn't question what he called the 'wealth of evidence' but argued with Sikorski that nothing could bring back the dead.) The Polish Cabinet in London, meanwhile, was demanding an enquiry from the International Red Cross, but the Red Cross replied that all parties must request any such enquiry. The USSR would obviously sit this one out, and took the opportunity, further, to sever relations with the Free Poles and blame the massacre on the Germans. More than 40 years later the Soviets admitted that, yes, they *had* done the ghastly deed. What they had done, in murdering most of the Polish officer corps, was to ensure that those men would be unavailable to oppose *Soviet* domination after *German* domination had ended. Back in 1943, though, with the Red Cross effectively blocked on Katyn, and Sikorski effectively silenced on the matter, did Sikorski need to be permanently silenced because of Katyn? By the Soviets? By the *British*?

This last supposition is the thesis of a play written in 1967 by Rolf Hochhuth. Hochhuth's villain in *The Soldiers* is no less than Winston Churchill, who decides in the play to have the Polish general murdered because Sikorski was alienating Stalin so thoroughly (about Katyn) that this ally of Britain might well make a separate peace with Germany. In Hochhuth's view, Churchill's action was for the greater good of the war effort. But the idea that Stalin would seek a separate peace in the summer of 1943 strikes me as unlikely. Stalin's armies had tipped the balance and were starting to win; Stalin wasn't interested in any deals.

If *anyone* planned Sikorski's death, logic suggests that the Soviets did; they stood to gain far more from his removal than did Britain. Perhaps it was a false-flag recruitment; John le Carré, in his introduction to *The Philby Conspiracy*, asks, 'If Sikorski *was* assassinated, is it conceivable that Philby planned the operation on behalf of his Russian masters, and that the assassin whom he hired believed he was working for the British?' Yes, it is conceivable.

Hochhuth claimed to have 'proof' of British involvement, this proof to remain locked in a Swiss bank for 50 years. But we don't need to wait. The Hochhuth thesis was demolished in an extraordinary book by the late Argentine actor and writer, Carlos

Thompson. A friend of Sir Laurence Olivier's, Thompson first read the play when Olivier was considering it for the National Theatre. Thompson offered to bring Hochhuth and Olivier together, translating for them, to allay Olivier's concerns. Thus began Thompson's own quest for the truth, culminating in 1969 in *The Assassination of Winston Churchill* (by which he meant character assassination).

Passionate and literate, the Thompson book shows Hochhuth to be manipulative and self-promoting, wholly without scruples in acquiring and presenting 'facts.' The one person, among dozens, whom Thompson couldn't interview (and the others completely undermined Hochhuth's theory) was the retired MI6 officer whose deposition is supposedly in that Swiss bank; this is the man who supposedly told Hochhuth in a 'slip of the tongue' about British involvement in Sikorski's death! Learning of Hochhuth's many deceits and inventions, one finally doubts whether the MI6 officer ever existed. Thompson's dazzling book persuades even a sceptic like me that the Sikorski crash was *probably* simply an accident.

The Soviets *might* have killed Sikorski to prevent his return to Poland before they could occupy that country. But as it worked out they didn't *need* to. In 1944 the Warsaw uprising saw the Polish resistance annihilated by the Germans as the Red Army stood by – outside Warsaw – and waited for the non-communist Poles to be massacred. And in 1945 the Yalta Conference extended the Soviet frontier westward into what had been prewar Poland and abandoned the Poles to Stalin.

Contemplating the valiant efforts planned here in the Rubens Hotel on behalf of Polish liberation, one can only be sad and angry. Britain and France had entered the war over Polish independence and the Poles had pinned their hopes on the West to guarantee a democratic and independent postwar Poland. But the Poles were sold out. The Western democracies were unwilling to be as tough with Stalin about Poland as they had been with Hitler, and thus the people of Poland (like the people of Hungary, Romania, Bulgaria, Yugoslavia, Albania, Latvia, Lithuania, Estonia, and later Czechoslovakia and East Germany) endured decades of communist enslavement. Stalin, it is often said, was the only winner of WWII.

Cross Buckingham Palace Road and turn into Lower Grosvenor Place. Take the first L, a narrow street called Victoria Square. Just before the tiny paved square, look to the R for

Site 15: **16 Victoria Square.** From 1953 until 1964, when he died at age 56, Ian Fleming lived here with his wife Anne and their young son Caspar. The first of the Bond books, *Casino Royale*, was published a month after the move here from Carlyle Mansions (*see Site 33*). The last of Fleming's Bond books, *The Man with the Golden Gun*, was published after his death. More than 20 million of his books sold during this time.

But, throughout these years, Fleming was often depressed, chasing an elusive happiness. Anne was witty and charmingly outrageous but essentially unsupportive ('those dreadful Bond books,' she called them). In this house she gave frequent dinner parties for people with possibly more literary pretensions, and certainly more literary achievements, than Fleming. He often spent those evenings hiding out at his club. 'The marriage survived one of its rockier moments,' Henry A. Zieger tells us in *Ian Fleming: The Spy Who Came in with the Gold*, 'when Fleming came home one night to find Cyril Connolly reading page proofs of the first Bond book aloud to the assembled multitude with heavily theatrical emphasis which the guests evidently found amusing.' Fleming's friend Malcolm Muggeridge would occasionally be included in Anne's gatherings and, finding them as distasteful as Fleming did, would retreat with him to what Muggeridge calls 'a sort of private apartment at the top of the house' where Fleming kept his 'masculine bric-a-brac.' Here the two would exchange Fleet Street gossip and sip highballs, writes Muggeridge, 'like climbers taking a breather above a mountain torrent whose roar could still faintly be heard in the ravine below.'

Fleming's was a flawed personality. Reviewers have noted the strong connection, in his books, between sex and cruelty. His attitude may have been formed at Eton; the British public school atmosphere is said to consist equally of sadism, snobbery and sodomy. For all that, Fleming seems to have grown up enthusiastically heterosexual – not always the case among fellow alumni. (He attended Sandhurst too, graduating from neither institution, although encouraging people to believe otherwise.)

Very ambitious, he was fortunately very skilled at self-promotion. He made a special effort to get into President Kennedy's good graces and the Bond books only sold well in America after Kennedy included one in a list of books he had enjoyed. Kennedy would obviously have relished these books. Like his father he was a great admirer of arrogant phallicism. Unlike his father he was a great Anglophile.

Fleming was an extraordinary story-teller, his talent more than compensating for his ignorance on many subjects. Whenever he discussed a subject I knew anything about, he was either partially or totally wrong. Like most British writers he was abysmally ignorant about firearms (undoubtedly a consequence of Britain's restrictive laws on firearms). He was also wildly ignorant about American speech. And I've been told by people close to British intelligence operations that he was no more accurate in that area. One can only admire the self-confidence that enabled Fleming to write so blithely those compellingly well-written stories that are no less compelling for being chock-full of howlers. My favourite of his short stories is 'For Your Eyes Only' (which has nothing to do with the film of the same name), probably because it is set in Vermont and because Bond uses a Savage 99, for years my primary deer-hunting rifle. Fleming acquired his knowledge of Vermont by visiting the Vermont home of his friend Ivar Bryce a few miles from my own home. But Fleming knew nothing about Vermont in the late autumn, just before deer season, and seems never to have fired (or even loaded) a Savage 99.

Fleming was driven by complicated love-hate feelings towards America. Undeniably, he felt uneasy about America's wealth and power. In *From Russia with Love*, he has the Russians say that America's bloated intelligence effort is ineffectual while Britain's low-profile service is as successful as it is small − surely a distorted picture of both services. (In 1992 a former head of KGB intelligence listed the top Western intelligence services and didn't even *mention* MI6. Customary disinformation? Or rare candour?)

Leave the square at its SW corner. Turn L into Beeston Place, which becomes Ebury Street. At the SW corner of Ebury Street and Lower Belgrave Street, among the residences-turned-hotels, is

Site 16: **18B Ebury Street.** Robin Winks, professor of history at Yale, tells me that OSS maintained a safe-house here during WWII for X-2, the outfit that provided liaison between the counter-intelligence activities of America's OSS and Britain's SIS. The name X-2

probably echoed (in admiration) Britain's XX or Double Cross or Twenty Committee, which played back dozens of German agents in Britain against their Berlin handlers.

This was a good area for a safe-house, Winks writes in his *Cloak and Gown* (about American scholars in the secret war), in part because 'the general neighborhood, being filled with rooming houses, would not be suspicious of transients.'

Several doors down, at the large Doric columns, is

Site 17: **22A Ebury Street.** In this odd building, described by Ian Fleming's biographer John Pearson as 'a setting rather than a home', the young Fleming spent his first years in London.

The place wasn't a home at all for most of its existence, having started out as a Baptist chapel (in 1830), then becoming successively a school for boys, a nightclub, and a furniture store before being turned into flats during WWII. But it was said to be haunted and the fun-loving Fleming found it irresistible. He redid the central portion with the help of 'a lady interior decorator from Berlin.' His bathroom was in an alcove that once held the altar. His bedroom and dining area were in the gallery. Workmen painted the windowless chapel grey, installed indirect lighting, and filled the skylight with dark-blue glass. Into the centre of this room Fleming moved a large black sofa, and in this gloomy space he kept a fire burning year-round. 'It must have been a lonely and oppressive house,' notes Pearson. But here Fleming pursued the obsessions so clearly manifest in his novels: womanizing, gourmandizing, and gambling. He didn't pursue them long here. When the Blitz damaged the adjacent building (No. 20), Fleming moved to the Dorchester Hotel; it was relatively bombproof and very social besides.

Fleming was then a junior partner in a stock-brokerage firm but said he didn't like finance, didn't understand it, and wasn't good at it. The *idea* of wealth fascinated him (many of his villains have immense wealth) and one detects a hostility mixed with envy, in Fleming/Bond, for such persons. But he had neither the skill nor the desire to acquire great wealth himself − that is, to earn money with money − and when his books brought him undreamt-of riches he was probably as surprised as anyone.

A previous occupant here had been Sir Oswald Mosley of the BUF (*see Site 8*). And after Fleming left, still early in the war, the building became something of an annexe to the Ebury Court Hotel (*see Site 18*); Yvonne Rudellat and several other women who worked there slept here. I don't know whether they changed the decor.

Farther down the block is

Site 18: **the Ebury Court Hotel, 26 Ebury Street.** Still home to the Ebury Court Club and still serving excellent food in a new restaurant named Tophams, this building is much as it was during WWII. Lifts and fire doors have been added and a 'gentle refurbishment' undertaken, but the hotel still has an old-style charm and − like grand hotels such as Claridge's and the Savoy − a coveted 'Red Star' rating from the Automobile Association.

This was a home-from-home during the war for a number of undercover agents. At least 15 hotel guests and club members − possibly more − were with naval or military intelligence, espionage, counter-espionage, Laurence Grand's 'Statistical Research' department, and SOE, writes Stella King in *'Jacqueline': Pioneer*

Site 18: **the Ebury Court Hotel, 26 Ebury Street.**

Heroine of the Resistance. The place had a kind of approval from British Intelligence.

Staff turnover at the hotel was high, as young women left for the wartime forces. The hotel sought a middle-aged secretary for the club, thinking that a woman of this age would not go to war. Yvonne Rudellat was hired. But in the peculiar way that war transforms ordinary people into heroic figures, Rudellat was recruited to SOE by a club member and became, at 45, the third female agent sent into France by SOE – the first sent in by clandestine means. Code-named 'Jacqueline', this native of France did the difficult work of receiving parachute drops and transporting explosives. She was one of two agents who set up and ran the Adolphe sub-network of the Prosper/Physician circuit. When the Germans penetrated Prosper, nearly 1,000 men and women, British and French, were arrested. Many, like Rudellat, died in concentration camps.

I had the pleasure of meeting Diana and Romer Topham here

recently. Mrs Topham came to London just before WWII to help with her brother's bed-and-breakfast place at 24-26 Ebury Street. She never left, buying out his interest when he enlisted, then with her husband (after the war) buying the houses down to No. 32 for the expanding hotel. The Tophams retired in 1989 but stayed on. They tell me that a radio transceiver of unknown provenance was found in the attic of the adjoining No. 34 in the 1970s. Who might have owned and used that equipment? A German agent never caught by MI5? A Soviet 'illegal' transmitting on behalf of some never-discovered *apparat*?

Turn R at Eccleston Street. Two blocks farther, turn R again into tranquil Chester Square. Midway up the street, on your R, is

Site 19: **71 Chester Square.** Hoping that the pen might do what the sword couldn't yet do, HM Government in 1938 created the Joint Broadcasting Committee to send propaganda broadcasts into Germany. JBC operated from this building, producing scripts well before the war and possibly setting up transmitters even inside Germany.

JBC antedated SOE but came from the same impulse and involved some of the same people. It also exhibited the same quaint sense of security; one of its top people, the ebullient Major Laurence Douglas Grand who headed Section D at its inception, wore civilian clothing and called himself 'Major Douglas' whenever he visited here. And very quaintly, JBC's first year was funded in cash – gold sovereigns.

Guy Burgess lived across the square then (*see Site 22*) and is said to have worked on anti-Hitler programmes for JBC, his Soviet handlers having instructed him to drop the pro-Nazi views he had pretended to hold a few months earlier.

How effective was JBC? Even SOE, able to raise a secret army throughout occupied Europe, was unable to foment anti-Hitler activity inside Germany. Despite JBC's earnest efforts, most Germans supported Hitler or at least acquiesced in his rule.

Several houses farther on, at the head of the square, is

Site 20: **77 Chester Square.** Much of the Dutch government-in-exile, including its *Centrale Inlichtingen Dienst* (Central Intelligence Service), worked out of this house during WWII. The building was Queen Wilhelmina's in-town residence; here, an admiring

countryman reported, she 'personally received everyone, regardless of rank or social position, who made it to England from occupied Holland.'

Like most of the governments-in-exile, the Dutch depended on SOE for everything – for all equipment, documents, radio communication with resistance groups, and transportation of agents in and out of the occupied homeland. Imagine the uneasiness of intelligence officers who must depend upon the kindness of strangers in such matters.

And imagine the anger of the Dutch towards the British when, in 1944, it was discovered that the Germans had fully penetrated SOE's Netherlands effort. Many agents and civilians had been captured. Few survived. The *Englandspiel*, as the Germans called this operation, involved every last one of SOE's radio operators in the Netherlands (*see Site 75*).

The Dutch had no alternative but to continue working through SIS and SOE. Now, however, they demanded a real partnership with the chastened British. More agents soon went into the Netherlands (along with weapons, ammunition, and explosives), and the resistance groups of the strengthened Anglo-Dutch partnership were highly effective when the Allies invaded the Netherlands.

Retrace your steps to Eccleston Street and turn R into 'Upstairs, Downstairs' territory. At Eaton Square turn L. On the L side of the street is

Site 21: **32 Eaton Square.** The eminent journalist Arnaud de Borchgrave tells me that this was probably the WWII site of Belgian Military Intelligence; 'most of Eaton Square' was taken up by the Belgian government-in-exile.

Belgium had 65,000 to 70,000 men and women in active resistance in WWII. But operating in Belgium was especially difficult, writes David Stafford in *Britain and European Resistance, 1940-1945*, because of 'the closely guarded coastline, the density of German air defence and security surveillance, and the thickly populated countryside.' For most of 1942, SOE's Belgian networks were completely penetrated by the Germans.

Belgian patriots encountered still another difficulty. The

Site 21: **32 Eaton Square.**

government-in-exile had two distinct services for intelligence and subversion – the *Sûreté de l'Etat*, reporting to the prime minister, and the *Deuxième Section* of the army, reporting to the minister of defence. According to Philip Johns, head of SOE's Belgian Section, each service had direct links to SOE and to SIS. Understandably, writes Johns in *Within Two Cloaks*, there was an 'almost paranoiac suspicion and jealousy' between the two Belgian intelligence services. Nevertheless, the Belgians accomplished two notable successes, each of which helped to shorten the war. They prevented the retreating Germans from destroying the port of Antwerp, and they supplied the uranium for the atom bomb.

Arnaud de Borchgrave's father, working in the *Deuxième Section*, helped to organize the shipment of uranium to the US from the Belgian Congo. (The world's only uranium mine was then at Shinkolobwe in Katanga province.) This capable man, Count Baudouin de Borchgrave d'Altena, also ran a team that selected and trained intelligence agents for Nazi-occupied Belgium. Arnaud de Borchgrave tells me how he discovered his father's activities. He volunteered for intelligence work himself and was summoned to

London to be interviewed by the board headed by his own father! At 15, young de Borchgrave had lied about his age in order to join the Royal Navy — he carried a certificate from his grandmother saying he was the required 17½. In the London interview, he tells me, 'I lied again about my age and my father winked as I stood at attention before his panel.' Rejected as too young to be parachuted behind the lines, young Arnaud reluctantly went back to his ship, the secret of his father's employment now his own secret as well.

Continue down Eaton Square, to Elizabeth Street. Turn L. At Chester Square again, on the L near the church, is

Site 22: **38 Chester Square.** One of Guy Burgess's friends at Cambridge was Victor Rothschild of the great banking family. In 1935, Rothschild persuaded his mother to employ Burgess as an investment adviser for £100 per month — big money then. Burgess

didn't even have to do the work. The financial advice came from Rudolph 'Rolf' Katz, a friend of Burgess, an economist, and (not incidentally) a Comintern agent.

Burgess moved into the top-floor flat here in 1935. Like his friends and fellow communists Maclean and Philby, he now pretended to have abandoned communism in favour of fascism. The Comintern had big plans for these young men, expecting them to rise to positions of power in government. Why didn't they pretend to be Liberals or Labourites or non-politicals? Because the Soviets were convinced that any European governments not already fascist, like Germany and Italy, would soon become so. The Soviets wanted their agents in on the ground floor, so to speak.

Burgess decorated his flat in patriotic red, white and blue. The place was always filthy; even in his early twenties he exhibited the gross personal habits that would continue throughout his life. According to his friend Goronwy Rees (*See Site 23*), Burgess would cook up a loathsome stew of whatever he found in his larder, would take to his bed for the weekend (the malodorous stewpot and some wine bottles on the floor beside the enormous bed), and here he would eat, drink, read and entertain any friends who dropped by.

Burgess at this time was more than an invincibly charming, superficially brilliant (and possibly psychopathic) eccentric. He was already working for Soviet Intelligence, recruiting up-and-coming intellectuals to a growing network. In this flat, he made recruiting pitches to Rees (later in military intelligence) and to Stuart Hampshire (later a brilliant code-breaker). Both denied spying; Hampshire's innocence is now fully accepted, but historians continue to be sceptical about Rees's.

Here, too, Burgess was already acting as a Soviet paymaster. He went to Spain at least once to replenish Philby's funds. And he may have been servicing other agents; Rees noticed 'thick wads of banknotes' in the untidy cupboards.

Leave Chester Square, turning L into the pleasant shopping area of Elizabeth Street. In two small blocks, at Ebury Street again, turn R. On your R is

Site 23: **136 Ebury Street.** During the 1930s this was the home of

Site 23: **136 Ebury Street.**

Goronwy Rees, a young Welsh intellectual and long-time friend of Guy Burgess; in *A Chapter of Accidents*, Rees tells of the many evenings the two spent drinking and talking far into the night, at Burgess's flat (*see Site 22*) or here. His book is less an autobiography than an account of this friendship.

One evening in 1936, Rees recalls, the two were sharing a bottle of Jameson's here when Burgess announced, 'I want to tell you that I am a Comintern agent, and have been ever since I came down from Cambridge.' He then tried to recruit Rees, telling him that Anthony Blunt, whom Rees admired, was also a Soviet agent.

Rees says he declined the invitation. Further, he says, he came to believe that Burgess had lied about being a Soviet agent — or that if Burgess *had* been a Soviet agent, he wasn't one any longer. Rees tells an odd story in this connection. As a military intelligence officer in WWII, he was entrusted with the final plans for D-Day, assigned to take them round to the commanders-in-chief of the British services for initialling. As he travelled across London (by taxi!), he realized that he could easily make the detour to Burgess's flat in Bentinck

Street (*see Site 83*) and place this Every Spy's Dream squarely in his friend's hands. *Then* he would find out whether Burgess was a Soviet agent! He didn't do it, he says, mainly because he had already decided that Burgess was above suspicion. What convinced him? For one thing, Burgess didn't conceal his Soviet sympathies; for another, 'an extremely important member of the security services' often present in the Bentinck Street flat 'on terms of the most intimate friendship' — Liddell, undoubtedly — seemed to have no concern about Burgess. (Indeed!) Can we believe any of Rees's story? Rees was never 'a consistent witness', Penrose and Freeman tell us in *Conspiracy of Silence*. Spy memoirs often shed new darkness on the past.

A number of people have been convinced that Rees became a Soviet agent. John Costello has quoted novelist Rosamond Lehmann as being certain that Rees was working for the Soviets. (Good leftist that she was, she kept her own counsel for decades. Only after the 1951 defection of Burgess and Maclean did she tell the authorities of Rees's 1936 claim that Burgess had tried to recruit him.) More recently, with access to NKVD files, Costello has named Rees as a founding member of an Oxford ring operating in the 1930s. Anthony Blunt, who probably headed the Cambridge ring, told Nigel West that Rees had indeed been recruited but had resigned in 1939 after the Nazi-Soviet Pact, promising not to betray his comrades to MI5. West believes that Rees maintained contact with the KGB until at least 1964. Whatever the date, would the Soviets have let Rees simply resign? Once a person worked for the communists, he was theirs for life.

Did he keep any promise not to talk? In April, 1951, shortly before Maclean and Burgess disappeared into the Soviet Union, a drunken and disintegrating Maclean confronted Rees in a London bar and said, 'I know all about you. You used to be one of us, but you ratted.' Whether Rees talked to MI5 *before* Burgess and Maclean fled, he surely did so *afterwards*. But first he talked with an old friend of Burgess — Anthony Blunt! Blunt tried to dissuade Rees from telling MI5 of Burgess's connection to Soviet Intelligence, eventually invoking (according to Rees) 'E. M. Forster's famous statement that if he had to choose between betraying his country or betraying his friend, he hoped he would have the courage to betray his country.'

When Blunt couldn't dissuade Rees, the two friends parted; in a masterpiece of understatement, Rees writes that Blunt 'did not disguise his disapproval of what I was going to do.'

After Burgess and Maclean appeared publicly in Moscow, leaving no doubt as to their geographical or ideological whereabouts, Rees wrote anonymously and sensationally for a popular tabloid about his relationship with Burgess. Subsequently revealed as the author, Rees was dismissed from the University College of Wales (where he was principal). I think he lost his job not because his academic colleagues thought his claim of innocence was a lie but because he had told some discomforting truths.

Site 24: **Ebury House, 39 Elizabeth Street.**

Retrace your path to Elizabeth Street. At the SE corner of Elizabeth Street and Ebury Street is

Site 24: **Ebury House, 39 Elizabeth Street.** Many extraordinary personalities worked in MI9, Britain's escape-and-evasion organization in WWII, and none more extraordinary than Airey Neave. Wounded and captured during the British retreat to Dunkirk, Neave failed twice to escape from POW camps before he broke out of 'escape-proof' Colditz. He made his way to neutral Switzerland and hurried back to Britain. Debriefed by MI9, he was immediately taken on by the organization and soon became chief organizer of MI9's escape networks, exfiltrating some 5,000 Allied personnel from occupied Europe. During his service with MI9 he lived here and interviewed agents in a flat belonging to his wife's aunt.

Neave later became a Member of Parliament. He wrote easily about his world; his most engaging books are about the escape from Colditz (*They Have Their Exits*) and the achievements of MI9 (*Saturday at MI9*). His writing reflects a modesty and understatement one thinks of as typical of his class and generation.

He was killed by an IRA car-bomb in 1979.

Turn R at Elizabeth Street. You'll pass the lower end of massive Victoria Station on your L. Six short blocks later, on St George's Drive, you'll reach Warwick Square. Turn L. At the head of the square, on Belgrave Road, is

Site 25: **76 Warwick Square.** The identity of the elusive Fifth Man was finally revealed in 1990 by Soviet defector Oleg Gordievsky and confirmed by the man himself, Glasgow-born John Cairncross.

The West had long speculated about the identity of the fifth member of the Cambridge ring. The first and second, as usually identified, were Maclean and Burgess; the third and fourth were Philby and Blunt. With newly opened NKVD files, however, it would appear that Philby and not Burgess was the principal recruiter. Burgess was simply the scapegoat. Thus, John Costello and his collaborator Oleg Tsarev (formerly a KGB colonel, now a consultant to Russia's Foreign Intelligence Service) establish a new order of

Site 25: **76 Warwick Square.**

recruitment in their 1993 book *Deadly Illusions*: Philby, Maclean, Burgess, Blunt, Straight, Cairncross. (Cairncross will remain the Fifth Man in the public perception.)

MI5 had known something about Cairncross as early as 1951, when his handwritten notes were found in Burgess's flat. Cairncross was allowed quietly to resign his government post and leave the country – 'greatly to the discredit of MI5,' writes Chapman Pincher. Then came Blunt's secret confession in 1964. 'It was no doubt because Blunt rather despised Cairncross,' writes Pincher, that he delivered the socially inferior Cairncross to MI5 'while doing all he could to guard his real friends.' Cairncross, in his own 'confession' to MI5 at this time, stuck by his earlier story that he had given information to the Soviets only during the war.

In 1979, when Barrie Penrose and David Leitch revealed Cairncross's spying in *The Sunday Times* (after remarkable sleuthing by Penrose), it was assumed that he had been 'small fry' as Pincher writes in *Their Trade Is Treachery* (1981). Exactly how big a fish he was, however, was revealed by Andrew and Gordievsky in *KGB: The Inside Story* (1990). Cairncross was definitely part of the

Cambridge ring recruited in the 1930s, they write; his achievements were 'the equal of any of the Five except Philby.'

Yuri Modin, former controller of the ring, spoke up a year later from Moscow: Cairncross played only a minor role as one of the Cambridge spies and in any case 'the Five' weren't a team at all. They were simply the five singled out in 1943 to receive top priority in processing their information. And now Cairncross spoke up from the south of France. Yes, he was the Fifth Man. But the label was less important than the details: he had worked alone, he had merely helped a wartime ally. Modin, alas, had disclosed that he was running Cairncross *until 1951* (when, he said, the sudden disappearance of Burgess and Maclean made it too dangerous to continue – actually, when someone tipped off the Soviets that Cairncross was being watched). All right, said Cairncross, amending his fishy story of years earlier, he had given the Soviets some 'gossip' after the war but he hadn't been a dedicated communist since 1936.

John Cairncross had been a scholarship student at Cambridge, brilliant in languages, an overt communist until he was spotted by Blunt and recruited by Klugmann. In 1936, still at Cambridge, he was instructed to quit the Party and drop his plans for an academic career in favour of a career in the Foreign Office. When he entered the FO in 1936, he lived here in Warwick Square.

For the next 15 years Cairncross served his government *and* the Soviets. At the FO the awkward Glaswegian made a point of asking people to lunch and giving detailed notes to the NKVD about the long luncheon conversations (he ate very slowly). In 1938 his controller told him to move to the Treasury; apparently the NKVD hadn't yet penetrated that department, and in any event Cairncross's social ineptness would hamper a diplomatic career. At the Treasury, the reports he passed to the NKVD through Burgess included descriptions of various officials, Pincher tells us, 'written as though by a talent scout giving information about character weaknesses and other features that might be exploited.' (These handwritten notes, later found in Burgess's flat, went by chance to an MI5 officer whose secretary recognized the hand – she had been Cairncross's secretary!)

In 1940 Cairncross became private secretary to Lord Hankey, who had access to all Cabinet papers and chaired a number of committees on secret matters. 'The earliest intelligence on the Anglo-American decision to build an atom bomb probably came from Cairncross' at this time, Andrew and Gordievsky assert. (This assertion has been disputed on both sides of what was once the Iron Curtain.) Moving to GC&CS at Bletchley Park in 1942, Cairncross seems to have supplied Ultra material to the Soviets, thus (with others) compromising the great secret of Britain's code-breaking success. In 1944 he moved to MI6 (suggesting that the USSR had other assets at Bletchley) and provided crucial information on Allied plans for Yugoslavia. After the war he returned to the Treasury to leak documents on defence until 1951.

Now past 80, Cairncross has spent more than 40 years outside Britain. He had been induced to come back, briefly, to help MI5 in its efforts to get confessions from Klugmann and others; if the efforts had succeeded, Cairncross would have been allowed to stay permanently. The efforts 'failed miserably,' reports Wright, 'and Cairncross was forced back into exile.' (Klugmann continued to help the USSR in every way he could within the CPGB, until his death in 1977, and two others whom Cairncross identified as KGB assets were still in positions of prominence when Pincher referred to them − anonymously − in 1981.)

Some MPs have demanded the extradition and trial of Cairncross, but I suspect he will be the fourth of the 'Magnificent Five' to die in exile. Only Blunt lived out his life in London and, as any number of outraged citizens and embarrassed officials know full well, none of the Five ever came to trial. I am glad that at least one of them lived long enough to see the downfall of Soviet communism and the end of the Soviet empire.

You are equidistant, here, from Pimlico and Victoria tube stations. For the next walk, choose Victoria: one stop to Sloane Square.

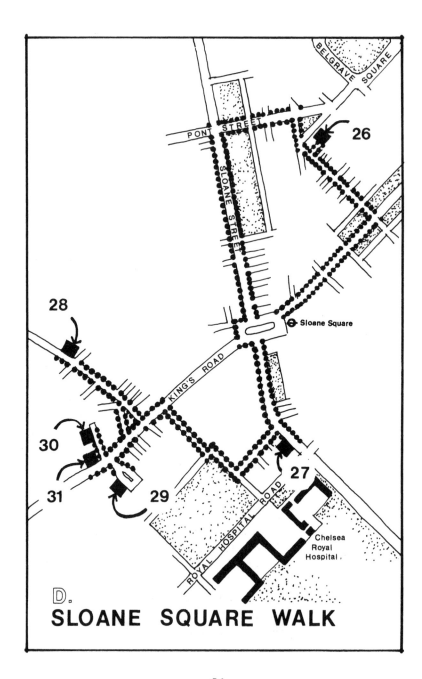

26

Sloane Square

28

PONT STREET

SLOANE STREET

BELGRAVE SQUARE

KING'S ROAD

30

31

29

27

ROYAL HOSPITAL ROAD

Chelsea
Royal
Hospital

D.
SLOANE SQUARE WALK

D. SLOANE SQUARE WALK

From Sloane Square tube station, turn immediately to your R. Cliveden Place becomes Eaton Gate as you approach Eaton Square. Turn into Lyall Street and continue four or five small blocks to Chesham Close. Step into the ample courtyard of

Site 26: **Chesham House, Chesham Close.** This was the Soviet Embassy in the late 1920s when the Comintern was interfering heavy-handedly in Britain's internal affairs. Astonishing as it may seem now, communists then expected the rest of the world to fall into their hands as easily as Russia had. True believers expected merely to nudge the Forces of History along by sharpening the class conflict and by engaging in a little military and industrial espionage.

Diplomatic relations between Britain and the USSR were complicated by the fact that the Soviet Union had a controlling link to a British political party. The USSR subsidized the Communist Party of Great Britain and was often caught recruiting intelligence agents from Party membership. Complicating things further was the fact that the Soviet Union viewed its commercial relations with the world as an extension of its subversive and intelligence activities. Britain couldn't pretend that the USSR was like any other nation with which it had diplomatic and commercial intercourse.

And Britain resorted to action not customary with any other nation. In 1927 when decrypted messages showed that the All Russian Co-operative Society (Arcos) and the Soviet Trade Delegation were involved in subversive activities, the Secretary of State for War obtained permission to search their combined premises (*see Site 92*). The ensuing 'Arcos raid' provided firm proof of subversion and of the use of diplomatic cover to conceal it. Britain immediately broke diplomatic ties.

When the embassy reopened in 1929, the Soviets promptly stepped up subversive activity again, producing the mutiny at the Royal Navy base at Invergordon barely a year later.

Site 26: **Chesham House, Chesham Close.**

Keep to the L side of the triangular 'square' where Lyall Street joins Chesham Place. Turn L into Pont Street and L at Sloane Street. Enjoy the upscale shops, and the gardens bounded by Cadogan Place. Sit a while in Sloane Square. Continue into Lower Sloane Street and marvel at the symmetry of this architecture: if a turret or griffin's head appears at one end of a wide façade, expect to see a repeat at the other end, and at suitable points in between. Somewhere along here is an address I know simply as

Site 27: **Lower Sloane Street.** A British intelligence network in Holland – the WL Bureau – was headquartered in Lower Sloane Street during WWI. I do not know precisely where, but my guess is the large building now occupied by the Sloane Club; all other buildings nearby would seem to have been exclusively residential.

Headed by Major Edmund A. Wallinger and based in London (hence its name, WL), this intelligence service was one of two serving the British Expeditionary Force. The other, headed by Major Cecil A. Cameron, was based in Folkestone (hence *its* name, CF). And each of these was separate from the Secret Service. In theory, the more services the better – competition would produce better results, and compartmentation would limit any damage from enemy penetration. In actuality, there was such 'poaching on each other's preserves' (as historian Michael Occleshaw reports in *Armour Against Fate: British Military Intelligence in the First World War*) as to produce warfare among the services almost as bitter as the larger warfare among nations. An observer noted unhappily that Wallinger and Cameron 'seem to be running the same show only separately. This was not the original idea.'

The idea, of course, was to get as much information out of Europe as possible, not only on the location and movement of enemy troops but also on enemy morale. This information came from some 80 spy rings in occupied Belgium, France and Luxembourg. (Wallinger noted that his 'best transmission is by a Belgian who has a hold on a German officer in Brussels. The latter goes to Holland once a week for unnatural purposes, and our Belgian got to know of this, and threatens to denounce him.') Then, too, Britain exploited the German soldier's interest in morphine and cocaine. Obtaining the approval of no less than the Prime Minister, British intelligence agents distributed drugs liberally to the guards on the Belgian-Dutch frontier. The border became altogether porous. People crossed easily from occupied Belgium to neutral Holland; propaganda materials made the reverse trip.

Information left Belgium in false bottoms of milk churns, in the axle-box of the lone train that crossed daily into Holland, and most ingeniously in lengths of knitting: plain stitches for the coaches carrying soldiers, and purl stitches for the coaches carrying horses. Train-watching was a vast (and vastly important) operation.

During these years the Dutch assisted the British greatly by giving British agents covert access to some 90,000 interned German deserters. Vital information on the situation in Germany came also from British infiltration of German refugee groups in Holland. But the efforts of GHQ services in neutral Holland during WWI were costly, giving the Nazis a ready excuse to invade neutral Holland in 1940.

Turn in at Turks Row, then R at Franklin's Row. For a detour, turn L at Franklin's Row to visit Christopher Wren's Chelsea Royal Hospital, home of the Chelsea Pensioners. Scan the surrounding wall for the loose brick behind which the KGB's Yuri Modin placed messages and cash for his agents. Guy Burgess didn't care for this 'dead letter box' (I can see why: it was far too exposed) and Modin often had to retrieve the stuff himself. Allow time, too, for the National Army Museum, one block farther along Royal Hospital Road. To skip all detours, follow Franklin's Row to Cheltenham Terrace and turn L at King's Road, the street that launched the mini-skirt and still purveys the styles that shock. Turn R at Anderson Street. On Sloane Avenue, just beyond Whitehead's Grove, is

Site 28: **Nell Gwynn House.**

Site 28: **Nell Gwynn House.** The capable Philip Johns, who was unusual in having worked both for SIS and SOE, lived here during the 1940s. He had served with SIS outside Britain, then was brought back to London to head SOE's Belgian Section. After the *Englandspiel* disaster (*see Site 75*) his responsibility expanded to include Dutch Section. He also served with the Air Raid Wardens on the roof here, during the Blitz, ready with sand buckets to smother incendiary bombs.

SOE was compelled to employ at least some SIS people, because of their experience in intelligence work or their knowledge of the target countries, but many in SIS considered SOE a bunch of bungling amateurs and many in SOE considered SIS a pack of tradition-bound incompetents. In fact, a real and substantial conflict of interest existed between the two organizations. 'Their functions were different,' Nigel West writes in *MI6*; 'SIS was the information gatherer who felt that its role was "to watch enemy troops crossing a bridge" whilst SOE's brief was sabotage, "to blow up the bridge to prevent army movements." ' SIS people would necessarily be put at risk by SOE people. A notable lack of cordiality prevailed between the two organizations.

Retrace your steps down Sloane Avenue. Turn R into Elystan Place and L into Tryon Street to return to King's Road. Two small blocks down King's Road, on your L, are the grand terrace houses of Wellington Square. Facing the centre of the square, on the R, is

Site 29: **30 Wellington Square.** Ian Fleming never specified where James Bond lived, beyond placing his flat in a little square in Chelsea off King's Road. It was John Pearson – who was commissioned after Fleming's death to write Bond's authorized biography (an interesting literary conceit) – who located Bond at this address. If, in fact, the sleek and soigné Commander Bond had lived here during the 1950s or 1960s, he would scarcely have enjoyed the place recently. Imagine his thoughts on walking out his front door and finding himself among scores of aggressively unattractive young people, their hair hideous in shape and colour, their ears and noses pierced with safety pins. Knowing enough about truly violent people, and being one himself, Bond might not have been alarmed by these spaced-out punk-rockers

Site 29: **30 Wellington Square.**

(who are mostly rather well-behaved working-class kids). I wonder, though, whether Bond might not have moved his residence before long.

Like the area around Wellington Square, Bond also changed over the years. In the first of the Bond books, Fleming sought to make 007 as bland as possible. In successive books he developed Bond's quirkiness, giving him preferences and opinions that were mostly, I suspect, Fleming's own (preferring martinis shaken and not stirred, disliking shoes that lace). In the last books, Fleming expressed through the Bond character his own depressive morbidness, revealing an attitude unimaginable to the younger Bond — or to the younger and healthier Fleming.

The books changed in other ways. The early ones were akin to the tales of Somerset Maugham, Phillips Oppenheim, and other British writers of spy fiction of that era, with some verisimilitude as to the scale of Bond's organization and its operations. But as the Bond books became trendy and 'mass-cultch' they began to resemble the worst of science fiction. The plots (and for that matter the locales and characters) are increasingly grotesque. The first book, *Casino*

Royale, is possibly believable. *Live and Let Die* is less so. By the time we get to *Moonraker*, we must suspend disbelief almost totally, and *The Man with the Golden Gun* finally goes so far beyond the believable as to be almost uninteresting.

The film Bond (whether portrayed by Connery or his successors) is the later Bond. What happened, I think, was that Fleming wrote his first book without having the movies in mind. By the time he sold *Dr No* to the film producers, he was thinking very much of the film audience, writing a far more gaudy character – leeringly lubricious – and a far more gaudy book. The movies, of course, are deliberate spoofs. Fleming would probably have preferred to have the movies as serious as his earlier books, but he was not the sort to argue with money or success, and the Bond films had the formula for both.

With all the trappings removed, the Bond books are basically about a Briton who *wins*, at a time when Britons were not winning. When Fleming has Bond defeating Le Chiffre at the gambling casino (thereby defunding him), he is putting into print one of his more telling fantasies. After the war he encouraged acquaintances to believe that he had tried to defund some German agents in Lisbon but had failed. Significantly, he doesn't let Bond fail. Looking at all the defeats, major and minor, of the British intelligence services – at the hands of Nazis, Soviet agents, Irish nationalists, and anti-British elements throughout the Empire and Commonwealth – one sees Bond's fictional victories in a new light.

Across King's Road is Bywater Street, its pastel-coloured houses suggesting a climate more southerly than London's. Mid-block, on the L, is

Site 30: **9 Bywater Street.** Only two fictional sites appear in this book (to the best of my knowledge!) and this is the second one. According to *Smiley's Circus* by David Monaghan, this is where George Smiley and his unfaithful wife lived from about 1950 to about 1973. It is here that Ann has several affairs, usually (but not always) while George is overseas. After their separation George stays on in the house.

Site 30: **9 Bywater Street.**

Some reviewers have conjectured that John le Carré (David Cornwell) modelled Smiley on Sir Maurice Oldfield, head of MI6 between 1973 and 1978. Indeed, Smiley and Oldfield shared the same podgy and bookish appearance, the same mild and self-effacing manner, the same habit of playing with their eyeglasses. And when Alec Guinness was preparing for the television version of *Tinker, Tailor, Soldier, Spy*, Cornwell introduced him to Oldfield. Guinness was fascinated by Oldfield's mannerisms but apparently drew his interpretation of Smiley from deeper sources. Cornwell himself explains that the model for Smiley was someone else entirely, a teacher of his at Oxford.

Cornwell, however, surely based his fictional organization (The Circus) on his own experience. He had done his National Service with the British Army of Occupation in Austria; fluent in German, he was posted to Intelligence. Afterward, he taught at Eton and was a free-lance artist (illustrating Maxwell Knight's *Talking Birds*, among other things), before being recruited to MI5 (possibly by Knight). He was then a case-officer for MI6 under Foreign Office cover. Not until the 1963 publication of his third novel, *The Spy Who Came in from the Cold*, did he feel able to spend all his time writing.

Le Carré obviously wanted to create an alternative to Fleming's *oeuvre*; le Carré's books are more realistic, less glamorous, more novelistic. They have character development and insight. They are simply better written. But while I admire le Carré's novels as literature, I am uneasy about his acquiescence to the notion of moral equivalence between the Western democracies and the communist dictatorships. And I am irritated by his anti-Americanism. Still, he is a good story-teller, and if one reads his works as entertainments, not documentaries, one is seldom disappointed.

Back on King's Road, just W of Bywater Street is the building-society branch that was, until a few years ago,

Site 31: **the Markham Arms pub, King's Road.** This was Kim Philby's habitual pub, his 'local' when he lived in Carlyle Square. And it was probably the site of an important meeting with Anthony Blunt in 1954. The Soviets waited three years after Burgess and Maclean fled

before re-establishing contact with Philby. They made subtle contact first with Blunt at the Courtauld (*see Site 82*). Blunt then made a lunch date with Philby; reasonable enough: the two had known each other for years. The restaurant where they met was crowded so they walked down King's Road and had a pub lunch, almost certainly here. Over drinks and lunch, Blunt gave Philby the details for Philby's subsequent meeting with Soviet intelligence officer Yuri Modin — a meeting at which Modin gave the unemployed Philby £5,000 and, I imagine, as much encouragement as their hurried street encounter would allow.

To conclude this walk, return on King's Road to Sloane Square underground. In the 1960s, so Spycatcher *tells us, an unfurnished upstairs flat in a mews house in Pavilion Road served as headquarters for the unprecedented MI5 investigation of its deputy head, Graham Mitchell. Elsewhere in this area (in an 'MI6 safe house near Sloane Square',* Spycatcher *tells us), Philby was interrogated in 1955. Well, not really interrogated: he was taken 'gently over familiar ground' by former colleagues from MI6, supplied with acceptable answers, and virtually whitewashed preparatory to Macmillan's clearance of him in the House of Commons. The interview was recorded by equipment under a floorboard, and the signal was fed by telephone back to Leconfield House where selected MI5 officers listened in outrage. If you have stamina for the next walk, leave the erstwhile Markham Arms and walk farther down King's Road, following Oakley Street to the river. Donald Maclean had a bed-sitter somewhere in Oakley Street, I am told, when he came down from Cambridge and started his twin careers with Moscow Centre and the Foreign Office.*

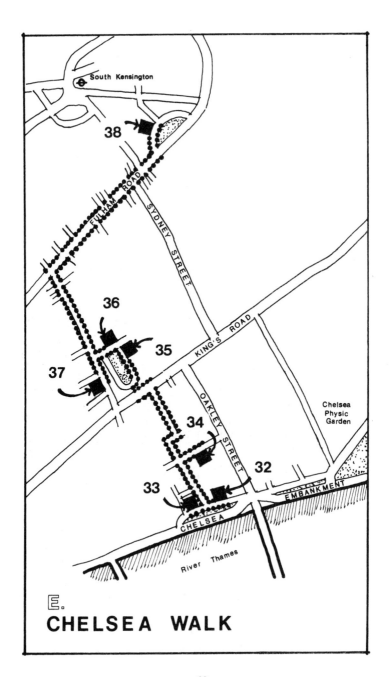

South Kensington

38

FULHAM ROAD

SYDNEY STREET

36

35

37

KING'S ROAD

34

OAKLEY STREET

Chelsea
Physic
Garden

33

32

EMBANKMENT

CHELSEA

River Thames

E.
CHELSEA WALK

E. CHELSEA WALK

Artists, writers, and other notables have long been drawn to the attractive neighbourhood of Chelsea. Take a bus down King's Road and walk towards the river on Oakley Street. Turn R into Cheyne Walk. Behind a 16th-century garden wall is

Site 32: **Shrewsbury House, 42 Cheyne Walk.** More than 40 years after the retirement of Guy Liddell (who lived here), 'a strong circumstantial case can be made' that this man who was deputy director-general of MI5 from 1947 to 1952 was nothing less than 'the most successful mole of all.' The accusation is John Costello's in *Mask of Treachery* (1988) and he is not alone. Richard Deacon, in *The Greatest Treason: The Bizarre Story of Hollis, Liddell and Mountbatten* (1989) argues that the highly placed Soviet agent inside MI5 was not Hollis but Liddell. In Costello's view, the 'probability'

of Liddell's guilt doesn't absolve Hollis, or Mitchell either, because of 'anomalies' occurring after Liddell's retirement. In fact, Liddell brought both Hollis and Mitchell into MI5, as also (what a record!) he brought Blunt and Harris into MI5 and indirectly (with Blunt and Harris) brought Burgess into MI5 and (with Burgess and Harris) brought Philby into MI6.

What are the 'anomalies' in Liddell's 33 years in counter-intelligence (first, briefly, with Special Branch and then with MI5)? Costello's 'partial list' includes an astounding 21 items: 'operational mishaps' and a 'puzzling string of failures' for which the only explanations suggesting themselves to Costello are 1) bad luck approaching the incomprehensible, 2) incompetence bordering on criminal negligence, or 3) treachery.

Costello's 21 items include both active and passive acts that can be laid at Liddell's door: alerting Arcos to the impending raid (*see Site 92*); failing to arrest Maly and Brandes (*see Site 79*) who ran the Woolwich Arsenal ring; failing to keep track of Jürgen Kuczynski and Klaus Fuchs (*see Sites 95 and 90*), although warned by MI6 that both were communist activists; failing to apprehend the Soviet agent who was running Captain King in the FO (*see Site 50*); failing to put 'Sonya' under surveillance in 1947 (*see Site 95*); failing to make a proper search for the mole identified by Gouzenko as 'Elli' (*see Site 54*); taking two years to look for 'Homer' in the FO in Washington (*see Site 78*); leaking the news to Blunt about the imminent interrogation of Maclean (*see Site 120*); colluding with Blunt to keep Rees from talking to MI5 after the Burgess-Maclean disappearances (*see Site 23*); and alerting the Soviets to the surveillance of Cairncross in 1951 (*see Site 25*). And these account for less than half of Costello's 'partial list'!

Deacon, who concurs in many of these, adds a few more: failing to find 'Scott' in the FO (*see Site 50*), ensuring that Foote was isolated (*see Site 58*), and using his influence 'to smear and destroy' anyone looking for Soviet agents inside MI5. More recently, from *The Observer* in 1991, comes a crucial item pointing to Liddell; an early 1950s investigation of security risks among Eastern European immigrants turned up information that the 'art adviser to the King' had worked for Soviet Intelligence. A reference to Blunt, of course. Nothing new there. But this information about Blunt went nowhere after it reached *Liddell*. (Much earlier, it was also probably Liddell who was silent when told that Blunt had bragged about giving every MI5 name to the Soviets.)

Sir Maurice Oldfield, head of MI6, strongly suspected Liddell; he would have put Liddell 'at the top of the list' in the molehunt within MI5. But Sir Dick White, who succeeded Liddell in MI5 both as director of counter-espionage and as deputy director-general (and who went on to head MI5 and later MI6), called the accusation 'the most awful rotten nonsense.' Nor do defectors resolve the matter. Clues from would-be defector Volkov and from actual defector Gouzenko make Liddell 'a better "fit" than either Hollis or Mitchell' for the mole within MI5, thinks Costello. But another defector, Oleg Gordievsky, puts Liddell among the 'mistakenly accused' in Britain's extensive molehunt.

One can't prove (or disprove) a negative. And since Liddell didn't defect, didn't leave notes in his own handwriting in the flat of someone who did defect, didn't have his duplicity revealed by someone who defected from the other side, and didn't confess, one can't prove that he was anything but a loyal (although 'very odd') public servant with a very odd choice of friends (*see Site 83*).

Peter Wright has written that the detection of espionage is mostly a matter of intuition, since evidence is so often lacking. Wright never really looked at Liddell. (Why not, one wonders.) Looking at Liddell today and applying Wright's criterion, I am more than attentive to Costello's conclusion that Guy Maynard Liddell may well have been 'the "grandfather" Soviet mole.'

Continue W on Cheyne Walk. The grand Victorian building just past Cheyne Row is

Site 33: **Carlyle Mansions, Cheyne Walk.** Newly married, Ian Fleming moved into a river-view flat on the third floor (above T. S. Eliot) in 1952.

Fleming had known his wife for a dozen years, through many of his other love affairs. She was Lady Rothermere when she had a child by Fleming; the baby died at birth. She was pregnant again by Fleming when Lord Rothermere divorced her. This child, Caspar Fleming, also died young — of a drug overdose in his teens.

Site 33: **Carlyle Mansions, Cheyne Walk.**

Fleming joked that he began writing novels to take his mind off the shock of marrying at the age of 44. To call the Bond books a diversion is, I think, a classic piece of disinformation, part of the Old Etonian image that Fleming affected of immediate and effortless success at anything he touched. John Pearson observes in *The Life of Ian Fleming* that Fleming carefully built a network of literary people who would support his novelistic efforts when he was ready. Undoubtedly, too, the soon-to-be Anne Fleming exerted formidable pressure on the man she was marrying, to the end that he should make his mark in the field of letters and not the field of finance. (Fleming had been in journalism but primarily in the business end of it.)

In January, 1952, he and Anne were at his Jamaican retreat, her divorce imminent. Full of foreboding about the marriage, Fleming began writing *Casino Royale*. He finished a draft in seven weeks. In his bedroom here at Carlyle Mansions he revised the manuscript, with characteristic *panache* using a gold-plated typewriter ordered from America. The book went into its first printing, a cautious 7,000 copies, in April, 1953. By then Fleming had returned to Jamaica for his annual retreat and had finished *Live and Let Die*— in 12 fewer days than the first book. The characters were established by then. 'M' was modelled after Admiral John Godfrey, Fleming's wartime boss. Pearson reveals that Fleming often called his mother 'M' and that she gave young Ian the same 'grudging praise' and 'terrifying blame' dished out to Bond by the fictional 'M.' Miss Moneypenny was based on Miss Pettigrew, secretary to Menzies. And Bond owes his name to the author of a bird book on Fleming's breakfast table in Jamaica. Fleming had wanted a superlatively colourless name for 007 and happily appropriated this one. 'The name later became so associated with adventure and excitement,' Henry A. Zieger writes in his biography of Fleming, that the ornithologist's wife wrote to Fleming, 'thanking him for using it.'

The fictional Bond is not the real Fleming, despite Fleming's statement that with *Goldfinger* he was writing 'the next volume of my autobiography.' To John Pearson, the Bond character is 'Fleming's dream of a self that might have been – a tougher, stronger, more effective, duller, far less admirable character than the real Fleming.' Today Fleming might be described as an intelligence 'wannabe.' He carried a commando knife and a teargas pen during WWII while working safely behind a desk in London, and he subsequently encouraged people to think he'd been involved in wartime matters of great danger and drama. The plot of *Casino Royale*, for example, came from a gambling experience that Fleming said he'd had himself – Fleming pitted against a group of Nazis. The real evening was nothing of the sort: the 'Nazis' were Portuguese, the stakes were low, and Fleming played on in the almost-empty casino until he was completely cleaned out.

Farther down Cheyne Walk, Turner painted the Thames and Whistler painted his mother. Retrace your steps and turn in at Cheyne Row. At Upper Cheyne Row, turn R. On your R is

Site 34: **19 Upper Cheyne Row.** In this house, the British businessman Greville Wynne maintained his home and small exporting business. 'The company's main asset' (Nigel West tells us in *Seven Spies Who Changed the World*), 'the longest articulated truck ever built in England, had been paid for in full by SIS so as to provide Wynne with suitable cover: a mobile trade fair demonstrating British goods in Eastern Europe.'

It was Wynne who was approached by GRU officer Oleg Penkovsky in Moscow in 1961; Penkovsky's earlier approaches to several Americans and a Canadian had been rebuffed. It was Wynne who for almost 18 months helped the GRU officer deliver some of his material to Anglo-American Intelligence (*see Site 76*). Wynne was arrested on 2 November, 1962, in Budapest shortly after Penkovsky's arrest in Moscow. Sentenced in 1963 to eight years in the Soviet prison and forced-labour system, Wynne was exchanged a year later for Konon Molody (*see Site 88*). He returned to England a wrecked man.

During Wynne's service to SIS, the Soviet delegations visiting him here were impressed by his fitted carpet, his air-conditioning, his cocktail bar. They were impressed too by his business zeal and his ability to bring together British entrepreneurs and Soviet functionaries. Wynne enjoyed his dual role. He later wrote, 'What excited me more than anything else was the opportunity I was going to have to work closely with the "Establishment" and be one of the select individuals who are trusted with their country's secrets. Call it vanity, if you like. It was something akin to knowing that the most exclusive club in the world had accepted me for membership.'

Wynne had a 'tendency to invention' as Nigel West delicately puts it. Wynne apparently grew up in a poor Welsh mining village, his father a foreman in an engineering works that made equipment for the collieries. But he did *not* begin his espionage career by exposing a German spy in Britain in 1938; no such person existed, according to Nigel West in *Seven Spies*. (Nor did Wynne work for MI5 during the war.) He did *not* exfiltrate Major 'Kuznov' from Odessa in 1959; again, no such person existed. He did *not* attend a London meeting of 20 Soviet defectors supposedly gathered to greet Penkovsky in 1961; such a meeting would have been an outrageous breach of security. He did *not* escort Penkovsky to Washington to meet President Kennedy in 1961; such an expedition would have been quite inappropriate and, as Nigel West concludes, couldn't have occurred in the way that Wynne recounted. There's more. As Jerrold L. Schecter and Peter S. Deriabin reveal in their 1992 book on Penkovsky, *The Spy Who Saved the World*, MI6 did *not* plan to have Wynne exfiltrate Penkovsky from Budapest, much less in the supposed secret compartment of Wynne's mobile exhibition. And although Wynne doesn't mention it, SIS seems to have warned him against going to Budapest to meet Penkovsky in November, 1962. (Penkovsky hadn't been heard from in weeks; Western Intelligence rightly feared he had been arrested.)

Wynne wrote about Penkovsky in *The Man from Moscow* (1967) and about 'Kuznov' in *The Man from Odessa* (1981). The first book was ghost-written by his novelist brother-in-law; the second was written with help from another professional writer. Both are 'good reads' but are marred by Wynne's almost pathological propensity to embroider on the truth. Nigel West suggests that Wynne suffered not only from his Soviet prison ordeal but also from a 'post-usefulness syndrome.' When Wynne's grandiose claims finally began to collapse, he brought a series of lawsuits 'against almost anybody who wrote about him' (West observes), none of which he won and most of which he abandoned before they even came to trial.

Wynne's years after the Soviets released him were difficult – a physical and nervous breakdown; two divorces; several disappointing business ventures; a severe drinking problem. He moved from the Canary Islands to Malta to Mallorca, living on the $213,700 provided by British and American Intelligence. In 1990, when he died, he was growing roses for export.

Greville Wynne was part of what the CIA has called 'the most productive classic clandestine operation ever conducted by CIA or MI6 against the Soviet target.' Many people believe that Penkovsky 'saved the world from nuclear war' as the Schecter-Deriabin book proclaims. Penkovsky, who initiated it all, was destroyed – executed by the Soviets (he was not a suicide, as Wynne claimed). But Wynne paid a high price too.

Return to Cheyne Row and turn R into Glebe Place. Take Bramerton Street into King's Road. Opposite is Carlyle Square, entered through a small pedestrian gate. How far from the real world is this sheltered enclave! Farthest house on the R, and most remote of them all, is

Site 35: **18 Carlyle Square.** In 1944 Kim Philby and his growing family moved from his mother's crowded flat in Drayton Gardens to this 'surprisingly luxurious' house, as Malcolm Muggeridge describes

Site 35: **18 Carlyle Square.**

point Philby's income must have been substantially augmented from Soviet sources.') At the time Philby was still married to his first love, an Austrian communist named Litzi Friedman. Two years later he obtained a divorce and married Aileen, who had already borne three of his children and was now pregnant with a fourth. He then made a clean breast of this domestic untidiness to Valentine Vivian of MI6, his patron in the service. (Vivian learnt from MI5 that Litzi was a confirmed Soviet agent but promptly dropped the matter. It was a long time ago, after all, and the promising Philby should be allowed to get on with his career.) In this house that was notionally financed by Aileen's mother, a lodger took the top floor and Aileen ran a day nursery on the ground floor. The family lived here 'in cheerful disorder' while Kim Philby coldly and steadily climbed to power in MI6 (*see Site 113*).

At his death in Moscow in 1988, Philby had served the KGB for more than 50 years. After his 1963 arrival in Moscow he was debriefed at length but given little to do; he gave his first lecture at Moscow Centre only in 1977. His early years, though, had been helpful enough to the Centre. Was he the most damaging double agent in Britain's history? The historian John Keegan believes that Philby was less damaging than Fuchs or Maclean. True, Philby's treachery caused the deaths of many agents, writes Keegan, but it didn't harm 'the vital interests of Britain or the Western Alliance.' Christopher Andrew, however, writes that 'the longest-lasting damage' done by Philby was precisely to 'the Anglo-American intelligence alliance, then, as now, the most special part of the "special relationship" ' between London and Washington. Unquestionably, Philby jolted the British out of the idea that they could trust anyone whose *background* they could trust − and the idea that they could command a loyalty and devotion unknown in other countries. The damage to the national psyche was deep and devastating.

But he didn't do everything claimed by and for him. He didn't, for instance, warn Burgess and Maclean; this persistent claim is a transparent attempt to protect someone else (*see Site 120*). Nor was he single-handedly responsible for the failure of the Anglo-American effort to liberate Albania after the war; that operation was doomed from the start. Nor did he betray the postwar Baltic operation (*see Site 37*); he knew neither the landing zones nor the drop zones for these agents, writes Anthony Cavendish in his memoir *Inside Intelligence*, and to lay this at Philby's feet probably shields a traitor elsewhere in MI6 or in the navy.

Philby's own memoir, *My Silent War* (1968), carries some world-class disinformation. Philby claims, for example, that the Soviets couldn't believe his tales of the internal workings of SIS. The British must have *another* secret organization, they said; the *real* SIS couldn't be so inept, so chaotic. (Even those who didn't read the book got the message − the Soviets knew that the anecdote would be picked up by most reviewers, eager to trash SIS.) Philby, of course, was trying to establish that he was the first Soviet agent to penetrate SIS. I doubt it.

One of Philby's favourite pieces of disinformation, however, is finally coming apart at the seams. Several months before his death, he repeated it yet again, to Phillip Knightley: 'There was no Cambridge ring. It's a load of nonsense invented by journalists and spy writers.... If there was a ring of spies at Cambridge, why not one at Oxford?' But apparently there *was* one at Oxford, its existence revealed by John Costello in 1992. How much more of Philby's mischief will be exposed in the future? More archives will be opened and more *apparatchiki* will make statements, even while the authenticity of any new material will be debated. The coming years should be lively.

Many questions about Philby remain unanswered. In his six-day interview in Moscow with Knightley (the only Western journalist ever invited into his home), he simply didn't answer what he didn't wish to answer. And in the Soviet television programme *Comrade Philby*, made for export after his death, his role is so vastly inflated as to mark this 'documentary' as pure disinformation. The film tells us, for instance, that it was *he* who supplied the information enabling the Soviet Union to win the crucial battle at Kursk. What this does, very neatly, is to discredit the idea that the British were so clever as to outwit the Soviet intelligence services about the true origin of the information, which was in all probability the Lucy ring (*see Site 58*).

Who, ultimately, was the endlessly fascinating Philby? He wasn't a psychopath (like Burgess) or a weakling (like Maclean) or a lost spirit (like Blunt). He was, I believe, an imperialist, but for the *new* imperialism. He was precisely the sort who had built and sustained the British Empire − clever, resourceful, determined, ruthless, self-disciplined, arrogant, eccentric. He was simultaneously shrewd enough to see that the British Empire was declining, ambitious enough to go where he thought the power would be, and unscrupulous and unsentimental enough to put aside past loyalty to *nation* in favour of primary loyalty to *self*. And I am sure that anti-Americanism came into it. He was, after all, a British chauvinist, probably despising in the Americans exactly what he admired in the Soviets: they were new, energetic, challenging the old order, challenging Britain. However, the USSR and the US threatened different aspects of British tradition: the USSR would replace capitalism with communism, while the US would replace the class system with a class-blind meritocracy. And as much as Philby hated capitalism he loved the class system. He would have wanted a Britain bound by hierarchial communism, and he would have loathed a Britain disfigured by capitalism *and* meritocracy.

Any faith he may have had in the Soviet system in and of itself was probably long gone when he took refuge in the USSR in 1963.

If we can believe him (and I think we can, here), he told Knightley of unspecified doubts: 'You see, I never swallowed everything. I never took it *all* in.' Nigel West's judgment, as quoted in the American journal *Foreign Intelligence Literary Scene*, seems correct: 'To this day,' writes West, 'I am convinced that he was not an ideologist. Spying was just his way of being above lesser mortals.'

Just as Philby's own faith is open to question, so too is MI6's remarkable faith in him. Was it a firm belief in his loyalty or was it merely expediency? *Item*: In 1945, SIS overlooked the curious coincidence of the increased Soviet wireless traffic between London and Moscow and Istanbul immediately after Philby was briefed about the would-be defector Volkov (*see Site 53*). *Item*: In 1947, SIS sent him to an important post in Turkey soon after discovering the Soviet connections of his first wife. *Item*: In 1956, SIS didn't keep Philby in retirement, after the golden handshake given him when Burgess and Maclean fled, but re-employed him in Beirut as a case-officer. (Peter Wright recalls that the next chief of MI6, Sir Dick White, retained Philby 'even though he believed him to be a spy', saying that 'to sack Philby would create more problems inside MI6 than it might solve.' If this is true, it says some pretty terrible things about MI6; if not true, it says some pretty terrible things about Wright.) *Item*: In 1962, the way in which SIS confronted Philby with proof of his treachery, in Beirut, could only have encouraged him to defect.

Philby subsequently repaid MI6's faith in him with a monstrous ingratitude: he called the GPU 'an élite service' while withholding this compliment from MI6. To his former colleagues this may have been the most grievous betrayal.

At the head of the square, all but hidden by the neighbouring house and by foliage is

Site 36: **21 Carlyle Square.** In intelligence work, it's not all Minox cameras and a quick dash for the border. They also serve who only sit and administrate. In this modest house lived Victor Frederick William Cavendish-Bentinck (later the ninth Duke of Portland), who for most of WWII was chairman of the Joint Intelligence Committee.

The JIC had been formed in 1936 to co-ordinate intelligence from SIS and the three armed services. Only in 1940 under Churchill,

Site 36: **21 Carlyle Square.**

though, was it given real authority and by then its purview also included the new SOE and the intelligence agencies of Britain's new allies. The five-man JIC was served by a Joint Intelligence Staff only double that size. William Casey, chief of OSS's Secret Intelligence branch in London during WWII (and director of CIA 40 years later), was impressed. He considered the JIC 'typical of the British genius for having tight little groups handle functions that in the U.S. spawned huge bureaucracies.'

Eisenhower's top intelligence officer in SHAEF deemed Bentinck 'the outstanding intelligence officer of his time.' Excessive praise? Consider these two qualities mentioned by Patrick Howarth, Bentinck's biographer: his ability to elicit everyone's views no matter how many officers senior to the speaker might be present, and his ability to speak his mind to men at higher levels. Howarth contrasts wartime decision-making in Britain and in Germany; the best intelligence can count for nothing if subordinates fear their leader or distrust each other. But even Bentinck couldn't manage what he called 'this awful quarrelling between MI6 and SOE.' And he had his own difficulties with SOE. He had produced the report properly blaming SOE for the *Englandspiel* disaster (*see Site 75*) and he later said, 'SOE would gladly have murdered me. I arranged with Victor Rothschild that if I suddenly died he was to carry out an autopsy.'

Bentinck chaired a meeting of the JIC every Tuesday morning in the Cabinet War Rooms; as the war progressed he lived there. But Churchill, writes Howarth, 'having issued the directive which in effect established the JIC as the supreme intelligence body, did not himself rely wholly, or even primarily, on it as a source of information.' As Bentinck later put it, 'Churchill had a tendency to create his own intelligence', becoming increasingly dependent on Ultra decrypts.

Bentinck's observations were often accurate. He correctly predicted that Germany would invade the USSR (later calling it Hitler's greatest single mistake) and he early looked upon the USSR with unblinking realism. During his time with the JIC he had occasion to meet Philby, Blunt and the others. He thought Philby 'a queer fish', which seems reasonable enough, but he was wide of the mark when he thought Blunt 'rather a dull dog.'

Near the war's end Bentinck saw the necessity of keeping the JIC structure in peacetime. 'I'd noticed that there were junior officers in the intelligence divisions in the Air Ministry, the War Office and the Admiralty all doing the same job, writing the same things, gathering the same information, most of it not secret in any way. I thought this should be rationalized. I put it up to the Chiefs of Staff, and they took it. The departments didn't like it at all.'

Leaving Carlyle Square at the back, you'll come to Old Church Street, oldest street in Chelsea. Turn L. Between Mulberry Walk and Mallord Street is

Site 37: **111 Old Church Street.** Here, in the 1950s, SIS trained refugees from Estonia, Latvia and Lithuania to be intelligence agents. A British couple came to cook and clean, and former SOE instructors left retirement to teach at 'The School.' SIS hoped to infiltrate these Baltic nationalists back into their Soviet-occupied homelands, building networks of indigenous informants there and ultimately extending the intelligence-gathering into Russia itself. For their part, the Balts hoped (with British and American help) to

Site 37: **111 Old Church Street.**

liberate their homelands. Towards these grand ends, the chosen refugees diligently studied Morse code and radio procedures in the basement, and on the second floor learnt how to manage dead-drops, cut-outs, safe-houses, surveillance, interrogation.

The 20th-century history of the Baltic states is mostly a sad one. After the Bolshevik Revolution, they won their independence from Russia, as did Finland. But in 1940 they were occupied by the USSR as part of its 1939 deal with Germany. (When the Soviets tried that with Finland, the Finns fought them to a standstill.)

The Soviet occupation was accompanied by the mass killings, deportations to prison camps, confiscation of businesses and property, and collectivization of agriculture that have characterized all communist takeovers. Some Baltic nationalists were so fiercely anti-Soviet that they actually welcomed Hitler's armies in 1941. But the German occupation was similarly murderous and oppressive. And the Balts could expect no help from Britain and America, who had reassured Stalin that the new Atlantic Charter (guaranteeing self-determination) wouldn't apply to the Baltics. Soviet rule returned to Estonia, Latvia and Lithuania in 1944-5.

When the Western democracies saw that Stalin was fast replacing Hitler as the primary threat, MI6 re-established its anti-Soviet section (with Philby at its head!) and made contact with nationalist groups in Estonia, Latvia, Lithuania, the Ukraine, and elsewhere in the Soviet empire. In all these areas, partisan groups were engaging the NKVD in open battle.

SIS hoped to duplicate SOE's modest successes of WWII. But the new adversary was smarter than the Nazis, tougher, more ruthless, more experienced; the Soviets had been in the Totalitarian Surveillance State business for 30 years. Then too, the Nazis had considered counter-intelligence merely a sideline, while the seizing and keeping of power was the very essence, the *raison d'être*, of the communist state: the only thing the communists understood or cared about or were any good at.

Even without Philby's help, the Soviets would still have penetrated Western attempts to liberate the Baltics. The Soviets had recruited some Balts, trained them, and 'dangled' them to SIS – that is, allowed them to flee, along with genuine nationalist émigrés, and waited for SIS or CIA to recruit them. Most teams returning to their homelands were met on the beaches or landing zones by the NKVD, and agents not already working for the communists were persuaded to co-operate or were executed. Any agents not immediately caught were soon betrayed to the NKVD by the terrorized populace.

Later in the 1950s, U-2 reconnaissance planes did much of the information-gathering on Soviet military and industrial activities. SIS seems to have stopped training Baltic émigrés by then, at least here in Old Church Street.

Go N on Old Church Street, then E on Fulham Road. Turn L at Pelham Crescent. Facing the green at mid-block is

Site 38: **22 Pelham Crescent.** Two Belgian officers lived here during WWII, working tirelessly with MI9 to exfiltrate Allied military personnel from western Europe.

By 1944 the large number of escapers and evaders on the Continent could no longer be hidden in the cities. And the escape networks of MI9 were increasingly subject to *Gestapo* infiltration. Airey Neave of MI9 met with the Belgians in this building to plan a string of

Site 38: **22 Pelham Crescent.**

hide-outs in the French countryside where Allied personnel could shelter until they could be exfiltrated. Only one such camp was established, but hundreds of Allied servicemen were protected in it until Allied troops arrived three months later.

Georges d'Oultremont and Baron Jean de Blommaert, who lived in this building when they were not moving in and out of German territory, were part of a generation that would never have scuttled off to a neutral country to avoid military service. If your country was at war you fought as resourcefully as possible and as long as necessary. These two brave and high-spirited men, and their cohort, were the finest (and perhaps the final) flowering of what M. R. D. Foot may be the last to call 'the officer class.'

Exit from Pelham Crescent at tree-lined Pelham Place. Turn L at Pelham Street for South Kensington tube station. From here you can return to home or hostel. To proceed instead to the next walk, turn into Old Brompton Road.

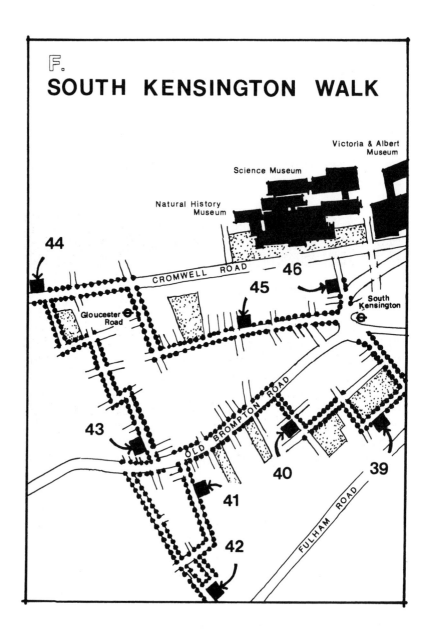

F.
SOUTH KENSINGTON WALK

Victoria & Albert Museum

Science Museum

Natural History Museum

44

CROMWELL ROAD

46

45

South Kensington

Gloucester Road

OLD BROMPTON ROAD

43

40

39

41

FULHAM ROAD

42

F. SOUTH KENSINGTON WALK

This walk meanders through one of London's most pleasant villages. From South Kensington tube station, turn L into the street called Onslow Square. In two blocks you'll reach the square itself. At the far side of the green turn R. Near the end of the street is

Site 39: **24 Onslow Square.** Here, on the steps of his London home, the pro-Nazi MP for Peebles was arrested on 23 May, 1940, three days after the arrests of Tyler Kent (*see Site 81*) and Anna Volkov (*see Sites 41 and 45*). Never charged or tried, Captain Archibald Henry Maule Ramsay remained in Brixton Prison for four years, his detention the result of broad new powers of the Defence Regulations enacted after the Kent/Volkov arrests.

Ramsay had been outspokenly Judeophobic since the 1920s. In the

1930s he supported the respectable Anglo-German Fellowship. In 1937 he co-founded the Link, a more extreme group devoted to friendship between England and Hitler's Germany. A year later he started the clandestine Right Club, which continued to function after war broke out and the other groups were disbanded.

Through Anna Volkov, his avid follower, Ramsay met Tyler Kent and gained access to the documents Kent was stealing from the US Embassy (some of which seemed to indicate that Churchill was going behind Chamberlain's back in dealing with President Roosevelt). Kent wanted Ramsay to raise a question in the Commons about the correspondence; by embarrassing both Churchill and Roosevelt, Kent and Ramsay hoped to keep America neutral and achieve a negotiated peace. Ramsay was arrested before he could make any documents public.

Ramsay's wife was also busy in the Axis cause during Britain's desperate days of 1940. She too was never charged with any crime. But in this very house she suggested to MI5's Joan Miller that the young woman change her fictitious job so as to get better information for the Right Club. Miller seemed to take the suggestion; Maxwell Knight gave her 'chickenfeed' to pass along.

A total of 1,373 people (almost the entire Right Club and about 800 members of the British Union of Fascists) were arrested after the Kent/Volkov arrests. Most were freed within the year. Many testified for Volkov and Kent, with Ramsay displaying (in the words of Muggeridge) 'the benighted innocence of the crazed' as, outside the courtroom, Ramsay's 'putative allies tried to blow the Old Bailey, along with all the rest of London town, to smithereens'. (Some of the most prominent pro-Nazis during WWII – Ramsay, Mosley, Pétain – had fought the Germans bravely in WWI but now saw Germany as the model, not the enemy.)

During Ramsay's long incarceration, his constituents sought unsuccessfully to have him relinquish his seat and the unrepentant Ramsay sought continually to be released from prison. Finally freed in September, 1944, he was back in Parliament the next day, meeting now in the House of Lords because of German bomb damage to the other chamber. Ramsay's parliamentary career ended at the next general election, but his anti-Jewish diatribes continued until his death in 1956.

Fanatic Judeophobes like Ramsay were perfectly comfortable with the idea that 'the Jews', in a vast international conspiracy, were behind communism *and* capitalism *and* the Masons *and* the Vatican. He had no difficulty with the obvious contradictions in this theory. Nor was he alone. His obsession dovetailed neatly with Hitler's national socialism – which was similarly anti-capitalist, anti-communist, anti-Jewish – and his Right Club of fewer than 500 members included a dozen MPs, four peers, four sons of peers, and many others prominent in British society. Ramsay himself was the scion of a distinguished Scottish family distantly related to the royal family.

Turn R into Sumner Place. At the end of the green turn L. In another block you'll reach Cranley Place. Just before the mews on your L is

Site 40: **20 Cranley Place.** Vera Atkins, who virtually ran SOE's F Section (*see Site 72*), tells me that this picturesque studio was an SOE

safe-house. To avoid wholesale damage from any single air-raid, SOE dispersed its safe-houses. Many were in the Baker Street area but others were in neighbourhoods like this, where bourgeois propriety could be counted on to give a certain security: the odd-looking foreigners, if noticed at all, would tend to be discreetly ignored.

Continue on Cranley Place to Old Brompton Road. Turn L. Enjoy the small shops for several blocks. Turn L again at Roland Gardens. On your L is

Site 41: **18 Roland Gardens.** Not far from her father's Russian Tea Room where the pro-Nazi Right Club held its meetings lived Anna Volkov, convicted in 1940 of activities useful to the German enemy. Her fellow-conspirator and probably her lover was Tyler Kent (*see Site 81*), a code clerk in the American Embassy. Their arrest was MI5's first major counter-intelligence triumph of the war.

The short, stocky, and (by all accounts) unattractive Anna Volkov – 38 when she was arrested – had been in London since the Russian Revolution. Her hatred of Bolsheviks and Jews assured her of friends among the Russian émigrés and the British élite; the Duchess of Windsor, for instance, was one of her dressmaking clients. Volkov became naturalized in 1935 but grew increasingly enamored of fascism, especially after visiting Germany in 1938 and meeting Hitler's deputy, Rudolf Hess. In London, she worked in the Anglo-German Fellowship and the Link, and was secretary of the underground Right Club (*see Sites 39 and 45*).

Volkov's activities on behalf of Germany were limited for a while to booing Churchill in newsreels and putting up sticky-back labels denouncing what she called the Jews' war. By late 1939, however, she had met the like-minded Tyler Kent. They often spent weekends together outside London; she had transferred her car to him because he, with his diplomatic credentials, could get the petrol coupons that she, a civilian, could not. In town, she occasionally went alone to his flat to study his growing cache of documents purloined from the embassy.

Through her, some of this material ended up in Berlin, a fact soon known to the British. Soon afterward, MI5's surveillance of her conduit (who worked in the Italian Embassy in London) and then of Volkov herself, led to Kent. Volkov and Kent were tried separately in 1940. Little was made public; at stake were no less than Churchill's leadership and Roosevelt's re-election. Her trial transcript remains closed until the year 2015.

Continue down Roland Gardens. Turn R where it turns. Your footsteps may be the only sounds you'll hear in these quiet streets. Take a L into Thistle Grove. At tiny Holly Mews turn R. Cross the street at Drayton Gardens to appreciate the full stature of

Site 42: **Grove Court, Holly Mews.** Philby's mother, Dora, bought the basement flat in this building in 1937. For the next seven years Kim Philby lived here intermittently.

He was already working for the Soviets during the Spanish Civil War, covering Franco's side for *The Times* and for Moscow Centre. He then covered Germany's invasion of France and the Low Countries for the same two employers. In 1940 his friend Guy Burgess recommended him for a job with MI6.

Philby was initially assigned to Section D at Caxton Street (*see*

Site 42: **Grove Court, Holly Mews.**

Site 5), but with that section's absorption into SOE he was posted to SOE's 'finishing school' at Beaulieu to set up instruction in propaganda and subversion. (SOE knew nothing of his excellent qualifications for the job!) But he was eager to get to the centre of Britain's intelligence activities and by 1941 had manoeuvred himself into counter-intelligence at SIS. When this section relocated from St Albans to London (*see Site 113*), Philby moved back here to Holly Mews with his growing family, which included his 'wife' (to whom he was not married), their two children, and a pair of terriers named MI5 and MI6.

As Philby rose in the ranks of MI6 during WWII, he was increasingly valuable to Moscow Centre as a manipulator of British policy in the interests of the Soviet Union. He was, for example, in a position to counteract the Germans who were opposed to Hitler (particularly those in the *Wehrmacht* and the *Abwehr*) in their efforts to remove Hitler and make a separate peace with the Western allies. Such an arrangement would have enabled a new German régime to turn its full attention to conquering the Soviet Union or, later, to keeping Stalin's army out of Central Europe. Naturally, Philby did his best to discredit the peace feelers extended by these anti-Hitler elements. He and his fellow communists scattered throughout HM Government were less interested in winning the war for Britain than in winning a good postwar situation for the USSR.

Philby's primary wartime mission for Moscow Centre, though, was providing inside information about MI6 and its anti-German operations. Consider the case of Dr Erich Vermehren, the *Abwehr*'s number-two man in Turkey. Vermehren contacted MI6 in Istanbul in late 1943, claiming a crisis of conscience over working for Nazi Germany. (I wonder whether his crisis of conscience was precipitated by the realization that Hitler was losing the war. After all, Hitler had been just as evil in, say, 1940 when he was winning.) SIS appears to have honoured Vermehren's unusual terms: his defection must be made to look like a kidnapping, and he must not be forced to work actively against Germany. (After all, Hitler might *not* lose the war.)

Vermehren and his wife were spirited to London. While SIS tried to decide what to do with them, given the unusual terms negotiated in Turkey, Philby invited the couple to stay with him. One can almost hear Philby in his charming and diffident way saying to Vermehren, 'But my dear fellow, of course you must stay with us.' And one can imagine the deft and patient (but unrelenting) interrogation that followed, disguised as exchange of gossip between intelligence professionals. Bear in mind that Philby was conducting *two* interrogations, on behalf on his *two* employers. And Moscow Centre, while eager to know about the internal affairs of the *Abwehr*, was even more eager to know about Britain's penetration of the *Abwehr*. Did Philby learn from Vermehren the identities of renegade *Abwehr* and *Wehrmacht* officers who may have been co-operating with SIS and/or trying to negotiate a separate peace with the Western allies? If so, he certainly gave that information to the Soviets, who certainly passed it subtly on to Himmler. Himmler's *Sicherheitsdienst* was in deadly rivalry with the *Abwehr*, and Himmler was thus doubly motivated to eliminate the *Abwehr* from the scene. Shortly after Vermehren's arrival in London, the *Sicherheitsdienst* took over the *Abwehr* and dismissed its chief, Admiral Canaris. Barely a month before the war ended, the Germans executed Canaris for conspiring against Hitler. He was assuredly guilty — as he was almost assuredly guilty of collaborating with the British.

When Philby moved to Carlyle Square (*see Site 35*), Dora Philby continued on here, drinking her way to an early death in 1956. But the year before her death the basement flat here was the site of her son's famous press conference.

He had come under suspicion as a Soviet agent when Burgess and Maclean fled in 1951. Many in MI5 thought he was the 'third man'. Many in MI6 thought he was innocent, and many in Whitehall and Fleet Street thought he was being persecuted by a British McCarthyism. They knew Philby personally; he *couldn't* be a Soviet agent. (Some Americans still say the same about Alger Hiss.) At CIA insistence London recalled Philby from his Washington posting as SIS liaison with FBI and CIA. When MI5 turned its most skilled interrogators to the task of getting him to confess, Philby realized that only his own words could betray him. He managed not to incriminate himself. Despite its failure to catch Philby out, MI5 wanted MI6 to fire him. And despite its belief in his innocence, MI6 agreed to fire him for the sake of inter-service amity. He was ostensibly separated from SIS in November, 1951.

In the autumn of 1955 a Labour MP accused the Tory Government (accurately) of covering up Soviet infiltration of the government in general and Philby's involvement in particular. Harold Macmillan, the Foreign Secretary, then engaged in a further cover-up by denying that Philby had ever acted against Britain's interests. Philby promptly called a press conference here. With stunning audacity, he denied that he had ever been a communist (let alone a Soviet agent) and claimed that he had not knowingly spoken to a communist since 1934; he indicated that he would sue for libel anyone mentioning his name speculatively in connection with these matters. (It was not allowed, at this press conference, to ask him about Burgess and Maclean. The American reporter Edwin Newman recalls that his own questions on the subject were considered McCarthyite.) Curiously, Philby's habitual stammer was, for once, absent; he stuttered not at all during this, his greatest performance. And within six months of the Grove Court press conference, he was again working for MI6, this time in Beirut under cover of a newspaper job. (He was still working part-time for MI6 when he escaped to the USSR in January, 1963.)

In Beirut in 1957 Philby learnt that his second wife, whom he had virtually abandoned in London, had died. He hung up the phone and announced to his cocktail party guests, 'You must all drink to my great news. Aileen's dead!' At the time he was having an affair with the wife of a *New York Times* correspondent; he soon married her. In Moscow, he discarded this third wife and took up with Donald Maclean's wife, ultimately discarding her too and marrying a young Soviet woman doubtless provided by his employers.

Late in 1961 a high KGB officer defected and, *inter alia*, convinced even Philby's friends in MI6 that good old Kim had been a Soviet mole all along. Incredibly, the government didn't even *try* to bring him to London for questioning. Instead, a former colleague from MI6 (Nicholas Elliott) was sent to Beirut late in 1962 to tell Philby that MI5 finally had the goods on him. This was practically an invitation for Philby to flee to the Soviet Union. He promptly did so, after exonerating Blunt in a confession that took MI5 a year (writes Nigel West) to recognize 'for the fabrication it was'.

Philby worked for the KGB in Moscow whenever they asked him. He died in 1988, regrettably of natural causes.

Walk N on Drayton Gardens to Old Brompton Road. Two small blocks to the R is Rosary Gardens. Early in this street, on your L, is

Site 43: **3 Rosary Gardens.** In *The Climate of Treason*, Andrew Boyle identifies this as the probable site of Philby's recruitment to Soviet Intelligence. In *Reilly: The First Man*, Robin Bruce Lockhart notes that a man named Rostovsky ran moles in the British government from here. Nicholas Kelso, however, sounds a cautionary note on such speculations in *Hostile Action: The KGB and Secret Soviet*

Site 43: **3 Rosary Gardens.**

Operations in Britain. This was the Soviet consulate, writes Kelso. 'As such it was probably watched by the British police and MI5, and was a highly unsafe place in which to arrange a meeting with a potential secret agent.' We don't know what may have taken place here. The Russians still own the building. I imagine they would deny any recent use of it for intelligence work: all they've done here is publish an English-language magazine. (*Novosti*, the Russian press agency, works from here.) But don't miss the television camera constantly watching the front door. And I'll bet the basement has a superb darkroom.

Continue up Rosary Gardens and jog L into Ashburn Place; the 30-storey Forum Hotel will hit you like a graffitoed obscenity. Just before the hotel, turn L at Courtfield Road and immediately R into Ashburn Gardens. Ahead is busy Cromwell Road. Across the street to your L is

Site 44: **124-126 Cromwell Road.** MI5 grew from 19 people to 844 during WWI but was back under 25 again by the early 1930s. Such fluctuations are common in a democracy; when things seem calm, nobody wants to spend money preventing espionage, sabotage and subversion. In the 1930s MI5 had its headquarters in these 'relatively tiny' quarters, as Costello's *Mask of Treachery* describes this 'front-line command post in the secret war'. (It was tiny compared to the already vast Soviet OGPU.) In 1937, still very small, MI5 moved to Thames House (*see Site 10*).

'Hundreds of Christmas cards were sent out by this secret

department in 1919,' according to John Bulloch's early book on MI5. Very soon, he adds, 'this easier atmosphere had to go.' Straining MI5's limited resources during the inter-war years were the continuing IRA violence, the growing export of the Russian Revolution and the sudden rise of European fascism.

Heading MI5 for all its years at Cromwell Road was Sir Vernon Kell. Indeed, he had headed the organization since its inception in 1909, when it occupied one desk and one filing cabinet in the War Office. (It was MO5 then, for Military Operations; it became MI5 with the creation of the Directorate of Military Intelligence in 1916.)

Kell was an unusual man, not as eccentric as the founding chief of MI6 but not a run-of-the-mill army officer either. His maternal grandfather was an émigré Polish nobleman, and on visits to his mother's family throughout Europe, young Kell became fluent in German, French, Polish and Italian. He graduated from Sandhurst to join his father's regiment but was dissatisfied with army life. He went to Moscow to learn Russian. With the outbreak of the Boxer Rebellion he saw active service in China, following which he became an intelligence officer in China and then a railway officer near the Manchurian border (at the juncture of the Russian and British portions of the railway). When the railway went back to Chinese control, he went back to England. When ill health prevented his going to India with his regiment, he worked at the War Office. He was not yet 36 when chosen to start MO5. Within two years he had pressed for a tougher Official Secrets Act, and within five years his department had uncovered all but one of Germany's spies in Britain.

Kell was 'very much a product of his time, of the last flush of British imperialism,' writes Bulloch. 'But he had the breadth of mind to change when change was needed, and to adapt himself to new conditions.' Here at Cromwell Road, for instance, Kell began the infiltration operations by which MI5 agents worked inside every organization whose aims or allegiances were inimical to Britain's security. He was probably the first Western intelligence officer, writes Bulloch, to understand that Britain's enemies could and should be fought with their own weapons.

Until more open recruiting policies prevailed, the Kell years saw basically two types of people enter the Security Service. The 'clubman' had been to the better public schools and to Oxford or

Cambridge. The 'flatfoot' had rarely been to university but had served in the military or the colonial police. The clubman looked down on the flatfoot for class reasons, of course, and thought the flatfoot too literal, too unimaginative, to be up to the job (too lacking in sophistication, for instance, to understand the ideology of communism). It is worth noting that all of the known Soviet moles in MI5 were clubmen. To Kell's credit or not, he didn't value intellectuals; he boasted that he had never knowingly hired a university graduate.

Walk E one block on noisy Cromwell Road and turn R into Gloucester Road. Turn L at Stanhope Gardens. Just E of Queen's Gate is a hairdressing salon, formerly

Site 45: **the Russian Tea Room and Restaurant, 50 Harrington Road.** The last naval attaché at the Imperial Russian Embassy in London was Admiral Nikolai Volkov. When the Tsar fell, the Volkov family stayed on in London and opened this special place; it served the best caviar in London, and vodka too, long before the drink became fashionable in England. In the flat above, the pro-fascist Right Club held committee meetings. Active in all of this was the Admiral's

daughter, Anna, helping her parents run the tea shop, helping Captain Ramsay run his clandestine Right Club (*see Site 39*), and helping Tyler Kent get his stolen documents out where they could assist the Axis (*see Site 81*).

MI5 had already infiltrated two women agents into the Right Club when one of them reported to Maxwell Knight that the club was eager to recruit someone from the War Office. Knight's choice for the job was young Joan Miller, previously employed in the display department of the cosmetics firm Elizabeth Arden and freshly assigned to his counter-subversion section from MI5's transport section. She was very pretty, very daring, and very taken with Maxwell Knight (*see Sites 12 and 49*). For her first assignment, Knight asked her to get a list of Right Club members. She began frequenting the Russian Tea Room and befriending the wary Anna Volkov, to whom she mentioned casually that she worked at the War Office. She invented a pre-war romance with a Nazi officer to explain her fascist sympathies. Before long she was invited upstairs where her performance before a dozen members of the Right Club earned her an immediate invitation to join.

'I had to keep reminding myself that I'd seriously wanted to be an actress,' Miller writes in her memoir *One Girl's War*. Club members soon trusted her completely, even consulting her as to which Britons should be hanged when fascism arrived. By now she was looking for more than a list of club members; MI5's surveillance had identified Anna Volkov as the link between Tyler Kent and the attaché at the Italian Embassy who was sending to Rome the Churchill-Roosevelt correspondence stolen from the American Embassy. (From there, Kent's material went on to Berlin where it was picked up by British 'eavesdroppers.')

The 11-year-old Len Deighton witnessed Anna Volkov's arrest here in May, 1940; his mother worked at the tea room. For two violations of the Official Secrets Act, Volkov received a ten-year sentence. If she hadn't been a woman, says one historian, she'd have gone to the gallows.

She returned here briefly upon her release in 1947, but the tea room soon closed when her father died. At the risk of being accused of indulging in the cheapest pop psychology, I think Anna Volkov had a classic Elektra complex. Early in life she took on all her father's attitudes and values; given his class and upbringing, these would naturally have included a vehement Judeophobia. Then came the revolution. Until Stalin killed off most of the key revolutionaries, Bolshevism was readily identifiable with Jews. Anna Volkov would have been furious that her father had been toppled from his position by what she considered a pack of lowly Jews. As to why she wanted to aid Germany during its non-aggression pact with the Soviet Union, only a better pop psychologist than I might be able to explain. Perhaps, like any true fanatic, she had room in her mind for only a very few ideas.

Until her death in 1969, she eked out a living from her dressmaking, saw only a few old friends, and clung bitterly to her hatred of Jews and Bolsheviks. She never harmed Joan Miller, despite her courtroom threats to do so. Miller found it all 'pretty harrowing'. She had not even disliked the woman. Afterward she threw away a dress that Anna had given her — but she saved the buttons for her 'memory box'.

Continue on Harrington Road to South Kensington tube station. Turn L into Cromwell Place. Just past Cromwell Mews is

Site 46: **14 Cromwell Place.**

Site 46: **14 Cromwell Place.** Claude Dansey was born in this house in 1876, when South Kensington was just developing. He entered the modern secret world when it, too, was new and he grew with that world, ultimately becoming the second in command in MI6 – some say, the power behind the *first* in command (*see Site 117*). When he retired at the end of WWII he had become what his biographers Anthony Read and David Fisher in *Colonel Z* call 'one of the most important, influential, and colourful figures in the history of espionage and secret intelligence'.

Many people have described Dansey less flatteringly as 'the most unpopular snake in the business' and the 'only truly evil man I ever met' and 'an utter shit' (this last, the view of historian Trevor-Roper). Others have called him Uncle Claude, out of respect and even affection. But admirers and detractors alike have found him well suited to the clandestine life. His biographers mention that he may have been the inspiration for Somerset Maugham's spymaster in *Ashenden*, who was (according to Maugham) 'one of those men who prefer devious ways to straight, for some intricate pleasure they get in fooling their fellows'. Dansey relished this pleasure and was expert at fooling his fellows; some of his secrets are still his secrets almost 50 years after his death.

One of his best-kept secrets involves the origin in 1936 of his secret Z Organization (*see Site 96*). Did he create this independent intelligence service on his own, having been banished from SIS? Or did he do it with the blessings of SIS? Historians disagree.

Another of Dansey's secrets involves the passing of Ultra decrypts to the Soviets through their Lucy ring in Switzerland (*see Site 58*). People who believe that this was done believe that Dansey did it; he was called in by Menzies (then 'C'), who was called in by Churchill to find a way to give German secrets to the Soviets without revealing that Britain had cracked Germany's most secret code. Did this happen? Again, historians disagree. But in *Operation Lucy*, Read and Fisher note that Dansey was knighted immediately after the Soviets won the massive tank battle at Kursk, a victory probably made possible by information from the Lucy ring. Dansey's knighthood, say Read and Fisher, was 'a reward, perhaps, for a job well done'.

Dansey's knighthood came precisely when SOE suffered one of its greatest catastrophes: the destruction of the vast Prosper/Physician network in northern France (*see Site 18*). In this, too, Dansey may have had a hand. As Read and Fisher write, 'he maintained to the end that SOE was filled with undisciplined amateurs who were more dangerous to his agents than they were to the enemy, and were therefore to be avoided and frustrated at every opportunity.' But did he frustrate them to the extent claimed by Robert Marshall in *All the King's Men*? Did Dansey coldly allow Henri Déricourt, a known Nazi agent in the network, to bring down the entire network, hundreds of whose members died in concentration camps? Did Dansey perhaps even work with Déricourt to that end? Marshall makes 'a strong argument', writes Nigel West, and West concedes 'some circumstantial evidence to support the contention that Déricourt had been an MI6 agent,' but he is not convinced. 'If Marshall is right,' West adds, 'it would reveal a particularly unpleasant and ruthless aspect to MI6. In short, what Dansey's many detractors have talked of for so long.' What is the truth? This is Dansey's secret.

I have another question about Dansey. He was of vital assistance in the creation of America's first Military Intelligence Service in 1917. (Until then, US military intelligence had consisted of two officers and three clerks in the War College.) He was immensely helpful to the Americans again – and of course to the British – in getting the US to build a new and larger intelligence organization in 1940. The first American recruits in what became the Office of Strategic Services were trained in London under Dansey's direction. It was Dansey, 'almost single-handed' say Read and Fisher in *Colonel Z*, who established the so-called 'special relationship' between the intelligence services of the two countries. Penetration of the OSS by MI6 would have been right up Dansey's alley. And since the CIA's founders were mostly OSS people, so close to the British by training and experience as to be accused of having divided loyalty, the CIA may have been penetrated as well. The special relationship may even have been sustained over the years *because* the American services were penetrated by the British. Did any of this penetration occur? And if so was Dansey behind it? Another of his secrets.

Here was a man who was part of the world of intelligence for almost 50 years. He joined the Field Intelligence Department in 1900 in South Africa when the Empire's intelligence efforts were expanding rapidly. He saw important changes in the methods of intelligence-gathering: the beginning of signals intelligence at the turn of the century, the beginning of aerial photography in WWII. But he held to his belief in the necessity and value of the agent on the ground. Perhaps this is not unusual for a man born in the 19th century. But his view is also a modern one, surviving in our own day when the technology is beyond anything Sir Claude could have imagined.

Here ends this walk, back at South Kensington tube station. A block away you can visit the superb Natural History Museum where, during WWII, SOE worked secretly on the creation of special tools for its secret work. (The museum people know little of the so-called 'toyshop' today, and that is probably as it should be. I am told that one or two have heard of the existence of the room; 'it is said to have been in the southwest basement area, in what is now the Mollusca Section of Zoology Department'.) For the next walk, go E to Brompton Oratory.

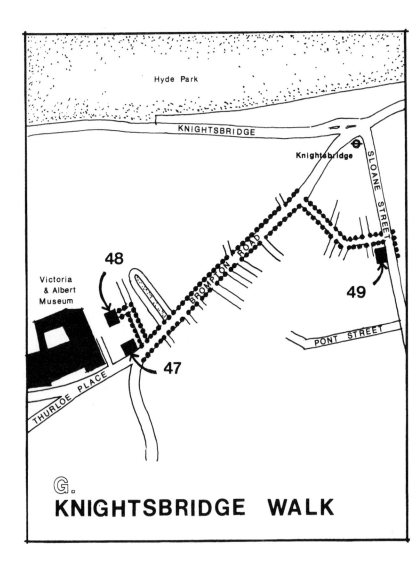

Hyde Park

KNIGHTSBRIDGE

Knightsbridge

SLOANE STREET

48

Victoria
& Albert
Museum

BROMPTON ROAD

49

PONT STREET

47

THURLOE PLACE

G.
KNIGHTSBRIDGE WALK

G. KNIGHTSBRIDGE WALK

Immediately E of the Victoria and Albert Museum is

Site 47: **Brompton Oratory.** Follow these tediously precise directions to the 'dead letter box' (dead drop, in American terminology) that one KGB officer considered the safest in all London: 'As you face the church from the street the entrance will be on the right hand side. Go into the church. Just to the right of the entrance is an altar. It is a memorial to Englishmen who were killed in the war and has a copy of Michelangelo's famous statue "Pieta" – the dead Christ in his Mother's arms. On the floor below the statue are the words *"Consummatum est"*. Just to the left of the altar as you face it, are two large marble columns which are part of the architecture of the

church. Both are very close to the wall. The DLB site is behind the column nearest to the wall (if you are facing them, it is the right-hand column), in a little space between the actual column and the wall.'

This description was sent by Moscow Centre to its top people in London in April, 1985. The top-secret message was copied for SIS almost immediately by Oleg Gordievsky, who had been working in the London *rezidentura* since 1982 and had been an SIS penetration agent since 1974. In May, 1985, newly appointed as *rezident*, Gordievsky was suddenly summoned to Moscow. Still there in July and aware that his double-agentry had been discovered, he made a run for the border – yes, such things do happen outside the movies – and escaped to the West by a still-undisclosed route. A collection of documents taken by Gordievsky over the years was published in 1991 as *Instructions from the Centre: Top Secret Files on KGB Foreign Operations, 1975-1985* (edited by Gordievsky and with commentary by the historian Christopher Andrew). The book is a dazzling collection of policy statements and tradecraft memos from the KGB.

Suggesting a DLB here, the KGB officer reported that the church wasn't watched round-the-clock since it wasn't state property. The chapel was observed to be seldom visited and poorly lit. 'I would be inclined to think that there is no safer place in Central London,' the officer advised Moscow Centre. I would be inclined to disagree. A visitor might suddenly enter this chapel, unseen until the last minute; an untended toddler might easily find the packet of film behind the column. (Much safer is a DLB not normally visible, even one as well-known as a magnetized box on the underside of the shelf of a telephone kiosk.) But bad as the Brompton Oratory DLB is, the alternate DLB selected by the Soviets is even worse (*see Site 48*).

Immediately E of Brompton Oratory, follow the path of lime trees along Cottage Place to

Site 48: **Holy Trinity Church.** This dead letter box – also revealed by Oleg Gordievsky – seems not just problematic but downright foolish. The drop is near the statue of St Francis of Assisi to the left of the church. 'The statue is surrounded by a small fence to protect the flowers planted round it,' according to Moscow Centre's

Site 48: **Holy Trinity Church.**

directions. 'If you stand facing the statue, there is a large tree growing just to the left. The fence passes close to the tree. The site for the DLB is on the ground at the base of the tree, between the tree and the fence.'

The KGB officer who wrote the above description mentions having tested this out-of-the-way spot: an empty film cassette remained 'exactly in place' all day. The spot is indeed 'fairly inconspicuous' and the path lightly travelled. But servicing this drop would seem risky; many windows overlook the place from the church and from nearby residences. Critics have argued for decades that communism discourages (or even extinguishes) initiative, enterprise, and excellence among its people. These two DLBs would seem to confirm such a theory.

We don't learn in *Instructions from the Centre* what resulted from SIS knowledge of these suggested DLBs. Within months, Gordievsky had defected (*see Site 47*) and the entire KGB operation in London was a shambles. But Gordievsky had been working for MI6 for a decade, one third of the time in this city. How many 'illegals' and their KGB support officers had been observed at similar DLBs in London? How many of these people had been 'turned' afterward by MI6 — or, in their innocence, used by MI6 to send disinformation to Moscow Centre or to uncover more KGB contacts in London? Identifying a DLB doesn't end the game but only begins a new round.

Walk E on Brompton Road towards Harrods; world-famous today, Harrods began here in 1849 as a small grocery shop. Enter to feast your eyes (at very least) upon the Food Halls. The public lounge on the fourth floor is also of interest; during WWII, 93 women volunteering for 'possibly dangerous work' were interviewed here. Those who were chosen soon entered Britain's Auxiliary Units (see Site 102), ready to do intelligence work should the nation fall to the Nazis. Leave Harrods, turning R at Hans Crescent and R at Sloane Street for

Site 49: **38 Sloane Street.** MI5's enigmatic Maxwell Knight lived here with a succession of exotic animals and baffled women. The animals

included a bear, a baboon, and a bush-baby, any one of which was likely to accompany Knight on his strolls through Chelsea. The women accepted his love for the entire animal kingdom (for bugs, snakes, everything) but suffered greatly from his behaviour towards the specific human female. He married three times and lived with at least two other women but consummated none of these relationships. The scandal that followed his first wife's suicide would have ruined the career of a lesser figure.

The dashing and capable Knight had unusual autonomy in his counter-subversion work (*see Site 12*). And his successes justified the freedom he was given: in 1938 he rolled up the Woolwich Arsenal ring (*see Site 51*) and in 1940 he captured Tyler Kent (*see Site 81*).

On the job he called himself 'Captain King' or 'Mr K' or 'M'. (He was not the model for Ian Fleming's 'M' but enjoyed the coincidence of names — as perhaps Fleming, who knew him, also did.) Off the job, he was 'Uncle Max' to millions of youngsters who listened devotedly to his weekly nature broadcasts on BBC radio and then, as instructed, went off in search of owl pellets or frogs' eggs or whatever. He was a serious ornithologist and zoologist, a prolific author (producing two passable thrillers and several popular books on natural history) and a skilled jazz musician. He had the same alloy of unfettered intuition and cold intellect that causes so many intelligence officers to excel at writing, music, and other creative efforts.

Knight had all the colourfulness (carefully cultivated, to be sure) of the Renaissance man, and all the colourlessness (just as carefully cultivated) of the counter-intelligence officer. 'He had an outer shell,' writes Anthony Masters in *The Man Who Was M*, 'so diamond-hard that it seemed impossible even to guess at what kind of person really lay beneath.' He also had 'charm of a rare and formidable order,' in the opinion of Joan Miller (an agent frustratedly in love with him), but he could make real connection only with the birds and animals he was so fond of.

He was also, unfortunately, capable of real error in his work, and the Ben Greene affair was the beginning of his undoing. Benjamin Greene was a pacifist, wrongfully imprisoned in May, 1940, as a traitor; one of Knight's agents had broken all the rules by playing *provocateur* with Greene and then giving false testimony against him.

111

The court case brought by Greene was a severe embarrassment to MI5. Masters writes that while the case broke both Knight and Greene, 'even more lasting damage was done to Great Britain's security'; Knight lost the credibility to convince his superiors of communist infiltration of MI5. Well before Knight's resignation from MI5 in 1956, his suspicions of that infiltration had proved only too accurate.

Walk N on Sloane Street past elegant shops. To begin the next walk, take the underground from Knightsbridge to Earl's Court.

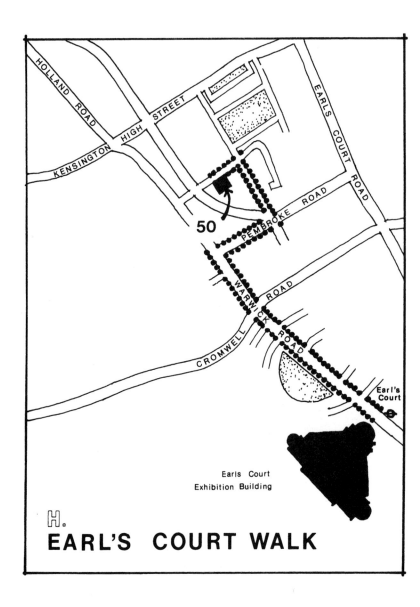

50

HOLLAND ROAD

HIGH STREET

KENSINGTON

EARLS COURT ROAD

PEMBROKE ROAD

WARWICK ROAD

CROMWELL ROAD

Earl's Court

Earls Court
Exhibition Building

H.
EARL'S COURT WALK

H. EARL'S COURT WALK

From Earl's Court tube station, follow the one-way traffic along Warwick Road. Turn R at Pembroke Road, then L into Pembroke Gardens and L again to

Site 50: **31 Pembroke Gardens.** The route you have taken to reach the home of Ernest Holloway Oldham is the route taken in 1930 by a dogged Soviet intelligence officer who found Oldham as one might find a needle in a haystack and who made Oldham (for a while) a Soviet agent. Oldham's story tells us much about the *Cheka*'s ingenuity and ruthlessness – and about Soviet penetration of HM Government.

Oldham was an unlikely spy for those days, motivated by greed and not ideology. After 17 years as a Foreign Office cypher clerk, he was poor and resented it. In Paris briefly with a trade delegation in 1929, he went to the Soviet Embassy and announced himself as 'Mr Scott' with a British cypher for sale. He was kept waiting while the OGPU's Vladimir Voynovich examined the material, and he was astonished to be cast out of the embassy within the hour, his documents thrown out with him. Voynovich denounced him as a *provocateur* and proudly sent the copied cypher to Moscow.

'Scott' went through nervous times back in London. A Soviet defector from the Paris Embassy had told the French of an amusing incident about an Englishman named Scott, and the French had told the British. The defector referred to Scott as B-3, suggesting that Scott was the third Briton working for the Soviets, but the British made little of any of it.

Now, however, Voynovich too went through nervous times. Moscow Centre had found Scott's material authentic and wanted him immediately as an agent. But his name was obviously fake and the embassy had compounded the problem by producing a surveillance report with the wrong address for his *pension*. (Moscow considered Voynovich a fool and later executed him in the Great Purge.)

To find their man, Moscow enlisted an 'illegal' based in the Netherlands, Dmitri Bystrolyotov, who used the name Hans Galleni and often presented himself as a Hungarian count. In London, Galleni exhibited the kind of resourcefulness that Stalin's purges would almost extinguish among *Chekisti*: he sought the aid of London's Metropolitan Police! He could do so, of course, only after eluding surveillance by the Soviet *rezident*, since to be seen contacting the British authorities would have earned him a one-way ticket to the Lubyanka.

At the police station, Galleni feigned difficulty speaking English and told the Bobbies a cleverly crafted tale. His sister's son had been injured in Paris, he said; the hit-and-run accident had been witnessed by a helpful Englishman whose name and address had, alas, been lost. The Englishman said he was with the Foreign Office. Could the Bobbies help? Galleni's sister needed the insurance money she would get if the Good Samaritan could be summoned to testify as he had promised. The Bobbies could indeed help. *They* telephoned the FO, *they* received the return call while

Galleni waited, and *they* supplied Galleni with the names of four persons who had been in Paris for the FO on the date specified.

Galleni eliminated two of the four — one was a woman, the other lived in too grand a street. He lay in wait for the person living in Pembroke Gardens, hoping that this one would match the photo taken surreptitiously at the Paris Embassy. When he saw his man at Cromwell Road, the exultant Galleni thrust into Oldham's hands an envelope containing £2,000 and instructions for a subsequent meeting. He darted away, leaving a stunned Oldham at the kerb.

At the designated meeting, Galleni persuaded Oldham to continue his espionage by giving him more money. The truth of Oldham's co-operation has been undisclosed for six decades, write Costello and Tsarev, the significance of the case underestimated. Oldham was 'not just a code clerk but a cypher expert' and between 1930 and 1932 he sent 'a great deal of information on security and secret traffic systems' to Moscow.

But Oldham had misgivings. He resigned from the FO, possibly as a way to end his relationship with Soviet Intelligence (even though Galleni had warned him against refusing to continue). And now the Soviets were worried. Oldham had helped to recruit John Herbert King in the FO communications department, thus compromising the principle of compartmentation whereby agents shouldn't know of each other's existence. The Soviets were worried that the disaffected Oldham would reveal Bert King's treason as well as his own.

As William R. Corson and Robert T. Crowley note mordantly in *The New KGB*, 'There were no live deserters from Stalin's secret army.' And indeed, on 29 September, 1933, a year after Oldham's resignation from the FO (and from Stalin's secret army), he lay unconscious on his kitchen floor here in Pembroke Gardens. The hospital pronounced him dead on arrival; the coroner's report indicated 'coal gas suffocation' and mentioned Oldham's 'unsound mind'. (Bert King later went to prison, his treason revealed by defecting *Chekist* Walter Krivitsky. In 1941 Krivitsky too was found dead — another 'suicide' — in his Washington hotel room.)

Twelve years after Oldham's death, MI5 asked Mrs Oldham to help in identifying Galleni (presumably by photograph, since Moscow had recalled him in 1936 and sent him to the gulag). The day before meeting with MI5 she fell mysteriously ill. She died before making the identification. Her timely death raises once more the question of Soviet penetration of MI5. Intelligence writer Richard Deacon hints that Guy Liddell (*see Site 32*), soon to become deputy director-general of MI5 and later suspected of being a Soviet mole, knew more than he should have about the deaths of Oldham and his widow.

Retrace your steps half a block and turn L into handsome Edwardes Square. Ahead is Kensington High Street: tube stations at Kensington (Olympia) and High Street Kensington. For the next walk, turn L on Kensington High Street. At Holland Road in Kensington High Street is the Olympia Hilton Hotel where Iraqi dissidents and CIA officers held secret meetings in 1992 to discuss an Iraqi plan to kill Saddam Hussein. The plotters in Iraq were ultimately betrayed in 1993, only days before the plan's execution, and Saddam arrested hundreds. Did the Americans betray them, as alleged by a leading Iraqi exile in London? Maybe not. Saddam would have learnt from the Soviet security services precisely how to infiltrate such a cabal — or even how to create one, attracting and then controlling the plotters.

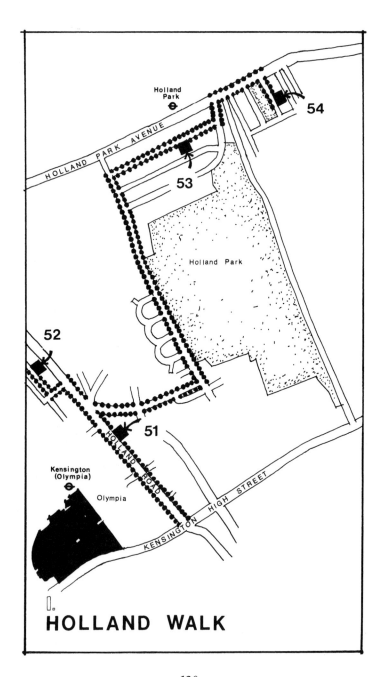

HOLLAND WALK

I. HOLLAND WALK

Arrive at Kensington High Street by bus or tube − nearest station is Kensington (Olympia) − and walk two longish blocks on Holland Road to

Site 51: **82 Holland Road.** In 1937 and 1938, Comintern agents round the world were busy gathering top-secret documents for Moscow Centre. Percy Glading, a leading figure in the CPGB, headed one *apparat* in London.

Glading knew that he needed a fixed location for photographing the material. He was clever enough to realize that the flat should be rented by someone unknown to MI5. He was clever enough to see that a young woman named Olga Gray, who had been recruited to secret Comintern work from a CPGB front organization, was the perfect person to help in renting and running the unprepossessing ground-floor flat here in Holland Road. Unfortunately for Glading and the others convicted in 1938 as the 'Woolwich Arsenal spies' he was *not* clever enough to know that Olga Gray was an MI5 penetration agent.

Gray was 25 when Maxwell Knight recruited her as 'a 50 shillings a week spy' (her words). She was well suited to spy work, explains Anthony Masters in his biography of Knight. She liked excitement and needed a sense of belonging; she had a strong (and even headstrong) personality. Her middle-class Tory background and even her membership in the bourgeois Ealing Ladies' Hockey Club caused no suspicion of her dual role. From 1931 to 1937 she worked with the Friends of the Soviet Union and the Anti-War Movement, doing typing, helping to produce the pacifist newspaper *War* (!), and attending cell meetings. In 1934 she smuggled a large sum of money to a Party member in India, concealing the notes in her sanitary pads. On her return, to Knight's delight, she was asked to work full-time at Party headquarters (*see Site 100*).

It was an exhausting and difficult life, and the need for watchfulness and secrecy troubled her. A boy-friend entered her life and she told Knight she couldn't continue. Knight pleaded, and when she broke under the strain he filled her hospital room with flowers and visited daily. Released from hospital, she returned to King Street; the boy-friend had gone. Early in 1937 she told the Party she wanted to resign, but two days later she acceded to Percy Glading's request that she run this safe-house. They shopped together to furnish it; 'the curtains are in my daughter's house now,' she would recall 50 years later.

To this flat Glading brought Teodor Maly, the NKVD's principal 'illegal' in England until Moscow recalled him during the purges. To this flat too came Maly's replacement, a Mr and Mrs 'Stevens' (*see Site 79*). In October, 1937, photographic equipment arrived. MI5 had already trained Olga Gray in photography but she pretended ignorance so that Glading and the Stevens couple could train her again. The three didn't always want her assistance. When an exceedingly nervous Mrs Stevens arrived one day with an oblong parcel, they ordered the young woman into the bedroom while they photographed the parcel's contents. From negatives drying over the bathtub, however, Gray discerned serial numbers on the blueprints – numbers that identified the documents as Woolwich Arsenal designs for a new naval gun.

The Stevens couple soon left for Moscow and, like Maly, were never heard of again. MI5 kept watch on the house from a flat across the street (and from the street itself with the odd 'letter-carrier' or 'street-cleaner') but waited two months to roll up the ring.

Olga Gray, testifying as 'Miss X', was the primary witness against Glading and the three Woolwich employees. The popular press invented an aristocratic background for their heroine. *Time* magazine depicted her as 'curvesomely sheathed in clinging black' and 'shifting her handsome fur piece with the sinuosity of Mae West.' She was actually in considerable turmoil; she had been close to Glading and felt uneasy at betraying him.

Years later, living in Canada under a new identity, Gray was still terrified of communist retribution and still bitter that her association with MI5 had ended so abruptly. She had been 'cast into the wilderness' writes Masters, perhaps too dramatically; she couldn't, after all, have expected to continue her undercover activities. Knight moved triumphantly into a senior position at MI5. His agent had exposed not only the CPGB activities but also the Soviet practice of subsidising CPs in countries like India. It was a great coup for Knight.

Today, the Woolwich Arsenal case 'does not seem to be quite the sensational counterintelligence coup it was made out to be at the time,' states John Costello in *Mask of Treachery*. True, the authorities ended an important espionage operation and sent Glading and two Woolwich men to prison. But at least three Soviet agents escaped arrest. 'Chance, miscalculation, or deliberate tipoffs are the only possible explanations,' writes Costello. He argues persuasively for the last of these possibilities.

Farther along Holland Road, turn L at Russell Gardens and R at Elsham Road, a street of deep front yards. Midway up this long block, on the R, is

Site 52: **18 Elsham Road.** In 1938 a relatively unpromising young man – an Oxford dropout, a failure in his intended career as a journalist, and most recently a tuberculosis patient – joined MI5 and moved

Site 52: **18 Elsham Road.**

here with his bride. He left Elsham Road for the Oxford area in 1940 when MI5 sought temporary safety at Blenheim Palace. In 1956, having been promoted several times beyond his abilities (as a good many saw it), he became head of MI5, a post he held until his retirement in 1965. The suspicions that dogged his later years stayed with him even after his death in 1973. It is still widely suspected that the late Sir Roger Hollis was a Soviet mole for all of his 27 years in the Security Service.

The case against him is wholly circumstantial, as it is bound to be without confessions, without witnesses, without solid evidence, without firm identification by defectors. But considering all that went wrong on his watch (*see Site 54*): the British ops that failed, the Soviet ops that succeeded, the many matters on which Hollis gave less assistance to the British than he might have (and more assistance to the Soviets), one is left with the suspicion that Roger Hollis was more than simply 'dour' and 'uninspiring.'

First, though, came the suspicion that something was amiss generally in MI5. The earliest clue came in 1962 when Philby in Beirut apparently expected the top-secret visit from Nicholas Elliott telling him he was under suspicion (*see Site 42*). There was also the accumulating evidence that someone in the upper reaches of MI5 had, for some time, been intentionally furthering Soviet aims. The Soviet defector Golitsyn had seen a card index of MI5 documents in Moscow and also knew of a technical paper by Peter Wright circulating there. Earlier Soviet turncoats (Igor Gouzenko who was successful in defecting and Konstantin Volkov who wasn't) had pointed to a still-unidentified Soviet asset in MI5 or MI6. Added to this was the growing realization that MI5 had achieved little success in attracting defectors or in running double agents and had only caught 'Lonsdale' and Vassall (*see Sites 88 and 12*) because they were probably discards. An unprecedented molehunt within MI5 began early in 1963 when MI5's Arthur Martin dug into the matter and came up with Graham Mitchell and Roger Hollis as his two chief suspects. Quite horrifyingly, these two were also the top two in MI5: Hollis the director-general and Mitchell (*see Site 133*) his deputy.

For obvious reasons, Martin went outside his own service – to Sir Dick White, head of MI6 – to discuss his findings. White sent him to Hollis, but only to report on Mitchell. Within the week Hollis had ordered Martin to investigate Mitchell. Joining Arthur Martin's team was Peter Wright.

By September, 1964, Mitchell had been virtually cleared (the charges against him unproven) and he had retired. Where did that leave the larger matter of the almost certain penetration of MI5? Hollis wanted the matter dropped. Wright circumvented him and requested that it be studied by an *ad hoc* committee from MI5 and MI6. This new committee, code-named 'Fluency' and headed by Wright, also included Martin – who had meanwhile been sacked by Hollis and hired by MI6.

Concentrating solely on defectors' allegations, Fluency took a hard look at material that 'pointed in Hollis's direction for the first time,' Wright relates in *Spycatcher*. The investigation faltered in 1966, however (Hollis having just retired), while MI5 pursued an investigation of someone else entirely. This new quest was a complete red herring; the Soviets had had Hollis's help, it is thought, in providing some initially believable disinformation.

The hunt continued. By 1967 the new head of MI5 (Martin Furnival Jones) finally agreed to an interrogation of Mitchell. When nothing conclusive emerged from that event, MI5's investigating branch (K7) recommended an immediate investigation and interrogation of Hollis as the best candidate. A ten-hour interrogation in 1970 was inconclusive: some people believed Hollis and some people didn't. Two years later K7 completed its first report on Hollis, finding him the primary suspect but ultimately giving him the benefit of the doubt. A second K7 report (ordered by Michael Hanley, MI5's new head in 1972) also failed to prove Hollis's guilt but did not precisely 'clear' him.

The molehunters now feared that 'the case was being shelved for political convenience,' as Pincher reports. Their efforts to keep it open resulted in an independent enquiry by Lord Trend, the choice of the Prime Minister. This one-man review ended with Hollis once again being given the benefit of the doubt – and the government, once again, considering the case closed.

It wasn't, of course. Chapman Pincher, with information from Peter Wright and others, wrote *Their Trade Is Treachery*, from which the daily press in 1981 produced excerpts. (The opening headline: 'MI5 CHIEF WAS RUSSIAN SPY SUSPECT.') Three years later, Pincher's *Too Secret Too Long* strengthened the case against Hollis. Peter Wright's own book, published in 1987 and immediately banned in Britain for breach of confidentiality, was almost an anti-climax.

'For ten long years,' Wright states, 'both sides had feuded like medieval theologians, driven by instinct, passion, and prejudice.' My brief recap cannot do justice to the truly wrenching impact of the molehunt. Morale suffered (as Hollis, for one, had predicted). MI5's reputation suffered. The Anglo-American alliance suffered. Individuals suffered. Some in MI5 judged Wright and the others to be as traitorous as any traitor sought by the molehunters. The matter of the Soviet mole high in MI5 is still unsettled. But I am persuaded, with Chapman Pincher, that 'the preponderance of probabilities' points to the enigmatic Hollis.

Retrace your steps to Holland Road, turn R, and follow Addison Crescent into Oakwood Court. At Abbotsbury Road turn L. (For a detour, turn R into Melbury Road where SIS occupied a villa in the 1920s. The move from Whitehall Court had been partially an economy measure; in 1924 the new Chancellor of the Exchequer, Winston

Churchill, found the money to return SIS to a central location, 54 Broadway.) To skip this detour, go N on Abbotsbury Road the length of Holland Park. Turn R at the second street named Holland Park. Towards the end of the block is

Site 53: **42 Holland Park.** At midnight on 13 April, 1983, an MI5 officer stuffed an envelope through the mail slot of this house; the envelope contained information of interest to the head of the Soviet intelligence effort in Britain, who lived here. At midnight on 12 June, 1983, the MI5 officer delivered an envelope of even greater value and again included instructions for contacting him. The traitor was 33-year-old Michael Bettaney. We know his name because he was arrested in September as he was about to deliver MI5's full counter-espionage plans against KGB and GRU operations in Britain. Bettaney's story highlights some of the problems faced by spies and spycatchers alike.

To begin with, Bettaney was a 'walk-in'; copying these documents and giving them to the Soviets was his own idea. The *rezident* (Arkady Gouk, by name) was suspicious. Surely this must be a British provocation to expose Gouk − supposedly a diplomat − as the KGB officer he really was.

When Gouk discussed the matter with his second in command, he had no idea that this trusted KGB man (Oleg Gordievsky) was secretly working for MI6. The British arrested Bettaney before he could do further damage, but *great* damage could still be done if the Soviets discovered how MI5 had learnt about him. Gordievsky must be protected. And he was, by a public report that was 'not entirely frank,' as Nigel West nicely puts it. According to this report Bettaney had drawn attention to himself by asking 'about sensitive matters, completely unrelated to his work.'

Convicted in 1984 under the Official Secrets Act, Bettaney was sent to prison for 23 years. Gouk was PNG'd anyway, sent home to become 'the laughingstock of Moscow Centre,' Gordievsky tells us: Gouk had had 'the first opportunity to recruit an MI5 or SIS officer for a quarter of a century' and had bungled it. Gordievsky himself, the defector-in-place who could have been undone by all this, actually improved his position with the KGB, becoming *rezident* to replace the expelled Gouk. Thus was played out an almost farcical drama, an elaborate minuet danced in a pitch-black room, with no music, with the partners wanting and not wanting to make contact with each other, with the dancers not even acknowledging that they are involved in a dance at all.

The Bettaney case has an interesting parallel in the case of Konstantin Volkov, the Soviet intelligence officer who sought to defect to the British in Turkey in August, 1945. In return for asylum, Volkov promised to name several Soviet moles in the upper reaches of Britain's intelligence services. He insisted that his offer be communicated to London via diplomatic pouch because he knew that the Soviets had broken many British codes. Unfortunately for Volkov, the case was given to Kim Philby, head of Britain's anti-Soviet intelligence operations and one of the very moles whom Volkov would be exposing. Philby imediately notified the Soviets, then delayed his trip to Turkey until Volkov and his wife could be drugged, strapped onto stretchers, and carted off to Moscow on the first available Aeroflot flight.

In both cases, a walk-in was betrayed to his employers by a mole within the service he wanted to aid. The difference, of course, is that Bettaney enjoyed a fair trial (and a standard of living in his British prison probably equal to that of the average Muscovite), while

Volkov was probably executed after the customarily ferocious torture.

Many questions were asked, at the time, about Bettaney. How had he advanced to such a sensitive position in counter-espionage, with his history of instability and public drunkenness? Why hadn't he been properly re-vetted? And was he really a case of 'auto-conversion'? The question that lingers in my mind, however, is how many others in MI5 may *not* have been discussed with a mole in the KGB and may *not* have been removed from MI5. One of Bettaney's jobs was to give lectures to new recruits and, as Chapman Pincher relates in *Too Secret Too Long*, Bettaney was fond of telling recruits that MI5 was no longer penetrated by Soviet agents. Have there been others, since Bettaney, saying the same thing to new recruits and smiling to themselves, knowing it wasn't true?

At the end of this street turn L for Holland Park Avenue. Walk E along this centre of Indian life to Campden Hill Square. Halfway up the far side is

Site 54: **6 Campden Hill Square.** Guilt, like beauty, can reside mainly in the eye of the beholder. And when a man is believed to have been

the most important Soviet mole inside British Intelligence, his every action can look suspicious. Sir Roger Hollis, who lived here from the time of his return from Blenheim in 1943 until his retirement as director-general of MI5 in 1965, invariably walked home from Leconfield House to this 'tatty bookless townhouse' (the description is Peter Wright's) even though he had a chauffeured limousine at his command. Why? To stretch his legs? Or to meet his controller in Hyde Park and perhaps signal his need to leave information somewhere? And he invariably stayed late at the office. Why? To avoid his wife and spend time with his secretary (who was his long-term mistress and later his second wife)? Or to do whatever he pleased in the virtually empty headquarters of MI5?

A full list of what Hollis is believed to have done in the Soviet interest is too long for this book. Chapman Pincher's *Their Trade Is Treachery* and *Too Secret Too Long*, each of which is heavily concerned with the probability that Hollis was a Soviet mole, run to a combined total of almost 1,000 pages. Some things are scarcely open to argument. It was Hollis who cast initial doubt on the defector Gouzenko, thus deflecting Gouzenko's allegations about a spy named 'Elli' in MI5 or MI6. (According to Pincher, 'the person who best fits the known information about "Elli" is, unquestionably, Hollis.') It was Hollis who failed to follow up when doubts about Harry Houghton first surfaced in 1956 (*see Site 94*). Houghton was arrested in 1961 with the rest of the Portland ring. It was Hollis who suspended MI5's Arthur Martin for a fortnight after Martin obtained Blunt's confession in 1964, even prohibiting Martin from seeing Blunt during this time and thus giving Blunt 'a completely free run,' suggests Pincher, to get advice from the Soviets, destroy evidence, or 'make any other dispositions.' It was Hollis who destroyed the tapes and transcripts of the early interrogations of Blunt, keeping only the summaries. It was Hollis who enabled Cairncross to return briefly to England in the late 1960s in exchange for helping MI5 (*see Site 25*). This offer was later construed as an 'inducement' that would have prevented any future prosecution of Cairncross. It was Hollis who, during his entire time as head of MI5, refused to allow naval spy Alister Watson to be interrogated (*see Site 119*). It was Hollis who, just before retirement, tried to destroy Liddell's diaries (*see Site 32*).

Other things about Hollis aren't so clear. Was he or wasn't he responsible for clearing Fuchs six times (*see Site 90*)? Some say that these security clearances can 'without question' be laid at Hollis's door, while others say that Fuchs slipped through the net 'despite Hollis's personal actions and not because of them.'

Was he or wasn't he the MI5 spy serviced by 'Sonya' in Oxford during the war (*see Site 95*)? He is 'the likeliest candidate,' says Pincher. For compelling logistical and organizational reasons, it wouldn't have been Blunt, whom the Hollis supporters offer as an alternative.

Was he or wasn't he the person in MI5 who made the 1947 interrogation of 'Sonya' a joke and then established the legend of her departure? Hollis was 'the leading figure' in the control of her case, notes Pincher.

Was he or wasn't he the person who tipped off Burgess, and therefore Maclean, about Maclean's impending interrogation (*see Site 120*)? 'Though not even deputy director then, he had been one of five people fully in on the secret,' writes Pincher.

Was he or wasn't he involved in MI5's decision to exempt itself from the positive vetting system instituted throughout the government in the early 1950s? As director of security at the time (head of MI5's C Division), Hollis must have been 'particularly influential' in this decision, writes Pincher. MI5 didn't adopt positive vetting until 1965, just before Hollis's retirement and 'after some indignant argument' from Hollis, writes Pincher.

Did he or didn't he pursue the Philby case with vigour – again people line up on both sides – and was it he or Mitchell or someone else entirely who told Philby that an offer of immunity would soon be extended to him in Beirut (*see Site 52*)?

Did he or didn't he delay the investigation of Mitchell (*see Site 133*), knowing that if Mitchell retired under a cloud then the suspicion hovering over Hollis himself might be dissipated?

The list could go on: the probable leakages, the botched cases, the peculiar coincidences. Is it coincidence, for instance, that the Soviets asked Blunt to get information from many sections of MI5 but never from F Division (which monitored political extremists) while Hollis headed it? Even Blunt thought this odd. Is it coincidence that almost immediately after Hollis went to Australia in the late 1940s to tell the

Australians of a major Soviet espionage effort there (but *not* to tell them that Britain had broken the Soviet codes), the KGB changed its codes? Is it coincidence that more than 50 attempts by MI5 to penetrate the KGB's effort in Britain all came to nothing? Is it coincidence that after Hollis left MI5, 'the leakages from MI5 seemed to have ended,' as Pincher states? The 1974 arrest of Willi Brandt's personal assistant as a Soviet agent would have been impossible, writes Pincher, if either of the British security services had been headed by a spy.

Hollis's defenders say that nobody could have succeeded against Soviet espionage and counter-espionage, in those times, with those resources, and in those circumstances (in a liberal democracy, that is, not especially alarmed about the Soviet threat). Thus argues Anthony Glees in *The Secrets of the Service: British Intelligence and Communist Subversion 1939-51*. No, runs another argument, the hunched-over and unforthcoming Hollis was unimaginative, dull, inept. No, runs another, he was fully aware of the Soviet threat. Looking at Hollis's words about the Anglo-Soviet Treaty of 1942, Sheila Kerr finds it 'impossible to believe he was a Soviet agent' and 'hardly plausible' that his warning about Stalin was 'an effort to maintain his cover.' Glees, too, claims that Hollis's words exonerate him: letters to his mother from his first job (with the British American Tobacco Company, in China) prove his 'complete loyalty' in China and argue against his having been recruited there by an active communist ring whose members he must have known. 'Why should anyone deliberately want to falsify their political views to their own family?' asks Glees. (I find this question both grammatically and intellectually wanting.)

Why, ask the defenders, does Gordievsky ridicule the charges against Hollis? John Costello has a reasonable answer: since Gordievsky wasn't told about Geoffrey Prime (the Soviets' long-time spy in GCHQ), he wouldn't have been told about Hollis.

Isn't it possible that everything attributed to Hollis can be explained by the presence of Philby and Blunt? Margaret Thatcher argued this to Parliament in 1981 when Pincher's *Their Trade Is Treachery* appeared. I understand Mrs Thatcher's reason for saying so, but no, it isn't possible.

Couldn't the Soviets have inspired the whole indictment of Hollis, asks Glees, perhaps even calling upon Philby to supply the well-crafted disinformation? This seems a desperate conjecture, and it doesn't begin to explain the almost certain existence of a Soviet spy *somewhere* in MI5. On top of everything else suggesting such a person, we have the word of the defector Golitsyn that the Soviet Embassy in London, almost uniquely in the world, needed no special department to prevent defections; their man in MI5 would warn Moscow, said Golitsyn.

Fears about Soviet penetration of MI5 go back many years. They were 'as old as the office furniture' when Peter Wright came onto the scene; early in the 1950s, MI5's Anne Last had entered the suspicions into a notebook and she had pointed to Hollis or Mitchell as the 'most likely' suspect. By the 1970s fully 16 of the 21 molehunters believed in the guilt of either Hollis or Mitchell. Since then, Pincher has been advised that 'many' in MI5 'now incline to the opinion that Hollis was a spy.'

One of Hollis's accusers concedes that he may have been the most ordinary of bureaucrats, wanting only 'to ingratiate the Service, and himself, with Whitehall. And that meant ensuring there were no mistakes, even at the cost of having no successes.' One of Hollis's defenders, on the other hand, concedes that he may have been 'the most ingenious liar of the twentieth century.' Which was he?

Here ends this walk, midway between two tube stations (Holland Park and Notting Hill Gate). To begin the next walk, continue E along Holland Park Avenue.

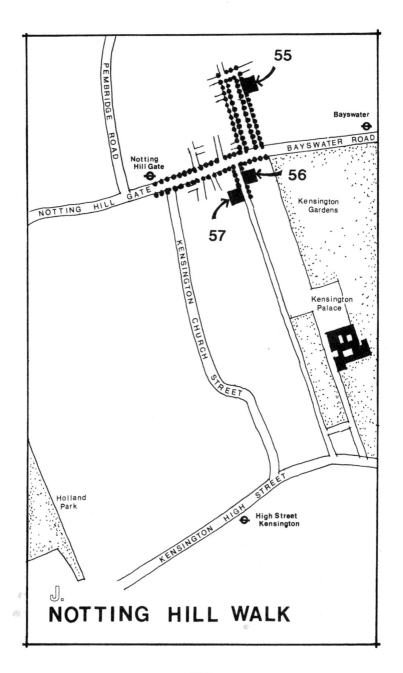

55

Bayswater

BAYSWATER ROAD

Notting
Hill Gate

56

NOTTING HILL GATE

Kensington
Gardens

57

KENSINGTON CHURCH STREET

Kensington
Palace

Holland
Park

KENSINGTON HIGH STREET

High Street
Kensington

J.
NOTTING HILL WALK

J. NOTTING HILL WALK

From Notting Hill Gate tube station, walk E. When the street called Notting Hill Gate becomes Wellington Terrace, turn L into Palace Court. On the R side is

Site 55: **30 Palace Court.** Anthony Blunt was recruited to Soviet Intelligence in 1937 by Burgess. Unlike the other Cambridge recruits, Blunt wanted to be an art historian, not a civil servant, and in 1937 he began working at the Warburg Institute in London. He was still talent-spotting for the Soviets while now trying to distance himself publicly from left-wing views – 'a rather difficult task,' he explained to Moscow. This prewar residence of Blunt's was a meeting place for the tightly knit little group of Marxists/intellectuals/Oxbridge graduates/homosexuals whom Blunt and Burgess tended to attract and exploit.

Shortly before WWII, the Soviets instructed Blunt to enter Britain's military intelligence. He received a commission in the military police and with his language abilities had a good chance of entering counter-intelligence. During the *Sitzkrieg* (or Phoney War), he served with the British Expeditionary Force in France and busied himself writing to influential friends who might get him into MI5 or MI6. After the *Blitzkrieg* and his safe return to England, a friend soon did pave the way for MI5 to hire him (*see Site 83*).

These were heady days for Soviet moles. They shared an optimism that things were going their way, that they belonged to an élite brotherhood even more exclusive than the Cambridge Apostles, that they were serving in the engine-room of history. As Anthony Glees points out in *The Secrets of the Service*, 'it was precisely because the British political class was so small, and so heavily dependent on a few select public schools and Oxbridge, that to penetrate it was so relatively easy and effective.' Crucial to the success of the Soviet

Site 55: **30 Palace Court.**

moles, Glees writes, were the informal networks based on their Oxford and Cambridge friendships – networks that included so many homosexual relationships as to earn this group its label as 'the Homintern'.

At the end of Palace Court, turn L into Moscow Road. (How they must have giggled!) At Ossington Street turn L again. Back on the high street, jog to the R into Kensington Palace Gardens. Once known as Millionaires' Row, it is now an embassies' row. On your L is

Site 56: **6-7 Kensington Palace Gardens.** The disastrous evacuation from Dunkirk in 1940 left Britain suddenly blind and deaf on the Continent. Along with their military conquest the Germans had rolled up all British intelligence networks there — those of SIS *and* those of the parallel Z Organization (which had been set up separately to prevent exactly what happened anyway). How did German counter-intelligence manage all this? By being very diligent, very resourceful, and very lucky.

Once Britain began acquiring prisoners-of-war (downed *Luftwaffe* aircrews, mostly), they were seen as a rich source of current information. They were screened in this magnificent mansion, which had been commandeered for the war effort and dubbed the 'London Cage'. More extensive questioning of officers, and of any enlisted personnel who seemed predisposed to co-operate, took place outside London.

The head of the London Cage, we learn from Richard Deacon's *Spyclopedia*, was a Lieutenant-Colonel Alexander Scotland who had served in the pre-WWI German Army while cattle-farming in German South-West Africa. The word was put out that he had recently infiltrated the German general staff and knew *everything*. The bluff worked: he soon *did* know everything from some very senior German officers.

Down the street, on your R, you will be watched from a pair of villas unidentified except as

Site 57: **18 Kensington Palace Gardens.** When Oleg Penkovsky told his debriefers in the early 1960s that fully 60 per cent of Soviet embassy personnel throughout the world were with the KGB or the GRU, he probably didn't surprise anyone. This particular embassy had long been under MI5 surveillance — from the upstairs bedroom of the house opposite one of the main gates, from the 'choke points' at either end of this elegant street, and from a safe-house in the next street.

MI5's mobile Watchers worked from cars repainted every three months. Number plates were changed even more frequently from a selection carried in each car. But the Soviets had good counter-surveillance, electronic and otherwise, and even without additional assistance from inside MI5, the Soviets could routinely outwit the Watchers. Some Watchers were so readily identifiable, Peter Wright tells us, that at one time they were systematically approached by KGB officers trying to suborn them – one KGB officer pressed an envelope stuffed with money upon a Watcher in a pub.

One remedy, of course, was to restrict the number of official Soviet personnel in London (Penkovsky had strongly recommended it), and in 1971 MI5 persuaded the government to do just that: 90 KGB and GRU officers were expelled from London and another 25 on leave in the Soviet Union were denied readmission. 'The expulsions marked a major turning point in the history of KGB operations in the United Kingdom,' writes Christopher Andrew in *KGB: The Inside Story*, his first book with former KGB *rezident* Oleg Gordievsky. 'The golden age of KGB operations' here was over. Because of these expulsions and because of the tighter surveillance that resulted, 'the KGB found it more difficult to collect high-grade intelligence in London than in almost any other Western capital.' By the 1980s the embassy was running 'only a handful of agents and "confidential contacts", none of major importance,' Andrew and Gordievsky write in *Instructions from the Center*.

During all these years, however, this embassy was paymaster to CPs throughout Africa and Latin America, according to recent revelations in Moscow by a former London *rezident*. A steady stream of 'guests' arrived here to collect the used pound notes sent by Moscow Centre via diplomatic bags. (Moscow Centre suffered some 'disillusion', *The Sunday Times* tells us, upon learning that 'an unnamed Communist party from Africa was spending Moscow's money on lavish entertainment for its leaders'.)

As to what else went on inside the embassy, perhaps MI5 picked it up by electronic means, perhaps not. Peter Wright describes a delicious plan devised by MI5 in the 1950s, using new technology to modify an ordinary object so that it would reflect sound waves; carrying no transmitter or receiver itself, the object was virtually undetectable. Why not modify some valuable object along these lines and give it to the Soviet ambassador? Wright consulted someone who knew the ways of the Soviet diplomatic community and had also been with MI5: Klop Ustinov, father of the actor. Ustinov suggested a bust of Lenin or a model of the Kremlin, something so sacred that the Soviets wouldn't be tempted to sell it. Lenin was vetoed ('the smooth contours of Vladimir Ilyich's skull were too rounded to be sure of reflecting sound waves,' Wright tells us) and ultimately the FO abandoned the project, for reasons we do not learn.

If the London embassy 'never recovered' from the expulsions of 1971, as Andrew and Gordievsky write, the KGB operation here was truly devastated by Gordievsky's escape in 1985: 'For the first time in Soviet history, a KGB officer already identified as a Western mole had escaped across the Russian border.'

Gordievsky's saga is better than the best fiction. Son of a stalwart NKVD man, brother of a brave 'illegal', he was raised among the privileged élite. He joined the KGB during the hopeful Khrushchev years but turned against the system after Moscow crushed the Prague Spring. By 1974 he was co-operating regularly with MI6 (in Copenhagen, then Moscow, then London), meeting sometimes twice a week with his case-officer until Moscow abruptly recalled him in 1985. Drugged, he somehow survived a hostile interrogation. Then, under constant surveillance, he managed to contact SIS *twice* in Moscow, elude his keepers again (while jogging), take a train to Leningrad, and evade KGB dogs and cars at the border. He had help. One can only imagine the details.

How was he discovered? Perhaps, thought Gordievsky, he erred in alerting the SIS to Bettaney (*see Site 53*); perhaps, with time on his hands in prison, Bettaney had deduced the truth about who had put him there. Gordievsky is confident that 'nothing leaked to Moscow' from MI5, MI6, or the FO. By 1994 he had a more likely prospect: the CIA's Aldrich Ames, for many years a Soviet agent.

After the abortive coup of 1991, the new head of the KGB finally allowed Gordievsky's wife and daughters to leave Russia and join him in England. Little outcry had come from human-rights campaigners during the family's six-year separation, writes Lord Bethell in a poignant column. 'After all, he is a traitor,' Bethell was often told by British friends. Even in the early 1990s, with all that was known by then about the Soviet Union, some people still couldn't bring themselves to oppose it.

NOTTING HILL WALK

At the end of this extraordinary street (guarded at both ends) is Kensington Palace, home to various royals. To begin our next walk, take the tube at High Street Kensington. Change at Paddington for Warwick Avenue.

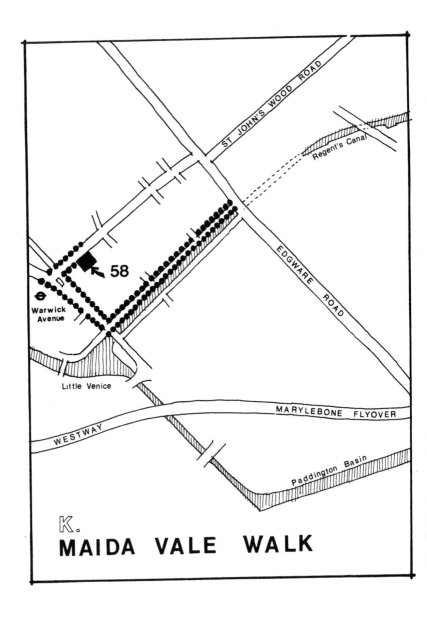

St John's Wood Road

Regent's Canal

Edgware Road

58

Warwick Avenue

Little Venice

Marylebone Flyover

Westway

Paddington Basin

K.
MAIDA VALE WALK

K. MAIDA VALE WALK

Adding this walk to the previous one, you'll arrive at Warwick Avenue tube station. Just E is Clifton Gardens. A preferred route, however, is by bus up Edgware Road. Get off at Blomfield Road and walk W alongside Regent's Canal (which reaches the Thames eight miles to the E, as the barge floats). Small boats here have names like 'Serendipity' on their hulls and sounds of chamber music coming from within. Where the canal widens at 'Little Venice' (named by Robert Browning), you can visit a floating art gallery or take a boat to the zoo or linger on one of the benches wishing you 'good health, good fortune and happiness'. It is a remarkable scene for typically sombre London, gone as soon as you walk N on Warwick Avenue. In the first block of Clifton Gardens, on the R, is

Site 58: **9-17 Clifton Gardens.**

Site 58: **9-17 Clifton Gardens.** Alexander Allan Foote, who spent his last years here in what was then a shabby hotel, was unique. Many have claimed to be loyal Englishmen while they were actually communist moles. Foote alone claimed to be a communist agent while he was actually a loyal Englishman.

Foote never admitted being a British agent; his *Handbook for Spies* calls the idea 'high farce'. But books by ex-spies are notoriously suspect. Foote later said that MI5 had 'mutilated' his book — deleting here, inventing there — and indeed the very style of writing suggests an author other than the unschooled Yorkshireman who was Allan Foote. In fact, the book was ghost-written by MI5 and contains 'deliberate misinformation' according to Chapman Pincher — perhaps to cover what Pincher calls the 'culpable negligence' of MI5 in the Foote affair.

The intriguing book *Operation Lucy: Most Secret Spy Ring of the Second World War*, by Anthony Read and David Fisher, makes a strong case for Foote having been recruited in 1936 to Dansey's Z Organization (*see Site 96*) and then, after two years in Spain with the communist-led International Brigades (establishing his leftist *bona fides*), going into Switzerland in 1939 as a British agent and a GRU officer. The Read and Fisher thesis is that Foote was one of four British access points to the Soviet network in Switzerland known as the Lucy ring, and that through this network Britain passed its top-secret Ultra decrypts to the Russians during the war. According to this theory, the British knew that Stalin wouldn't trust such material if he thought it came from *them*; also, since Soviet Intelligence was infiltrated by the Nazis, the Soviets mustn't learn that Hitler's 'unbreakable' cyphers had in fact been broken. Cited by Read and Fisher in support of this thesis are no less than Victor Cavendish-Bentinck, who headed Britain's Joint Intelligence Committee, and F. W. Winterbotham, who established the control system by which Ultra secrets were fiercely protected.

'There is, of course, no truth in this nonsense,' writes Phillip Knightley in *The Second Oldest Profession*. Poor reception from Germany (garbling the messages) and difficulty breaking that day's Enigma key, says Knightley, would have required far more time getting the material to the Lucy ring and then to Moscow than seems to have been the case.

Knightley relies on the word of F. H. Hinsley, official historian of British wartime intelligence; Hinsley's multi-volume work explicitly denies that Britain used the Lucy ring to pass information to Moscow. Hinsley describes the route by which Enigma decrypts *were* sent to Moscow. Messages from the individual intelligence branches were cleared with 'C' and then dispatched to the British Military Mission in Moscow. The information ostensibly came from 'an officer in the German War Office'.

Where *did* the accurate and detailed Lucy material come from? From members of the German High Command, according to one theory. But, say Read and Fisher, 'common sense alone' argues against any spy or spies working in the German High Command 'undetected through all the most difficult days of the war, surviving all purges and postings, and finding time to encipher and transmit vast quantities of information. Such a premise simply does not hold water.'

The debate will continue. Intelligence writer Richard Deacon names a member of the Bletchley operation who, unlike Hinsley, supports the Lucy/Ultra theory. And a recent scholarly article by Richard Àldrich in the journal *Intelligence and National Security* uses words like 'lurid' and 'exotic' to ridicule that theory. Even the CIA favours German sources for the Lucy material, as seen in its official history of Soviet intelligence networks in wartime Europe.

The CIA account agrees with MI5 in omitting any connection between Foote and British Intelligence. Who was the enigmatic Foote? He was ingenious, affable, hardworking (sometimes transmitting for days and nights on end). He was smart enough to avoid being outsmarted by German or Soviet agents. He *was* arrested by the Swiss, in 1943, but his ten-month incarceration was rather a joke. I have always wondered whether the British themselves didn't sell out the Lucy ring. It had already accomplished its work of saving the USSR (and therefore the Allies), and by 1943 the USSR enjoyed a position of strength worrisome to Churchill. Stranger things have happened.

Here's another wrinkle. For some time before the ring was broken, Foote had been in a power struggle with Sándor Radó over its control. After Foote's release by the Swiss, he and Radó were recalled together to Moscow, and on the trip Foote filled his colleague's mind with worries about how the Soviets would view Radó's various lapses. During their stopover in Cairo the frightened Radó sought refuge with the British. The British had no interest in him and gave him to the Egyptians, who let him be forcibly repatriated to the USSR in July, 1945. To historian Aldrich, such British carelessness undermines the Lucy/Ultra theory: if Radó had been part of a British-manipulated ring, wouldn't the British have tried to protect their secrets? (I have a hunch that the British hands-off policy towards Radó may owe something to Kim Philby or others in London.) Foote was actually *lucky* that Radó was returned to the Soviets; they thought Radó had been killed by the British because he was carrying news that Foote was a British agent! In Moscow, Foote slowly regained the trust of the Soviets. Radó spent ten years in the Lubyanka.

In Berlin in 1947, *en route* to Argentina for Soviet Intelligence, Foote suddenly crossed into the British sector of Berlin and surrendered. What had happened? He was worried about his ulcers, we know. He may also have been worried about his safety, since another member of the Lucy ring (another British agent, Rachel Dübendorfer) had just been recalled to Moscow.

MI5 interrogated Foote for ten weeks. And now the British exhibited some very odd behaviour. They didn't ask him to continue working with the Soviets. Why? And they didn't maintain surveillance on 'Sonya' (*see Site 95*), who had trained him for his work with the communist *apparat*. Why? She was inexplicably allowed to slip away to East Germany. Read and Fisher believe that 'someone somewhere effectively blocked all [Foote's] efforts to make the authorities listen to what he had to say'. Foote felt certain in his later years that traitors existed at high levels in both MI5 and MI6, but he found nobody to listen to him. Why? Perhaps, say Read and Fisher, because he was only an adventurer, a maverick, the son of a failed poultry farmer, and because 'a double agent can never be trusted, even by his own side'. Did highly placed moles encourage this dismissive attitude?

Although Foote wanted to work for MI6 as a consultant, he was given a minor job in the Ministry of Agriculture and Fisheries. If HM Government believed his loyalty was to the communists, why give him a job at all? And if HM Government believed his loyalty was to Britain, why not take advantage of his knowledge of Soviet Intelligence? 'MI5 had something on him,' say Read and Fisher, and Foote was left to rot – 'and rot he did with the help of alcohol'.

The Soviets decorated Allan Foote four times and promoted him to the rank of major; the Lucy material, whatever its sources, had been critically important to them (even though they hadn't believed one of its earliest items, about Hitler's invasion of the USSR). But Foote was tossed away by what I believe was – the whole time – his own side. At the age of 51, he left his room here in Clifton Gardens for his final trip to hospital. There, with half his stomach gone and his condition hopeless, he resolutely tore off his dressings, removed his tubes, and died.

To call it a day, take the bus down Edgware Road. (Near the bus stop, Clifton Road is the kind of neighbourhood shopping centre that gives this vast metropolis the sense of being a collection of small towns.) To proceed with the next walk, take the tube from Warwick Avenue to Marylebone – same line, two stops.

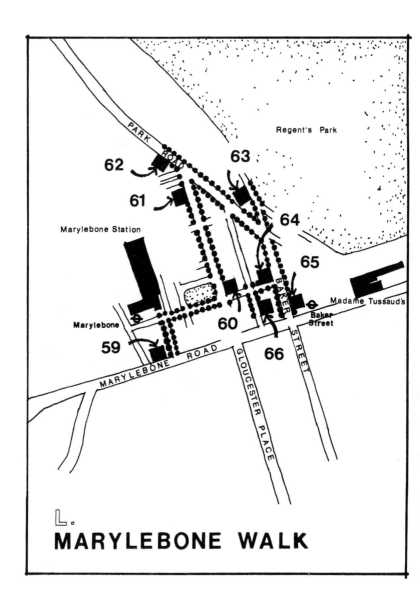

Regent's Park

62

63

61

64

Marylebone Station

65

60

Madame Tussaud's

Marylebone

Baker Street

59

66

PARK ROAD

BAKER STREET

MARYLEBONE ROAD

GLOUCESTER PLACE

L.
MARYLEBONE WALK

L. MARYLEBONE WALK

Marylebone tube station is in the cavernous Marylebone railway station. The original cast-iron canopy leads directly to

Site 59: **the old Great Central Hotel, Marylebone Road.** This grand pile, requisitioned by the War Office during WWII, was used in part to debrief Allied military personnel returning from occupied Europe.

For the last two years of the war the chief organizer of escape networks for Britain's wartime exfiltration organization was the impressively capable Airey Neave (*see Site 24*). He was debriefed here himself following his own escape from maximum-security Colditz Castle. Wearing a hand-me-down uniform without insignia, he had been constantly questioned by military police on the train down from Scotland. Britain was still obsessed with German saboteurs and Neave must have been quite a sight. But things were different at the Great Central:

> We were directed to the reception desk where two years before a splendid blonde in black had been on guard.
> Now there was a sergeant at the desk.
> 'What is this place, sergeant?'
> 'The London Transit Camp, sir.' He studied me politely. 'Where are you from, sir?'
> 'Germany.'
> He did not bat an eyelid.
> 'Quite so, sir. Then it will be MI9 you want. They are on the second floor.'

This building never resumed its function as one of London's four major railway hotels, disappointing many who, like Neave, had gloried in its 'magnificent dullness and solidity.' For a time British Rail used the building for offices. It is now the Regent Hotel.

Walk through Melcombe Place to Dorset Square, first site of Lord's cricket ground (established in 1787 by Thomas Lord). Walk the length of the square. Ahead is

Site 60: **1 Dorset Square.** On 19 July, 1940, the day Hitler announced England's impending collapse, Churchill created the Special Operations Executive 'to co-ordinate all action by way of subversion and sabotage against the enemy overseas.' Before year's end, SOE had formed its F Section (*see Site 72*). But the French were not wholly grateful. All the governments-in-exile were wary of the British; General de Gaulle, head of the Free French in London, was especially so. He was enraged at F Section's early recruitment of French citizens (whom he considered his property); when France was liberated he gave SOE agents 48 hours to leave his country.

Early on, however, SOE recognized de Gaulle's strength in France and formed another French section to work with his military intelligence in London (*see Site 73*). The new section was called RF, 'a name that echoed, by a delicate compliment, that *République*

Site 60: **1 Dorset Square.**

Française which de Gaulle felt he personified,' writes M. R. D. Foot. The agents of RF were mostly French, as the agents of F were not, and French was spoken exclusively in RF until English-speaking officers produced such abominations (*un vrai fil vivant* for a 'real live wire') that the rule was mercifully allowed to lapse.

SOE's ubiquitous Bickham Sweet-Escott served here briefly in 1943 as head of RF Section. In his *Baker Street Irregular* he describes the place: downstairs, an operations room; on the top floor, a flat where staff checked the 'authentic Gallic appearance of those about to cross the Channel'; elsewhere, the various training, dispatching and intelligence units. RF's tenancy here succeeded the directorate of the Bertram Mills circus, and Sweet-Escott mentions a large room on the *piano nobile* where Mills himself had worked: 'innumerable dirty rhomboids on the wall showed where had hung the signed photographs of the lion tamers, the jugglers and the men on the flying trapeze.' Critics of RF Section enjoyed thinking of RF's officers sitting where the managers of clowns had recently sat, but nobody ridiculed the dangers of RF's work − far greater than putting one's head into the mouth of a docile lion or setting forth on a safety-netted high wire.

For RF's task involved nothing less than (in Foot's words) 'to stimulate, guide, and service the creation of a unified resistance movement and a secret army inside France.' F Section had more limited objectives, mostly involving demolition and industrial sabotage. But the demarcation was not so sharp: 'inevitably, some of F's best men ranged far outside a narrow saboteur's brief,' Foot writes, and some of RF's agents performed 'highly distinguished' acts of sabotage.

RF's orders were prepared jointly by SOE and by de Gaulle's *Bureau Central de Renseignements et d'Action*. SOE had veto power (rarely used) and controlled the flow of information. SOE kept the French in the dark about D-Day plans, for instance. When BCRA planners came up with the same date and many of the same beaches, Baker Street initially (and wrongly) suspected a leak from RF Section – then had to hope that the Germans weren't as accurate in *their* assessment of tides and terrain.

F and RF were only two of the six sections of SOE involved in France. These two were the largest, though, supplying more than 400 agents each. AMF Section, which began after the North African landings in 1942, sent in another 400; the Jedburgh teams, which began as support for the Normandy invasion, almost 300. (DF Section sent in few agents but built excellent escape lines, and EU/P dealt solely with the large number of Polish refugees in northern France.) And these six sections were only *some* of the Allied secret organizations working in France. 'Gaul was certainly divided into many more than three parts,' observes Sweet-Escott, citing the activity of the Czechs, Poles, Belgians, Dutch, British, and of course the French. With each group somewhat isolated from the others, he writes, 'the scope for muddle was immense.'

The potential for rivalry was also great. 'Inter-section jealousies within SOE were endemic; between F and RF sections they raged with virulence,' Foot writes, although in his view this jealousy was mostly 'froth' and basically 'unimportant.' Every historian mentions the conflicts between F and RF. I gladly give Foot the last word: 'These jealousies were gradually resolved, as each came to accept the accomplished fact of the other's existence; in any case, they were always far worse in London than "in the field".'

In the end France belonged to de Gaulle (as he had known all along). He had feared the British, expecting them to impose a puppet government on France after the war, but the British involvement through SOE was essentially military, not political. He had also feared the French communists, and his basic distrust of the British was fuelled by the knowledge that SOE didn't believe in excluding anybody, of any political persuasion, from the war against Hitler. Nor was de Gaulle alone in his concern about the communists; many feared, with some justification, that the communists wouldn't stop fighting after the Germans were defeated but would use the postwar chaos to overthrow any democratic government. The communists, however, were no match for the Gaullists. Foot, again: 'The latter had bothered to read Trotsky, whom they rightly regarded as the leading expert on how to seize power in an industrial society; the communists, brought up to abhor Trotsky, had not.' (The failure to study Trotsky also contributed, I think, to the failure of the 1991 coup against Gorbachev.)

In the end, too, while France received a great deal of attention from SOE, Foot is not simply being gallant in saying that 'the French saved themselves; the British and, later, the Americans gave them the means to do so, but could not give them the will.' The (literally and figuratively) towering figure of Charles de Gaulle gave them a focus for their will. He was surely a difficult man; but for many of the defeated French and certainly for the agents of SOE's RF Section, he *was* France.

Walk the width of Dorset Square, and continue on Gloucester Place for several blocks. At Taunton Place is the modest apartment building known as

Site 61: **Ivor Court, Gloucester Place.** According to my friend Bob Iveson-Watt (a brave American who served with the British Expeditionary Force until he lost a leg at Dunkirk), OSS lodged its field operatives here while they awaited transportation into occupied Europe.

Contrary to the romantic stereotype, not all agents parachuted into Europe. Many did. But some went in on small airplanes (typically Lysanders), touching down on isolated landing strips and being greeted by welcoming committees composed usually (but not always) of resistance workers. And some went in on small boats; not all agents were in condition for parachuting.

Site 61: **Ivor Court, Gloucester Place.**

Immediately to the N is another prewar block of flats,

Site 62: **Rossmore Court, Park Road.** Here, too, Iveson-Watt tells me, were accommodations for OSS agents going into Europe to organize resistance units, to lead or co-ordinate units already in existence, to conduct sabotage, to wage partisan warfare.

Site 62: **Rossmore Court, Park Road.**

Some of the OSS people later became the nucleus of the Central Intelligence Group, which later still became the Central Intelligence Agency. For almost 40 years, some of the CIA's leading figures were former OSS officers. They viewed covert ops (sabotage, assassination, insurrection) as an integral part of intelligence activities – a view undoubtedly reinforced by their OSS experience.

Walk down Park Road and make a sharp L towards the Clarence Gate of Regent's Park. Overlooking the park is a series of elegant villas, their location and style set by the theatrical John Nash, architect to the Prince Regent. Named for the second brother of the Prince Regent is

Site 63: **Clarence Terrace.** When Western intelligence agencies built the Berlin Tunnel beneath the Soviet sector of Berlin in the early 1950s, they showed the kind of audacity and enterprise that had long typified communist ops. Here at Clarence Terrace, SIS and CIA planned the project together, Nigel West tells me. The 1,800-foot tunnel ran from the American zone in West Berlin to the Soviet zone in East Berlin. Sophisticated equipment tapped into all Soviet telephone traffic in East Berlin and recorded all Soviet communication with Warsaw and Moscow. Unfortunately, the

155

Soviets learnt about the tunnel even before it was built (*see Site 84*). After officially 'discovering' it in 1956, they took thousands of East Berliners on propaganda tours.

Site 63: **Clarence Terrace.**

Peter Wright in *Spycatcher* locates another activity in this building (which I assume to be his 'unmarked four-storey Georgian house in an elegant terrace in Regent's Park'). MI5 knew that if its Watchers operated from Leconfield House, they could be readily identified by Soviet counter-surveillance. Instead, therefore, they worked from an anonymous building in Regent's Park. Wright describes the scene: 'The central control room was dominated by a vast street map of London on one wall which was used to monitor the progress of operations. In the middle of the room was the radio console which maintained communications with all observation posts and mobile Watcher teams.' To imagine the wealth of electronic technology behind the graceful façade of Clarence Terrace is to know that such equipment, for such activities, could be anywhere. And probably is.

Back at Park Road, walk S into Baker Street. In 1930, when the two parts of Baker Street were united and the street was renumbered, a real 221B Baker Street came into existence for the fictional Sherlock Holmes. On your R, just above Melcombe Street, is

Site 64: **221 Baker Street.** In addition to 'country' sections, SOE had a number of 'technical' sections — 'dealing with security, clothing,

forgery, cipher, armament, air liaison, and so on,' as M. R. D. Foot rather casually enumerates them. The clothing section, located here, sought to provide agents with as convincing a civilian disguise as possible. Agents might be betrayed in many ways but mustn't be betrayed by what they wore, or what they *carried* in what they wore; before leaving England they would scrupulously empty their pockets of every tattered bus ticket, every flake of tobacco.

Two refugee tailors made clothes that were designed and detailed, to the last stitch and buttonhole, as if fabricated on the Continent. Agents also went into occupied Europe in clothing brought out by refugees. Mistakes happened, though. Two SOE agents were horrified to realize that they had dropped in identical clothes; their matching shirts, ties, raincoats, socks, shoes, and briefcases gave them the look of mismatched twins as they began their hazardous mission.

And sometimes the disguise was amusingly thin. Foot tells of two bolts of pyjama cloth brought to England by one of the refugee tailors; every male agent of SOE soon had pyjamas of this material. One agent, on his first night in occupied territory, was staying briefly with a colleague who looked in to make sure the newcomer was comfortable 'and said with a rueful smile, "Ah, *pyjamas maison*. I'd get some others if I were you. Good-night".'

Another story, perhaps apochryphal, concerns some two-way radios that were fabricated to resemble luggage. These 'suitcases' were identical – same colours, same stripes – and were instantly recognizable by any Gestapo man who had seen more than two. Baker Street realized the gaffe and diversified. Using a wireless in Nazi-occupied territory was dangerous enough without courting disaster simply by carrying one.

Below Melcombe Street, still on Baker Street, is the grandly symmetrical block of flats flanking the entrance to Baker Street tube station. Best appreciated from across the street is this massive block called

Site 65: **Chiltern Court, Baker Street.** SOE's Scandinavian sections (located here) faced very different situations in the three Scandinavian countries. The Danes quickly acquiesced to German occupation and were allowed to keep their king and parliament almost intact. The Norwegians resisted from the start, their king fleeing to Britain (with thousands of his countrymen) to set up a government-in-exile. The Swedes remained neutral, avoiding any offense to Germany until certain the Allies would win.

Site 65: **Chiltern Court, Baker Street.**

Denmark was the first to be invaded. Hitler tried to convince the Danes, and probably the British, that German occupation of a fellow Nordic country could be a model of civility. He wanted Danish foodstuffs and industrial goods for his war effort, so the Danes suffered rather little interference in everyday life. Hitler purported to be merely 'reuniting' Denmark and Germany (which prompted King Christian X to comment drily that he considered himself too old to rule both Denmark *and* Germany).

In the absence of a Danish government-in-exile, it was necessary for SOE to work with a small cabal of officers in the general staff of the Danish army (which Hitler had allowed to survive in reduced form). These officers, known as the Princes, advocated great caution, claiming that the actions proposed by SOE would bring massive

German reprisals. According to some observers, the Princes may have been more concerned with preserving private property than with protecting civilians. As elsewhere, SOE hoped to form a 'secret army' in Denmark to rise on The Day, but the Princes, astonishingly, considered this plan *illegal*. The Danish military even ordered help denied to British raiding parties, arguing (falsely, I think) that such restraint would encourage the Germans to move their troops from Denmark to Russia and thus make The Day easier for the Allies.

SOE was substantially frustrated in Denmark in the early days. The Princes promised that the Danish army would rise up when the Allies invaded Denmark, but meanwhile they didn't want to do anything against the Germans or help the British do anything. Since the Princes argued that they could help by means other than violent resistance, however, they were obliged to provide the British with intelligence. Almost all British intelligence activities in Denmark, and all escape and repatriation activities, were run through SOE (causing SIS some humiliation).

By August, 1943, the Germans had dropped their pretence of a friendly sojourn among their Nordic brothers; they disbanded the Danish military, prohibited the parliament from meeting, and put the king and queen under house arrest. Did this cause the Princes to lead, or at least approve, a massive uprising? No. Three of the four leaders fled to Sweden and the fourth was taken to Germany for questioning. Only then did the remaining lower-level Princes co-operate with SOE in a more active resistance in Denmark.

Norway's situation was altogether different. SOE trained 650 of the Norwegians who had fled to Britain; 540 ultimately saw service in Norway. (By contrast, SOE trained only 150 Danes from the smaller pool of Danish refugees; only 60 saw service in Denmark.) Norway's vast and crenelated shoreline was easily accessible by boat, unlike the closely patrolled coast of Denmark. Indeed, so many Norwegian seamen and fishermen escaped to the Shetland Islands that SOE's transport service between Norway and the Shetlands operated with such frequency and regularity as to be called the Shetland Bus.

Then too, the Norwegians were less subtle in their resistance than the Danes. When the Danish owners made their shipbuilding industry available to the Germans, the Danish workers responded by damaging their output to the extent that little of it could be used. The less sophisticated Norwegians were more forthright, mounting an enthusiastic and resourceful campaign against the enemy from the start. The Heavy Water raid is perhaps the best known of SOE operations in Norway; an SOE team overcame terrain, weather, and German defences to destroy the factory that was producing deuterium for an atom bomb. SOE-trained Norwegians later completely sank Hitler's hopes for the bomb when they sent the remaining deuterium to the bottom of Lake Tinnsjo. (These agents resuscitated SOE's flagging fortunes by succeeding where the RAF's conventional methods had failed.)

But the Norwegians were unsuited to the mindset of clandestinity, suggests Charles Cruickshank in his book *SOE in Scandinavia*. He mentions the 'simplicity of the people, who had a childlike confidence that no one would give them away' − they often did their secret work openly! The Norwegian resistance was further burdened, near the end of the war, by the need to shift gears; the *Wehrmacht*'s scorched-earth policy was designed to leave no building standing in their retreat, and the Norwegians, who had been single-mindedly blowing up factories, bridges, and rail lines now needed to prevent the enemy from doing exactly the same.

Sweden, the third of the Scandinavian countries in which SOE operated, maintained a scrupulous but synthetic neutrality. The Swedes grew rich selling minerals and industrial products on a cash-and-carry basis to anybody. But they worried about a German invasion. As long as Germany seemed to be winning, Sweden can fairly be described as having been neutral on the side of Germany.

SOE's predecessor (Section D) had cultivated Swedish industrialists and bankers before the war and still maintained good relations in military, financial and governmental circles. But sabotage against Swedish industrial output was out of the question, and even propaganda activities had to be polite and mild to avoid strengthening the already substantial pro-German and anti-British sentiment in Sweden. Some in the London Controlling Section urged a more assertive policy towards Sweden, in order to provoke a German occupation that would tie down vast numbers of German troops, also in order to spur a resistance movement that would diminish Sweden's contribution to the German war effort. But the

Joint Planning Staff in London considered a German occupation of Sweden neither likely nor desirable, and SOE confined itself in Sweden to support-and-supply for Norwegian and Danish ops. (MI6 in Sweden was involved in the usual information-gathering by any means possible, as we learn from an anecdote in Sir Peter Tennant's recent memoir, *Touchlines of War*. The service found a homosexual tennis-playing agent to debrief the homosexual tennis-playing German agents who were cavorting with the homosexual tennis-playing King of Sweden. All is possible, in love and war.)

Facing Chiltern Court on Baker Street is another solid mass of flats. Walk W on Melcombe Street and S on Glentworth Street for the entrance to the block-square

Site 66: **Berkeley Court, Glentworth Street.** This was another of the many residential blocks in the Baker Street area where SOE agents briefly stayed.

Parachuting agents into Europe was the most dangerous and difficult way of getting them there. But parachuting supplies was safer and easier than offloading them at a landing strip. SOE understood that any low-flying plane would pique the enemy's curiosity. These planes, therefore, often scattered hundreds of propaganda leaflets over any town near the drop zone – close enough to account for an overflight in the minds of the Germans but distant enough to draw attention from the real cargo, which would be long gone by the time the Germans had frantically gathered up the subversive material.

Here ends this walk. For points distant, go half a block S to Marylebone Road and one block E to Baker Street tube station. Or continue with the next walk immediately S of you on Baker Street. Or, if you've never been to Madame Tussaud's, this might be the day for it. The woman was as remarkable as her models; in her youth, she was forced to make effigies from the freshly-guillotined heads of victims of the French Revolution.

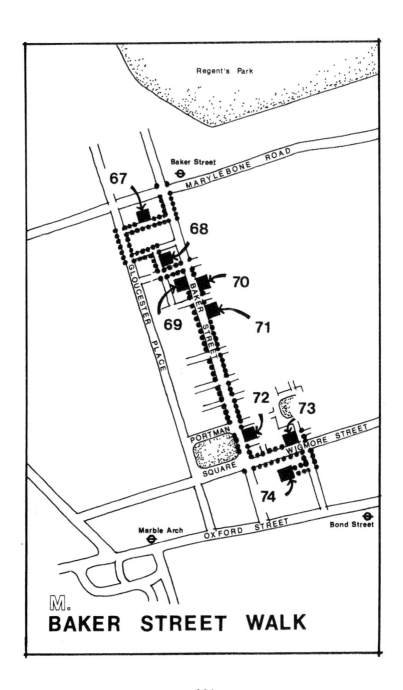

Regent's Park

Baker Street

MARYLEBONE ROAD

67

68

GLOUCESTER PLACE

BAKER STREET

70

69

71

72

73

PORTMAN SQUARE

WIGMORE STREET

74

Marble Arch

OXFORD STREET

Bond Street

M.
BAKER STREET WALK

M. BAKER STREET WALK

Start this walk from Baker Street tube station, which in 1863 was part of the world's first underground railway; the platforms here are restored to their original Victorian appearance. Walk S on Baker Street. Turn into Bickenhall Street. On both sides, mid-block, you'll see

Site 67: **Bickenhall Mansions.** In 1960, at government request, M. R. D. Foot began to research the history of SOE in France. Several hostile views were already in print; Foot's book was to be more balanced. His *SOE in France* is a monumental work, but Foot is more than the official historian of SOE; his vivid prose and intellectual rigour make his writing on this subject (including a later book, *SOE*) just about the best that anyone has done. He has given

us a wealth of data about the organization that came to be known as 'Baker Street' (for its heavy concentration of personnel in this area). Bickenhall Mansions, Foot tells us, was one of several Baker Street locations used by SOE.

Just why SOE's main archive remains closed, as I write, is still a mystery. Former SOE agents can't even see their own files. A good bit of SOE material has already been lost – destroyed by what Nigel West calls 'the mysterious fire' of January, 1946, or weeded out by what Foot calls 'inexperienced clerks'. Does the archive still contain important secrets? I had thought that anyone waiting for an answer to this question would be well advised to get comfortable, but with the promise now to open SOE's files, we may (or may not) get some answers.

Go through Bickenhall Street and turn L into Gloucester Place. Turn L again at York Street and immediately R into

Site 68: **Montagu Mansions.** By the winter of 1943-4, writes Foot, 'most of the western side of Baker Street, through to Gloucester Place, had been requisitioned by SOE under one or another of its cover names.' The various mansion blocks into which SOE expanded

included this one.

Most SOE agents had been ordinary civilians before signing up for sabotage and subversion work. They were hardly 'ordinary', to be sure; they had unusual ability at mountain climbing or other outdoor pursuits, or special experience with the languages and cultures of the occupied countries. But SOE was at pains to inculcate quickly in them the reasoned paranoia needed by an agent operating in hostile territory.

Disregard for the basic rules of security could easily bring disaster. One agent who had lived in Paris before the war promptly looked up all her old friends; for this indiscretion she was caught by the Germans, tortured and executed. At the other end of the spectrum is the SOE officer who kept his address in enemy territory a secret even from Baker Street – an extreme application of the principles laid down in his training but possibly the reason he lived to tell about it.

Security was important – but not all-important. Foot writes: 'Those who bothered incessantly about security survived, but few of them had much beyond survival to their credit. To strike and then to survive was the real test.' Foot knew what he was talking about. He served with Britain's famed Special Air Service during the years when SAS provided military personnel to stiffen resistance groups much as SOE's Jedburgh teams did. When the Germans captured Foot, Hitler's policy was the summary execution of all such personnel whether they served in uniform or not. But one of Foot's captors had taken his SAS patch for a souvenir and the enemy never connected him with that feared and admired unit. SAS operated in considerable numbers behind enemy lines after D-Day (and 'to great effect,' reports Nigel West in *Secret War: The Story of SOE*). Indeed, argues West, 'harrying the enemy before he had even reached the field of battle' was not so much SOE's doing as it was 'predominantly the work of irregular formations composed of SAS troops.'

Turn L at Crawford Street and R at Baker Street. On the W side of the street is

Site 69: **Norgeby House, 83 Baker Street.** This was one of the buildings that took up the overspill from SOE's headquarters. Passers-by noted only a small plaque for the 'Inter-Services Research Bureau'. Conflicting sources locate the plaque also at two other buildings (*see Sites 70 and 71*). The story I especially like about the plaque − wherever it was − concerns Maurice Buckmaster's dog. As head of SOE's F Section, Buckmaster divided his time between Orchard Court (*see Site 72*) and Baker Street, telling not even his wife where he worked. His dog was often with him. Once when his wife was walking the dog, it took a familiar turn toward a Baker Street building. Mrs Buckmaster saw the nondescript plaque and immediately knew one of her husband's secrets. The Germans, lacking this kind of assistance, thought all of F Section was run from the flat in Orchard Court. According to Foot, F Section took up considerable space in Norgeby House.

Site 69: **Norgeby House, 83 Baker Street.**

SOE didn't have German agents to contend with in the immediate area, but had plenty of other enemies, some within the organization itself. 'Pitched paper battles' attended SOE's first year, writes one observer, until the propaganda component of SOE became the independent Political Warfare Executive, and another component (involved in 'planning spelt with a very big P,' reports Sweet-Escott) 'duly planned itself out of existence'.

SIS was a foe of SOE's from the outset. Section D had been virtually 'snatched away' from SIS (Anthony Cave Brown's description) to create the new organization, and by 1941, SIS and SOE were engaged in 'full-scale and dangerous brawls the like of which Whitehall bureaucracy had rarely, if ever, seen before'. In 1944 the head of SIS threatened to resign when SOE was given priority in certain operational matters even though SOE's networks in several countries were almost certainly compromised. As late as 1944 SOE was still fighting efforts to merge it into SIS. Is there a case for separate organizations for secret intelligence and special operations? J. G. Beevor comments in his book *SOE: Recollections and Reflections, 1940-1945*: 'If SOE had been a mere branch of SIS, its chances of growth in the conditions of 1940-5 would have been poor.' But Beevor also acknowledges the case for unified direction; long after the war, the head of SOE himself wrote in favour of one executive head as the only way to 'enforce collaboration and co-ordination'.

Nor was SIS the only foe of SOE's. The war leadership considered SOE 'a wayward child alternatively to be neglected and then chastised for going its own way,' writes one historian. Junior diplomats regarded SOE 'with disdain, as an ungentlemanly body it was better to keep clear of,' writes another. And no less than the Chief of the Air Staff, on being asked for the first time to put SOE personnel into Europe, replied that 'the dropping of men dressed in civilian clothes for the purpose of attempting to kill members of the opposing forces is not an operation with which the Royal Air Force should be associated'. He was outraged by these 'assassins' – as much for their subterfuge, I've always thought, as for their mission. Soon, of course, the RAF worked closely with SOE.

Negative views of SOE have outlived SOE. In *The Times Literary Supplement* in the mid-1960s, a reviewer charged that many of SOE's higher executives 'displayed an enthusiasm quite unrestrained by experience; some had political backgrounds which deserved a rather closer scrutiny than they ever got, and a few could only charitably be described as nutcases'. Undoubtedly some truth adheres to that allegation and to other critiques, but I disagree with Richard Deacon's assessment of SOE as 'one of the most appalling espionage services ever launched'. I think he errs in more than one respect: SOE was not strictly an 'espionage' agency at all.

To be sure, SOE saw its share of espionage, but was on the *receiving* end in two cases we know about. In one, Captain Ormond Uren, who worked in this building, gave secrets of SOE policy in Eastern Europe (and a floor plan of Norgeby House) to the national organizer of the CPGB (*see Site 101*). Each was arrested in 1943 and imprisoned.

In the other, and far more serious, case of espionage within SOE − worth telling in some detail − the 15 million people of Yugoslavia paid a terrible price and the chief culprit paid no price at all, not even discovery and opprobrium during his lifetime. For years I have wondered why a card-carrying anti-communist like Churchill would withdraw support from the pro-Western resistance of General Mihailović in 1943 and provide vastly enhanced support to the communist guerrillas under Tito; this action ensured a postwar communist Yugoslavia. Until recently, Churchill's decision has been explained by the claim that since Tito was an effective and committed enemy of the Germans, while Mihailović was collaborating with the Germans (and interested only in defeating Tito), then Tito's Partisans were more deserving of support. A very respectable pair of recent books has now demolished that claim.

Each book − *The Rape of Serbia: The British Role in Tito's Grab for Power 1943-1944*, by Michael Lees, and *The Web of Disinformation: Churchill's Yugoslav Blunder*, by David Martin − makes use of SOE documents inexplicably released in the mid-1970s to the Public Record Office at Kew. Most important of these documents is the daily Operational Log from SOE Cairo, which contains excerpts from the reports sent to Cairo by British Liaison Officers serving with Mihailović and Tito. Martin's book shows that the reports sent on to London were 'outrageously and systematically falsified and even suppressed' by SOE's Yugoslav Section in Cairo (later in Bari, Italy). 'It can also be established,' Martin continues, 'that relations between Mihailović and the British government were sabotaged in many ways by SOE Cairo.' Primarily responsible in this matter was James Klugmann, whom Martin calls 'by far the most brilliant of the Communist group at Cambridge'. Klugmann was an open sycophant of Stalin's, yet became deputy director of SOE's Yugoslav Section (working out of Cairo and Bari); his MI5 file, which should have prevented his getting such power, had been destroyed in England by a *Luftwaffe* bomb. No less compelling is the documentation by Michael Lees on Tito's extensive collaboration with Hitler and Tito's false image as a patriot. (Tito cannot even be credited with driving the Germans back. The Red Army did the job while Tito was slaughtering thousands of his own countrymen with British weapons.) The betrayal of Mihailović is a sorry chapter in SOE's record.

It is sobering to consider SOE's lack of concern for the postwar power balance in the countries it was helping to liberate. Nigel West's assertion in *Secret War*, that SOE 'actively assisted despotic tyrannies to seize power in so much of Eastern Europe', is lamentably quite accurate. The desperate military situation of the British is often cited to justify Churchill's short-sightedness. But Stalin's military situation was even more desperate and Stalin never supported *non*-communists. (Think of the fate of the Polish nationalists.)

Farther down the street, on the E side, is

Site 70: **Michael House, 82 Baker Street.** As SOE requisitioned ever more space in Baker Street, the secret organization became known to those who needed to refer to it as 'Baker Street' − also as 'The Racket' and 'The Org' and 'The Old Firm'. SOE had the top floor here above the head office of the department store Marks & Spencer.

Staff came and went unobtrusively through the mews at the rear. The pub at the entrance to the mews would have been an ideal place, I think, for a Nazi agent to linger over a pint, but Foot declares categorically that no enemy agents loitered nearby. Good thing, because chatter 'about parachutes and boats and missions' could be heard in the Baker Street *patisserie* of Monsieur Richoux, writes Stella King in her book on SOE's Yvonne Rudellat. Papa Richoux, luckily, was as discreet as some in SOE were indiscreet.

The charge that SOE was guilty of amateurism came first from MI6. The charge was true to a certain extent: SOE's agents *were* amateurs at SOE's work − except for the few professionals who were brought in to do SOE's forgery work and to give instruction in lock-picking.

Recruitment was delicately handled. At the outset, candidates were told only in the second interview that perhaps they might do more for the war effort than be translators. By 1943, the informal sizing-up was replaced by a lengthy psychologists' assessment. 'This was a more scientific and perhaps a safer system,' Foot writes, 'but it was a less individual one; and there was less chance in it for men of eccentricity and panache to find their way into a body original enough to get the best out of them.'

Site 70: **Michael House, 82 Baker Street.**

Training covered everything from raiding and demolition tactics to methods of silent killing. Agents learnt how to be aggressive and self-reliant, how to live off the country, how to conceal their actions and personalities, how to deal with Gestapo interrogation. SOE also needed to change the self-image and world-view of these civilians very quickly — needed to empower them psychologically so they could do things that well-brought-up Britons wouldn't dream of doing.

Asian martial arts figured prominently in the training; both William Fairbairn and Eric Sykes, who had been with the Shanghai police during the days of the International Settlement (Fairbairn as head of the force), taught SOE's recruits (Fairbairn as head of combat training). The Fairbairn-Sykes knife was standard issue. It was good only for silent killing but it *looked* menacing enough and came to have a certain mystique – which is sometimes more valuable than anything real. The Fairbairn-Sykes knife did much to create the feeling of belonging to something important, even glamorous, and it helped to sustain the confidence and courage of people working alone and under constant stress.

Before Buckmaster's agents went into the field, he gave each one a valuable memento: a gold compact for the women, gold cuff-links for the men. Agents could pawn the item, if necessary, or keep it as a reminder of the organization behind them – an organization that believed in them and depended on them and had given them in a few short weeks, in southern England or in the wilds of Scotland, the skills and gadgets for their own survival and for the destruction of the enemy.

Below Dorset Street, still on the E side of the street, is

Site 71: **64 Baker Street.** When the new SOE almost immediately outgrew its Caxton Street offices (*see Sites 5 and 6*), this building in October, 1940, became SOE's 'main headquarters'. The Ministry of Works had been reluctant to give the new outfit so much space, but SOE filled it within a month.

Among military historians, it is a commonplace that every military establishment starts a new war by fighting the last one over again. Hitler and Churchill, however, were so traumatized by the grinding attrition of trench warfare in WWI that they approached WWII looking desperately for more mobile, more decisive, tactics. Hitler developed the *Blitzkrieg*, launching it in Poland, refining it in France, and applying it successfully in Russia until the failing German supply system allowed Russia to counter-attack. Churchill was especially eager to avoid a long war of fixed positions; on top of everything else, the high casualties would be politically ruinous. His desire to pursue almost any alternative to the horrors of WWI was behind the creation of SOE.

The 'godfathers' of SOE, as Foot calls them, were the

Conservative Neville Chamberlain and the Labourite Hugh Dalton. Chamberlain provided the organizational details and the name. Dalton became the enthusiastic first chairman of this new body that

Site 71: **64 Baker Street.**

would do its 'unavowable' work separate from any existing service. But Churchill supplied the concept – 'an army of the shadows' throughout enemy-occupied Europe, to 'set Europe ablaze'.

'To think up schemes of piratical daring in a war that opened with ceremonial dress and sword drill; to wage in the early forties a kind of warfare that did not become common till the late fifties; such feats argue some imaginative capacity,' writes Foot in *SOE in France*. And indeed, the imaginative leaders of SOE throughout the war advanced the tactics only barely glimpsed in the Boer War, in the Near East in WWI, in the civil wars in Russia and Spain, in the Chinese struggle against the Japanese, and in the Irish actions against the British. This was 'unconventional' and 'irregular' warfare – new to Britain in an official sense, but not alien to some of Britain's military and intelligence men and eagerly grasped by those SOE leaders who came from civilian life.

Major-General Colin Gubbins was perhaps the most impressive of the men who led SOE. (He was decorated after the war by all the Allies except the USSR.) Starting as director of operations and training for SOE, Gubbins was executive director from September, 1943, to the war's end. Without him, writes E. H. Cookridge in *Inside SOE*, the new organization would not have survived. Gubbins had already done some surviving of his own. He had built and led the first 'Striking Companies' (later to become the Commandos) and was active in their effort to delay the German advance in Norway. Immediately after his return from Norway, he organized Britain's own resistance forces, the secret 'Auxiliary Units' that soon stretched clockwise along the coast from north-west Scotland to central Wales (*see Site 102*).

We shall never know how well the Auxiliary Units might have done in Britain against a Nazi occupation. We do know the record of SOE. Surely, as Marcel Ruby states in *F Section, SOE*, 'the resistance would still have existed even if SOE had not'. But SOE's contribution to the war effort cannot be discounted – or negated by its great blunders and heavy losses. I particularly like Foot's comment: 'An effort that German as well as allied generals believe shortened the European war by about six months cannot have been quite devoid of strategic value.' (He then delineates the strategic value of SOE after the Allied invasion of Normandy: because of the secret forces that SOE had raised and armed throughout France, the enemy could no longer control its rear areas or its communication lines.) But everywhere that SOE operated, the exploits of its agents lifted the spirits of the people and sapped the spirits of the enemy. Such things are immeasurable. And for its size, SOE's impact was considerable. At its peak, with approximately 10,000 men and 3,200 women, it was 'about equal to that of a weak division' says Foot (5,000 of the total, mostly men, were agents). But 'no single division in any army exercised a tenth of SOE's influence on the course of the war.' Whatever was achieved by SOE, I believe the effort alone had significance. For Britain's own morale and the morale of the occupied countries, such things were important.

One of SOE's sharpest critics, the respected military historian John Keegan, believes that the psychological impact of the resistance in western Europe was virtually its only achievement. I think he overstates when he says that the programme of subversion, sabotage and resistance supported by Churchill and the governments-in-exile 'must be adjudged a costly and misguided failure', its major uprisings a disaster and its lesser activities 'irrelevant and pointless acts of bravado'. Really effective guerrilla activity, writes Keegan, could be sustained in only two areas, Yugoslavia and the Pripet Marshes of the Eastern Front; the popular notion that western Europe was 'ablaze' must be 'recognized as a romantic, if understandable, myth'. (According to Keegan, cryptanalysis was far more valuable to the war effort and far less costly – and the war could have been won without either.)

SOE ended abruptly in January, 1946, (although its Far Eastern operations continued until the end of June). Foot tells the story briefly. Clement Attlee was shown that SOE had, in Foot's words, 'a world-wide communications network, staffed by brave men and women dedicated to friendship with Great Britain: the makings of a priceless intelligence tool'. But the new Prime Minister was unimpressed. 'Attlee brusquely replied that he had no wish to preside over a British Comintern, and that the network was to end immediately. It was closed down at forty-eight hours' notice.'

Continue S on Baker Street to Portman Square. Just S of Fitzhardinge Street is

Site 72: **Orchard Court, Portman Square.** In a four-room flat on the second floor, officers of SOE's F Section met the new recruits before they began training and again before they left for France. Agents weren't to know the postings of fellow agents and were thus bundled from one briefing room to the next – even into the legendary bathroom – like 'characters in a French farce', the head of F Section would recall. The famous black bathroom was theatrical in its own right. It had a black-tiled bathtub, an onyx bidet, subdued pink lighting, thick carpeting, and peach-pink mirrors engraved with scantily-clad maidens. Redecorated in 1965, this bathroom still exists vividly in memoirs and memories.

F was SOE's 'independent' section for France, not to be confused with the Gaullist section known as RF (*see Site 60*). SOE had wanted to operate in France without de Gaulle and, for security reasons, without connection to the centrally organized Gaullist resistance in France. The separate RF Section was formed in belated recognition of de Gaulle's importance and, it must be said, in response to his fury over F Section's existence. F Section continued to build its many small networks unconnected to each other and to the larger resistance organizations in France. This did not eliminate security problems for F's agents in France, of course, nor did it eliminate the difficulties between F and RF in London.

The head of F Section tried to maintain perspective about these legendary difficulties: 'I always tried to have as little as possible to do with the politics of the Resistance both in England where I found them distasteful and in France where we were bound, by the terms of our mission, to avoid all interference in internal matters. Our job was, at all times, strictly military.' Not really. The OSS/SOE presence in enemy-occupied areas was inherently political. The communists weren't the only ones who fielded guerrilla groups. OSS and SOE officers on the ground often determined policy towards political parties, trade unions, religious groups, ethnic minorities, and the like. Giving or withholding support for these *other* politically partisan groups often had an impact on the postwar situation.

Leading F Section from September, 1941, until just after D-Day was Colonel Maurice Buckmaster. He had run Ford Motor Company's European department in Paris before going into France with the British Expeditionary Force. He was among the last to leave Dunkirk; because his French was so good (Marcel Ruby reports in *F Section, SOE*), his commanding officer told him he might have to stay there, pretending to be French. But he spoke little Italian, and in 1941, about to be sent to Libya as an intelligence officer to interrogate Italian prisoners, he sought another posting. SOE took him on as an information officer and within six months he was in charge of F Section – all eight staff members.

One of the eight was Vera Atkins, said to be 'the real brain of the French Section' and also its heart. A WAAF squadron officer before joining SOE; she became head of F Section in June, 1944 (when it had been 'reduced to a rear link'), and at war's end she spent a year in Germany tracking down 117 of the section's 118 missing agents. Those who hadn't died in action or in captivity were executed just before Germany surrendered. The one agent whom even the impressively capable Vera Atkins couldn't trace had apparently run off with three million francs of SOE's money – a singular act of misconduct among the section's 470 agents sent into France.

F's agents were not French. They were supposedly French-*speaking*, although at least one spoke French with a Scottish accent thick enough to endanger himself and others. They included Britons (many from the Anglo-French business community),

Mauritians, French-Canadians, dual-nationals, Americans, even, writes Foot, a few 'of enemy nationality' (mostly Jewish and therefore 'thoroughly anti-nazi').

A fair number were women, because women could often go unnoticed where men would be suspect. One of F's bravest agents was Yvonne Rudellat (*see Site 18*), originally considered for the job of receptionist at Orchard Court. Another was the American journalist Virginia Hall. (She had an artificial foot she referred to as 'Cuthbert'; when she radioed London expressing the hope that Cuthbert would not be troublesome during her escape over the Pyrenees, an unknowing radio operator replied that if Cuthbert became troublesome she should kill him.) Still another was the courageous Violette Szabo, who twice went into France and died there. Of 52 women sent into France by F Section, 12 were killed.

Agents practised derailment on a disused railway branch in the Midlands; they studied demolition on replicas of French factories and power stations (one large model almost filled a room here at Orchard Court). For industrial sabotage, agents learnt the trick of wrecking the same part on every machine and then wrecking the replacement parts before any could be installed. Agents also used blackmail, telling factory owners that their production would be halted one way or another – either by Allied bombing, which would ruin the plant and cause heavy civilian casualties, or by carefully targeted sabotage.

Each day the BBC's French Service sent scores of *messages personnels* to France, instructing agents to proceed with predetermined tasks or convincing the wary French to trust these visitors from Britain. (To verify an agent's legitimacy, a prospective recruit could make up his own message and expect to hear it on the radio within hours.) Instructional messages were prearranged: '*Charles est très malade... Marcel aime Marceline... Yvette a dix doigts...*' (German codebreakers sought in vain some meaning in the words and letters.) Most messages were phoney, not only inflating the size of the activity in the enemy's mind but also camouflaging the arrival of D-Day; on the eve of D-Day, all 306 messages were genuine.

'Ours was not a disjointed series of defiant and foolhardy acts,' Buckmaster writes, 'but a unified tactical and strategic operation'; (by 1943 strategically linked to SHAEF). London directed almost 100 independent networks large and small, which committed enough industrial sabotage to earn Foot's judgment that F Section's record 'compares favourably with that of the much less economical RAF bomber command'.

The triumphs were not without cost. Some agents were destroyed through their own foolishness or by SOE error. Some simply had the bad luck to be caught; the Germans were quite good at disabling networks, although they were themselves hindered by the fierce conflict between *Abwehr* and *Sicherheitsdienst*. In the end, one quarter of F Section's agents died in France — fewer than the one in two anticipated, but still a very high percentage — and some died after horrendous torture. Because of de Gaulle's bitter animosity towards F Section, it would be 50 years before a memorial would be unveiled in France to honour the fallen of F Section.

At the SE corner of Portman Square, turn L into Wigmore Street. At Duke Street turn L again. First doorway on your L is

Site 73: **10 Duke Street.** After some shuffling and reshuffling in 1940 and 1941, General de Gaulle's office of secret intelligence and special operations moved here early in 1942. The *Bureau Central de*

Renseignements et d'Action (Militaire) — BCRA(M) — became BCRA later in the year. The removal of the final word did not so much exclude military matters as it 'dislodged' (in Foot's terminology) the commissariat of the interior from direct contact with active operations. (Don't worry, it was French; you don't need to know more than this.)

What we must remember, however, is that the French military (of which the extraordinary Charles de Gaulle was an example *par excellence*) has always been highly politicized, with feuds and cabals the norm. It is no surprise that many of the Vichyite military regarded their own staying behind as more honourable than de Gaulle's leaving. Thus, although the Gaullists were at war with the Germans, they also felt threatened by their Vichyite countrymen, their communist countrymen, and their British hosts. Defeating the Germans would count for little, they felt, if postwar France were dominated by the Vichyites, the communists, or a British-led puppet government. The Gaullists saw traitors everywhere. We must remember, too, that even paranoids can have real enemies.

SOE trained all of BCRA's agents and transported them into France (*see Site 60*). In return, BCRA supplied (astonishingly, if we can believe this figure) 'approximately 80 percent of the military and naval intelligence on which the plans for invasion of the Continent were founded,' according to the wartime diaries of David K. E. Bruce, head of OSS in London. The bargain was no different from that struck by SIS with other Allied intelligence organizations — material assistance in exchange for shared information — but the arrangement between the British and the Gaullists was never easy: suspicion and rivalry constantly nibbled away at co-operation and mutual respect. One of the worst quarrels, writes Foot, ensued after the *Conseil National de la Résistance*, so grandiosely set up by the Gaullists, was (of course) uncovered by the Germans and its leadership destroyed. The British then insisted on decentralization for everyone's protection, but the French — while promising to comply — did not do so. The British discovered the French noncompliance only because all BCRA communications went through the British, who hastily cracked the French code in order to check on the precise BCRA message. 'This put everyone's back up,' Foot writes.

The near-paranoia of the French occasionally threatened serious embarrassment. In 1943 an agent suspected of working also for the Germans was found hanged in the basement here. He had been undergoing a 'hostile interrogation', writes Nigel West in *MI6*. 'It was only after SIS's intervention that the local police were persuaded to drop the matter.'

Later in 1943, when de Gaulle moved to Algiers, these BCRA offices in Duke Street became the much-reduced BRAL (*Bureau de Recherches et d'Action à Londres*). London was not sorry to see the General go.

Walk S now on Duke Street. In the large block before Oxford Street is an unmarked roadway behind Selfridges. Somewhere along this roadway, I understand, was

Site 74: **Selfridges Annexe.** Joseph S. Schick, of Terre Haute, Indiana, who served with US Signal Intelligence in WWII, tells me that a top-secret signals intelligence headquarters was located at the rear of the department store. Schick knew the facility only as 'Selfridges Annexe.' It was 'a one-story (ground-level) structure, outwardly unimpressive; it looked like a long-neglected storage warehouse, an

eye-sore. Inside all was military spit and polish. Although only the ground-level structure was seen above ground (and almost certainly it was windowless), there were four or five levels of floors into the ground.' Covering two whole floors was the voice encryption device operated by US Signal Intelligence for the telephone link between Roosevelt and Churchill. According to Schick, other intelligence units were also here.

A few steps will bring you to Oxford Street and the end of this walk. Here is Selfridges itself, once said to be the most luxurious business premises in London. You can take the tube from Bond Street (two blocks to the E) or from Marble Arch (three blocks to the W). If your legs hold out, you might stroll down New Bond Street to see some of the latest fashions, or down Park Lane to see some of London's most fashionable hotels. Or stop at Speakers' Corner to sample some of the current fashions in ideas, a few a bit threadbare. The next walk begins near Speakers' Corner.

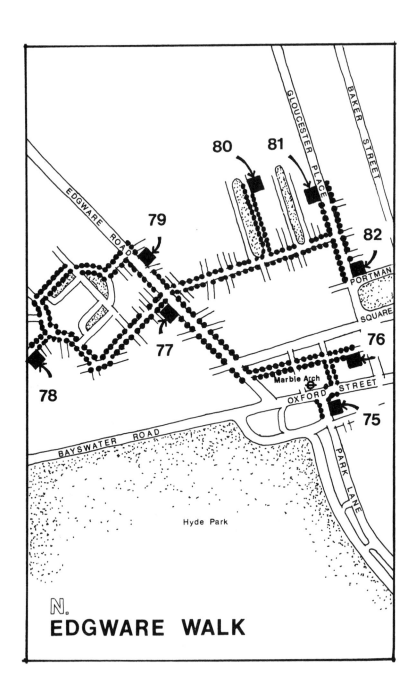

EDGWARE WALK

N. EDGWARE WALK

At the start of this walk, ponder the sad fate of Marble Arch. Built as a royal entrance to Buckingham Palace, it proved too narrow for the state coach; then, relocated here, it was left high and dry by road-widening. Ponder, too, the changes in Park Lane, once lined with the mansions of local landowners. Now the only view of London not spoiled by the Hilton on Park Lane is from the Hilton. In the first block of Park Lane is

Site 75: **140 Park Lane.** SOE's N Section worked here — but so inattentively and irresponsibly that for almost two years every SOE agent sent into the Netherlands was captured. To this day, the *Englandspiel* (as Germany termed its playing back of these agents) still arouses outrage, still arouses suspicion as to how this German operation lasted so long and whether some hidden British game was

behind it. Other secret organizations made mistakes. Indeed, the capture of an MI6 agent *with his cyphers* 'made the whole deception feasible', writes Nigel West. But the extraordinary malfeasance of SOE's Dutch Section seems unbelievable, even today, and one grieves afresh at the loss of some 60 Dutch and British agents, many of them barbarously executed by the Nazis at Mauthausen concentration camp.

The first to be captured (in March, 1942) agreed to continue transmitting, confident that London would pick up his warnings. Huburtus Lauwers properly omitted his 'security check' (which would have involved a mistake every 16th letter) and improvised false security checks to satisfy the Germans and still warn London. Amazingly, London paid no heed. Even when Lauwers transmitted 'worked by Jerry since...' and three times inserted the word 'caught', London didn't catch on. So great was his admiration for British Intelligence (he thought he was working for MI6) that he decided against escaping; he thought London must want him to be where he was for some larger deception. Only when several *dozen* captured agents began communicating with each other through the central heating system of their prison did they realize the magnitude of the disaster.

Warnings came also from England, reports Nicholas Kelso in *Errors of Judgement: SOE's Disaster in the Netherlands, 1941-44*. Leo Marks, SOE's chief cypher officer, reported his belief that all SOE radios in the Netherlands were under German control, but an MI5 investigation found nothing amiss. Repeated warnings came from a man in SOE's signal section but he was warned, in turn, to keep silent or risk being sent to the front. A garbled message from the prisoners finally reached Berne in May, 1943. MI6 warned SOE at once, amplifying an earlier SIS warning to SOE (on 5 April) that a Dutch SOE agent was under the closest *Gestapo* surveillance. Yet SOE sent more agents into Holland later in May. Supplies continued until October.

In August, 1943, two brave Dutch officers, Peter Dourlein and Johan Ubbink, escaped from their prison at Haaren and made their way through occupied Europe to Britain − where they were confined to Brixton Prison until after D-Day. (The Germans had used a captured set to tell London that the escapees were 'turned' and couldn't be trusted, and Dourlein and Ubbink only confirmed British suspicions by providing different answers to the seemingly trivial questions asked about their escape. To complicate matters further, the two were convinced of the treachery of an officer in London's N Section and seemed bent on disposing of him. It made perfect sense, unfortunately, to keep these two under British lock and key.)

When three more agents escaped in November, the Germans knew the game was over. In April, 1944, the *Abwehr*'s Hermann Giskes sent this stunning message to N Section: 'We understand that you have been endeavouring for some time to do business in Holland without our assistance. We regret this the more since we have acted for so long as your sole representatives in this country, to our mutual satisfaction. Nevertheless we can assure you that, should you be thinking of paying us a visit on the Continent on any extensive scale, we shall give your emissaries the same attention as we have hitherto, and a similarly warm welcome. Hoping to see you.' (The message was not even encyphered.)

The Dutch conducted a postwar enquiry. Had their agents been deliberately sacrificed in some deception operation? Or (a possibility the Dutch took more seriously) had SOE's N Section harboured a traitor? No evidence supported either theory – or a handful of other speculations. The official verdict of both the British and the Dutch was 'errors of judgment.' Kelso finds these words wholly inadequate to describe SOE's 'crass incompetence.'

His book, *Errors of Judgement*, gives details. Agents were told, incorrectly, that the Germans couldn't trace their transmitters. Agents were untrained in radio repair. Radios had crystals for very few frequencies (giving the Germans an easy job of monitoring). Radios required large and visible antennae. Agents were required to keep all previous messages (London often referred to them). London made no effort to verify a transmission's location. London had no alternate ways of confirming an agent's whereabouts, such as the innocent postcard or the walk-by.

And so on. And these 'technical' errors were in addition to other difficulties. The rigid compartmentation in SOE kept N Section from learning of a similar 'playback' in F Section. The lack of communication between SOE and Dutch Intelligence prevented the Dutch from seeing messages sent by their own agents. And the early leadership of N Section was ignorant or pig-headed enough to overlook every sign of trouble. To be sure, the *Englandspiel* benefited from the work of able Dutch collaborators (more than 50 of them) and brilliant German counterspies (the *Abwehr* and the *Sicherheitsdienst* co-operating fully with each other for a change). But SOE's contribution to the disaster was broad and deep.

The *Englandspiel* netted the Germans vast quantities of weapons, equipment and money. It also provided knowledge of British bombing routes over Holland; 12 bombers were lost. But the operation never provided information about 'military intentions' (specifically D-Day), writes Kelso. Disastrous as it was, it was successful for only part of the war and only tactically, while the British 'playback' of German agents in Britain was successful for *all* of the war and strategically.

After this débâcle, Dutch Intelligence demanded to see all orders for their agents and all messages from them. A hundred or so agents went into Holland in the last year of the war, most of them operating safely and effectively. 'Had SOE co-operated with the Dutch in 1942, as they were forced to do in 1944,' writes Kelso, 'the *Englandspiel* might well have been avoided.'

Walk E on Oxford Street for half a block. On the N side of the street you'll see the rear of

Site 76: **the Mount Royal Hotel.** In 1961-2, GRU Colonel Oleg Penkovsky gave Western couriers an immense number of secret Soviet documents − over 10,000 pages-worth − photographed with a Minox given him by the British-American team who 'ran' him. On several permitted trips to London and Paris, he provided information that filled another 1,200 pages of transcripts. His material was 'invaluable' according to many contemporary and later observers; he was 'the spy who saved the world' according to the 1992 book with this title by Jerrold L. Schecter and Peter S. Deriabin. He was probably the most important double agent we know about operating against the USSR.

But was Penkovsky a true spy, motivated by his belief that the communist system was fraudulent and harmful and that Khrushchev was provoking nuclear war? Or was he, knowingly or unknowingly, part of a calculated disinformation scheme — perhaps planned by a faction within the Kremlin? Or was he first genuine and *then* turned? Penkovsky has been a riddle for 30 years, although less so with the opening of important CIA files on him in 1988.

Site 76: **the Mount Royal Hotel.**

Colonel Penkovsky was not quite 42 years old when he walked into a third-floor suite here, in April, 1961, for his first clandestine meeting with MI6 and CIA. He was heading a six-man delegation that had come to London to acquire Western technology; as a GRU officer (with the State Committee for the Co-ordination of Scientific Research Work) he had the rare privilege of foreign travel. He also had an 'unreliable' background. His father had been a lieutenant in the White Army, dying in the siege of Rostov in 1919; the son bitterly resented being held back because of a father he had never known. Some think that if Colonel Penkovsky, after his 20 years in the Red Army, had become General Penkovsky, there would have been no Agent Penkovsky.

Penkovsky had been making reckless overtures to Westerners in Moscow since 1960. Was he a *provocateur*? Had he been observed and forced to be a 'postman'? MI6 and CIA took the risk of working with him (and working with each other, which multiplied the danger of leaks). Each night for several weeks in April-May, 1961, Penkovsky would sneak out of his room above the corner of Portman and Oxford Streets (Room 566) and walk quickly down to the Anglo-American team in Rooms 360 and 361. Here he would pour out his knowledge, his opinions, his passions, his worries. He 'gushed like a swollen stream,' writes Schecter. During one of these sessions Penkovsky said, 'This is an historic room. Someday there will be a memorial plaque here.' (There isn't, of course.) Each night Western intelligence officers would take the empty wine bottles away with them, removing all evidence of the lengthy meetings. (On a later trip Penkovsky stayed at the Kensington Close Hotel, off Kensington High Street, and the four-man team met him at a flat in the Little Boltons.)

Both the quantity and quality of Penkovsky's material argue against his being a plant, writes Schecter. Through Penkovsky, the West learnt that Soviet nuclear and missile programmes were in their infancy, that Khrushchev wanted war but wasn't yet prepared for it, that there was widespread disaffection in the USSR, that the military leaders were at odds with Khrushchev, that the Soviets had resumed atmospheric nuclear tests, and that the Soviets had developed an elaborate civil-defence plan and believed they could survive nuclear war. *In addition*, Penkovsky revealed secrets about GRU tradecraft, identified dozens of GRU and KGB officers working in the West, copied top-secret memoranda about Soviet military strategy, provided gossip about important figures, gave details about the lifestyle of the élite, supplied technical data on key Soviet weapons (including the missiles that went into Cuba), delivered the armed forces field regulations (which gave full instructions for the deployment of combat forces and arms), and even obtained the Kremlin telephone directory (which enabled the West to put together its first chain-of-command for the Kremlin).

With Penkovsky's information, President Kennedy stood up to

Khrushchev over Berlin in 1961 and over Cuba in 1962. In fact, Penkovsky's crucial role in the Cuban missile crisis has fuelled suspicion that he was serving an anti-Khrushchev faction. The 'amazing timing' of Penkovsky's arrest is mentioned by Knightley in *The Second Oldest Profession*: 'only by arresting Penkovsky [on 22 October, 1962, at the height of the Cuban missile crisis] could the Russians provide the final proof that the information he had been giving the West was genuine.' We now know, however, that the West didn't learn of the arrest until 2 November, by which time the Cuban crisis was over. I don't reject the possibility of an anti-Khrushchev faction. It could have paralleled the German opposition to Hitler, coming from the same sources (the intelligence services and the military) and for the same reasons (hatred of the Party and distrust of the adventurer at the top). But there are plenty of indications that the romantic and narcissistic Penkovsky acted on his own. I believe that he was the genuine article; if he was used at all, it was only after his arrest.

We have only supposition to explain the discovery of Penkovsky. The KGB wouldn't talk to Schecter about it (even late in 1991), the CIA hasn't released its extensive study about it, and 'a former KGB colonel' quoted by Phillip Knightley in 1993 may not be telling the truth. There are many possibilities. From the US, the leak could have come from a Soviet asset (Jack Dunlap) in the National Security Agency or another Soviet asset (William Whalen) in the Defense Department, both of whom saw Penkovsky's material, or from a US Army sergeant (Robert Lee Johnson) who gave the Soviets access to flight bags at the armed forces courier centre at Orly. From the British, the leak could have come from two spies inside British Intelligence (John Vassall, Frank Bossard). And the head of MI5 (Roger Hollis), long suspected of being a Soviet mole, had taken the unusual course of asking – and getting – Penkovsky's name.

Possibly, though, the culprit was George Blake (*see Site 84*). He had told the Soviets that Rauri Chisholm was an active MI6 officer; the two had served together in Berlin during the 1950s. When Chisholm turned up in Moscow in 1960 he would have come under full surveillance. When Chisholm's wife, Janet, became Penkovsky's contact in Moscow, she too would have been under the most careful scrutiny. Even such seemingly innocent contact as meeting casually in a park (Penkovsky seemingly offering chocolates to her charming children) is seen now as questionable tradecraft.

Or was there a mole — someone never uncovered in British or American Intelligence — who learnt of Penkovsky? A senior KGB officer smiled at this question from Schecter. 'No, no. This is sheer imagination.' We can be forgiven, I hope, for smiling at his answer.

Tom Bower, who produced a 1991 television documentary on Penkovsky with the assistance of *Novosti*, the Soviet press agency, suggests that Penkovsky was discovered because of two unauthorized meetings: one with Greville Wynne (*see Site 34*), the other with a British diplomat who might have been Rauri Chisholm. The Bower-*Novosti* documentary, *Fatal Encounter*, would be more convincing if Bower's same sources hadn't proclaimed only months earlier (to Schecter) that it was not Rauri but Janet Chisholm who led them to Penkovsky, and it was Penkovsky himself (confessing) who led them to Wynne. (Knightley's 'former KGB colonel' also points to the surveillance of Janet Chisholm as leading to Penkovsky, prompting Knightley to claim that the real betrayal of Penkovsky was by SIS: knowing that Blake had compromised Mrs Chisholm, SIS was 'cavalier' in its handling of Penkovsky because it was 'desperate to re-establish its reputation with the CIA'.) The Bower-*Novosti* documentary faults MI6 for dealing dishonestly with the CIA and irresponsibly with Penkovsky and it provides persuasive evidence for those accusations. But the fact that the Russians gave one version of this story to Bower and quite another to Schecter only reminds us that we probably know less about the Penkovsky affair than we will know in the future.

Penkovsky took extraordinary risks. Possibly, as his words suggest, he was constantly driven to prove himself to the West. Possibly, as his deeds suggest, he was psychologically unable to appreciate the danger; he was like a teenager driving at 140 miles an hour, said a CIA psychiatrist. Or did he know, early on, that he had nothing to fear from the Soviets? I don't think so. I think he was genuinely on the side of the West. At his request, the British and Americans made him an honourary officer in their armed forces and he kept photos of himself in British and US uniforms hidden in his home in Moscow. I imagine he looked at these photos often, in his lonely work.

After Penkovsky's death, the Soviet defector Anatoli Golitsyn convinced Angleton of the CIA that Penkovsky had been part of a vast Soviet disinformation effort. The Soviets themselves made a brief attempt in the mid-1960s to suggest that Penkovsky had been under GRU and KGB control the whole time. The KGB line today is that he was an unimportant agent who did nothing so grand as saving the world from nuclear war. In 1963, though, the Soviets thought enough of his treachery to mount a public trial and execute him. Penkovsky is rumoured to have been thrown alive and screaming into the Moscow city crematorium before a select gathering of GRU officers to whom the event would have been especially instructive.

Walk through Old Quebec Street to Bryanston Street and turn L. At Edgware Road turn R. On the L side of Edgware Road, past Connaught Street, is

Site 77: **Portsea Hall, Portsea Place.**

Site 77: **Portsea Hall, Portsea Place.** Anthony Blunt lived here on the sixth floor (flat No. 45) from 1974, when he retired from the Courtauld Institute as Sir Anthony, until a heart attack killed the disgraced scholar in 1983. He was living here when Mrs Thatcher answered a parliamentary question in 1979 and announced that Britain had known for 15 years of Blunt's role as a Soviet agent. This startling public disclosure must be credited to the writer Andrew Boyle, who had painstakingly discovered Blunt's confession and revealed it in his book *The Climate of Treason* (1979). Boyle got a few details wrong and didn't actually *name* Blunt, resorting instead to the pseudonym 'Maurice' for the so-called Fourth Man. But the cat was out of the bag. When the Prime Minister confirmed Blunt's spying and gave specifics of Blunt's deal with the government, MI5 was horrified.

Blunt had joined MI5 in 1940. Serving HM Government throughout WWII, he served the Soviets better. As Anthony Glees explains in *The Secrets of the Service*, 'The moles did not simply say, "we must do whatever the USSR wants," for the obvious reason that this would arouse British suspicions. Rather, they appear to have said, "what Russia wants in this specific case is absurd and should be rejected; as a quid pro quo, however, we must make sure that Russia gets what it wants in other areas".' The moles did more than pass on secrets; in subtle ways they subverted policy, as Glees is not the first to point out.

Blunt, of course, passed on a lot of secrets. Near the war's end, he told a superior that he had, with consummate pleasure, given the name of every MI5 officer to the Soviets. (This startling admission was followed by an even more startling response from MI5 – *no* response, at that time or any other time.) Information imparted by Blunt compromised every counter-espionage operation of MI5 during the many months he was in charge of the Watchers. He also routinely delivered information gleaned from his MI5 task of opening the diplomatic bags of other nations. (In so doing, writes John Costello, he 'helped facilitate the Soviet takeover of Eastern Europe'). Only the courier bags of the Soviet Embassy were 'immune to the activities of Blunt's team,' writes Costello; according to a rumour 'perhaps put about by Blunt himself,' the Kremlin's diplomatic bags were said to be booby-trapped. Blunt's treachery

194

also ended the work of two key MI5 assets: a secretary to Anastas Mikoyan inside the Kremlin, and Tom Driberg inside the CPGB. Blunt was far more valuable to the Soviet intelligence services than to his own, especially since the Soviets alone were looking beyond Hitler's defeat to the inevitable confrontation between their expanding empire and the West.

With his treachery made public in 1979, Blunt was obliged to give up his honours and prestigious affiliations. But he was not prosecuted. That was the deal struck in 1964: immunity from prosecution in exchange for Blunt's telling MI5 as much − or as little − as he liked. Defenders of MI5 argue that the government could do no better, lacking evidence for a trial. But does anyone believe that Blunt told the government everything he knew?

The Labour Party made political capital of the case. They couldn't denounce the Tories for a McCarthyite smear since Blunt had confessed. So they denounced the Tories for allowing an upper-class communist spy like Anthony Blunt to skate while a middle-class communist spy like George Blake did heavy time. They were absolutely right, of course. Blunt's press conference in November, 1979, was especially outrageous. Held at *The Times*, and including BBC, ITV and *The Guardian*, it excluded all newspapers hostile to Blunt. He wasn't asked any impolite questions; he wasn't required to apologize; he wasn't forced to name any of his contacts or recruits. The excluded newspapers were furious − and properly so. Blunt wouldn't have 'co-operated' at all (even to the extent he did) if he hadn't been betrayed by one of his own recruits.

Leave Edgware Road at Kendal Street. Just after Connaught Street pick up Tichborne Row, which leads into Hyde Park Crescent. The buildings hereabouts are new and unlovely. Turn L into Southwick Place. On your L is

Site 78: **6 Southwick Place.** Donald Maclean, the brilliant young British diplomat who fled to Moscow in 1951 and years later would still be remembered as 'such a good fellow', lived in a dark three-storey house here during his boyhood.

The family had moved to London when Maclean *père* entered Parliament. Young Donald, born in 1913, returned to Southwick

Place periodically from the reformist environment of Gresham's, one of the smaller public schools. He had little ease with his father, 'a figure of almost claustrophobic rectitude.' Depending on which partisan view we accept, the father was either 'one of the least-inspired Cabinet ministers of his time' or 'very near to being a great man.' He was a pillar of the Liberal Party, his reformism a secular expression of his Calvinism. But while father and son shared a puritanical dislike for the excesses (and successes) of modern capitalism, Maclean *fils* soon abandoned Calvinism for the secular religion of Leninism. His father's death in 1932, here at Southwick Place, released young Maclean from the need to lie to his father about the loss of one faith and the acquisition of another.

Site 78: **6 Southwick Place.**

The circumstances of Donald Maclean's recruitment to Soviet Intelligence have been unclear for 60 years. His best friend at Gresham's was James Klugmann (*see Site 69*). His first male lover, soon after he came up to Cambridge in 1931, was Guy Burgess. Was Maclean recruited by either of them? Newly opened NKVD files indicate that it was Philby who invited Maclean to serve the Soviets. The year was 1934; friend Burgess, not yet recruited himself, was disappointed in Maclean for breaking with the Party (as Moscow had ordered).

Under orders from Soviet Intelligence, Maclean sought entry to the British Foreign Service, abandoning his plans to drive a tractor in the USSR while teaching English to the peasants. Asked by the FO about his communist views at Cambridge he replied, 'I haven't entirely shaken them off.' This answer seems to have satisfied his questioner, for Maclean entered the FO soon afterward. A shining young man, he seemed destined for a distinguished diplomatic career. His first foreign posting, in 1938, was to the important embassy in Paris where, as John Costello has learnt from newly released KGB documents, Maclean was already delivering huge quantities of material to the Soviets.

He was sent to Washington in 1944 and reached the embassy's third-ranking position before leaving there in 1948. During this period of keen Soviet interest in America, Maclean was both British diplomat and Soviet agent − and in the latter capacity was 'both saboteur of the West and adviser to the East,' writes Verne W. Newton in *The Cambridge Spies: The Untold Story of Maclean, Philby and Burgess in America* (1991). Maclean's name is deliberately first. 'From Stalin's point of view,' writes Newton, 'Maclean was far more valuable than either Burgess or Philby.'

Nowhere was Maclean more valuable than on matters of US atomic capability. In Washington he served as the British representative to a high-level American-British-Canadian committee on atomic policy. He was allowed unescorted access to Atomic Energy Commission's facilities when even J. Edgar Hoover and members of the President's Cabinet needed escorts. From Maclean, the Soviets learnt that 'America's nuclear arsenal was nonexistent' after the war, writes Newton. During the 1948 Berlin crisis, Stalin understood that he had 'nothing to fear' from America.

Maclean aided the Soviets from Washington in a multitude of other ways: he supplied important Churchill-Truman exchanges concerning postwar policy towards Poland; he supplied the probable 'holdline' for NATO (the precise Soviet behaviour that would be considered an act of war); he supplied the names of Soviet citizens who had contacted British diplomats; he continually supplied the updated listing of personnel and weapons at every American military base throughout the world. And that's only *part* of it. In every possible way consistent with avoiding detection, Maclean put the Western alliance at a disadvantage while also causing difficulty *within* the alliance − all the while maintaining what one observer calls a 'reassuring concern for embassy security.'

In 1948 Maclean was posted to Cairo as head of chancery. The youngest counsellor in the FO, he was one of Britain's most promising young diplomats. And then he began to unravel. The conviction of Alger Hiss early in 1950 must have been unnerving. Hiss claimed never to have met Maclean but, as Newton reports, 'for nearly a year, the FBI listened in on many of their phone calls.' The arrest of Klaus Fuchs, also early in 1950, must have been doubly disquieting to Maclean. Drinking heavily, he now began doing things that even the most indulgent couldn't ignore. At a party given by King Saud, he urinated on a carpet. At a smaller party, he tried to strangle Melinda, his wife. After another evening of carousing, he and a friend wrecked the empty apartment of two American women, tearing their underclothes apart and hurling a large mirror into their bath (breaking the bath, not the mirror). It was time to leave Cairo. Maclean took medical leave in May, 1950, and returned to London. Had he been *trying* to end his career, as a means of getting out from under the communists? It's a charitable theory. More likely, I think, he simply couldn't help himself.

Medical leave could last only six months. To keep Maclean from being reduced to half-pay after November, the FO made this loose cannon the head of its American Department! The appointment must have struck the Soviets as quite mad: *their* diplomats would never be forgiven the indiscretions of Cairo. And now Maclean was of inestimable value to the other side. The Korean War had just begun. Maclean divulged the limitations placed on UN forces as to targets in North Korea and beyond. He also divulged early Anglo-American decisions not to retaliate against the Chinese, not to use atomic weapons, not to aim for a military victory or a unified Korea. With Maclean's information, Peking and Moscow could fight 'almost a risk-free war,' writes Newton.

The FO subsequently tried to conceal the fact of Maclean's access to such vital information, pretending that the American Department dealt 'principally with Latin-American affairs' and, in the US, only with tourism and British citizens there. Files going to the Public Record Office were suitably purged. But the attempt was bungled, says Newton; prior files of the American Department were *not* purged. In any case, Maclean had routinely seen highly restricted information about the Korean War from the Far Eastern Department.

Maclean's tenure at the American Department, and in the FO altogether, would soon end. The Americans had been working on a batch of intercepted messages sent during the war between Moscow Centre and its people in New York. In 1949 the cryptologists achieved a breakthrough, locating a spy called 'Homer' inside the British Embassy in Washington in 1945. By the end of 1950 there were 35 suspects; by April, 1951, only Maclean and one other. By May it was all over: Maclean had been tipped off and had flown the coop (*see Site 120*). Only the recriminations remained, with MI5 accusing the FBI of having acted too slowly on its information (J. Edgar Hoover having failed to advise the White House or State Department of the unidentified spy), and with the FBI accusing MI5 of having dragged its feet altogether (Guy Liddell having been perhaps the chief offender in the casual pursuit of 'Homer').

Maclean's last 32 years, in the USSR, couldn't have been easy. At first he had a teaching job 500 miles from Moscow, then he was allowed back to the capital to work in the foreign ministry. He wrote a book on British foreign policy: 'a boring, shallow polemic,' according to Newton. Eventually he drank himself to death, reveals Gordievsky (although more slowly than Burgess who predeceased him by 20 years). Eventually too, he came to see things somewhat differently: he sought out dissidents and read their *samizdat*, he had a sign on his door saying 'Anti-Semites not welcome here' and he abstained from voting (once, at least) in order to protest at the Soviet use of psychiatric hospitals for political prisoners.

Maclean was 'crippled by inner stress', write Page, Leitch, and Knightley in *The Philby Conspiracy*; driven by fury and a need for revenge, writes Newton in *The Cambridge Spies*. But he was the perfect spy, with an adolescent's desire for conspiratorial relationships and an élitist's desire to run against the herd — and with a sophisticate's ability to get away with a life of deception. He had a strong anti-American streak, as did the other Cambridge spies, stemming in part (I believe) from a British chauvinism gone awry: they hated the nation and culture that they viewed as surpassing Britain. Most observers deny that Maclean was a hard-core ideologue for the communist cause. In fact, as Newton argues, 'Had Maclean's ideological ardour been greater, the Soviets would never have recruited him.' The KGB avoided the really committed types as too volatile, too risky.

Maclean was, above all, successful. 'It is doubtful that any other agent in the postwar period,' writes Newton, 'served Moscow more ably than Maclean.' (Whoever protected him at the FO can be considered even more successful.)

His story has been a cautionary tale for more than 40 years, providing early evidence (with Burgess in 1951) that the communist threat was real. More recently, as Ronald Radosh argues in his review of the Newton book for *The American Spectator*, Maclean has provided evidence utterly discrediting the revisionists who suggest that espionage against the West was without harm during the Cold War and that Western counter-espionage effort was without purpose.

Site 79: **Forset Court, Edgware Road.**

Return to Hyde Park Crescent and turn L. At Cambridge Square turn R. Turn R again at Norfolk Crescent and follow its curve into Burwood Place and Edgware Road. Across the street to your R, often erroneously called Forset House, is

Site 79: **Forset Court, Edgware Road.** A Romanian couple named Brandes lived here, after replacing Soviet spymaster Teodor Maly in the early summer of 1937 and before they were themselves replaced in November, 1937. Under the name of 'Stevens' or 'Stephens' – both names appear in MI5 files – the couple worked with the Woolwich Arsenal spies to get weapons information for the USSR (*see Site 51*). Did the Brandes couple discover that MI5 had penetrated their operation? The couple fled from England only days after MI5 had observed them receiving classified plans from a Woolwich employee.

The official MI5 position is that the Brandeses were allowed to leave with good reason. As John Bulloch reports in his early book on MI5, they were only 'minor spies... little more than couriers' and MI5 preferred to wait for the person expected soon 'who was to be the chief of all the Russian spies in England.' Also, reports Nigel West, MI5 expressed the view that since Willy and Mary Brandes could claim diplomatic immunity, 'there would be little to gain by taking them into custody.' This view 'is made nonsense of,' writes John Costello in *Mask of Treachery*, 'by the recent recovery of the contemporary reports on the Brandeses' false Canadian papers. These show that MI5 cannot have been under any illusion that the couple had diplomatic immunity.... If MI5 officers were concerned about prematurely spoiling the stakeout on Woolwich Arsenal, they could have arrested the Brandeses on the false-passport charges at Dover without alerting the Soviets to the penetration of their ring.' It is 'surely not farfetched,' Costello believes, to think that the Soviets were tipped off – as they were probably tipped off about Maly who escaped to Moscow and was never heard of again.

Thousands of dedicated Leninists round the world were recalled to Moscow during Stalin's purges and never heard of again. Guides at the Lubyanka today speak of 20,000 GPU officers who fell victim to the purges; the true figure is probably higher. The devastation of Stalin's foreign intelligence structure by Stalin himself was more comprehensive than anything the West could have accomplished – or even attempted. Most of those who were recalled went willingly. Some, like Maly, had no illusions about their fate. All were given summary trials; many were tortured; almost all were executed. Some who refused to return were murdered on Western soil; Ignace Reiss in Switzerland, Juliet Stewart Poyntz and Walter Krivitsky in America. Were the Brandeses spared by traitors in MI5 only to be returned to the 'safety' of Stalin's Moscow?

MI5's Watchers were in the Edgware Road to see the Brandeses load their luggage into a taxi bound for Victoria Station and the Paris boat train. Eventually the journey would end in Moscow; for the Brandeses the journey (and their lives) probably ended in the cellars of the Lubyanka. Did the Brandeses suspect what awaited them? If so, why did they take all those suitcases full of British clothing?

Go S on Edgware Road. This was a Roman road, its straightness and width designed for ranks of marching soldiers. Turn L at George Street. Several blocks E is 19th-century Bryanston Square; towards the rear, on the R, is

Site 80: **18 Bryanston Square.**

Site 80: **18 Bryanston Square.** 'In spite of the adage that advises against changing donkeys in mid-stream,' writes M. R. D. Foot, 'SOE and the Free French adopted a major change-over in the command system on 1 July, 1944. From that date, all but one of SOE's sections working into France were thrown under a single large and confused staff in Bryanston Square.'

The *Forces Françaises de l'Intérieur*, ordained by de Gaulle in March of 1944, had its staff or *Etat-Major* here. To command the EMFFI, de Gaulle chose the distinguished French general Joseph-Pierre Koenig. Under Koenig were the heads of SOE's F Section and of BCRA (*see Sites 72 and 73*). Koenig himself operated under Eisenhower's orders, or, as de Gaulle preferred to say, 'served at Eisenhower's side.'

The EMFFI made sense. Important as were the myriad resistance plans for damaging power stations and communication lines, for tying up rail and road transport, 'it was just as important,' de Gaulle would write in his memoirs, 'that the local actions of the clandestine groups assume, at the desired moment, the character of a national effort; that they function with enough consistency to become an element of the Allied strategy; that they ultimately lead the army of the shadows to merge with the regular troops into a single French Army.'

The bureaucratic connections, however, were impossible. EMFFI was subordinated both to SHAEF and to Special Forces Headquarters (the new British-French-American unit for SOE and OSS in London). 'That it worked at all was a triumph for *système D*, the capacity for muddling through,' writes Foot, 'and it worked exceptionally badly.'

Part of the problem was the large number of new French staff from North Africa, 'high in rank and low in knowledge of the secret war,' as Foot describes them. Their constant concern was politics; British senior staff found Bryanston Square 'nauseatingly full of intrigue.' About the place altogether, Foot writes, 'there hung an inescapable flavour of that motto of amateur theatricals, "it'll be all right on the night".' And so it was, of course, as Foot explains, with SOE's secret army managing more than a thousand rail interruptions in the week after the Normandy invasion, and keeping German troops so busy that eight divisions never reached their designated battlefields.

Site 81: **47 Gloucester Place.**

*Continue E on George Street past the monstrous Portman Towers —
only 12 storeys high but so alien to the special scale of London as to
seem part of a different city. At Gloucester Place turn L. Halfway up
this longish block, on the L, is*

Site 81: **47 Gloucester Place.** Imagine the surprise of Tyler Kent, a
code clerk in the American Embassy in London, when his
second-floor flat was broken into on the morning of 20 May, 1940,
and the raiding party (composed of Maxwell Knight and
representatives from Special Branch and the American Embassy)
swept past him to search his two small rooms. Imagine the surprise
of the intruders when they discovered no fewer than 1929 documents
stolen from the embassy, including six top-secret messages between
Churchill and Roosevelt.

Tyler Kent was a presentable young man (29 at the time of his
arrest), well-educated, a descendent of the Alamo hero Davy
Crockett, and the son of an American diplomat. Convinced that the
world was being pushed into war by the Jews (whom he hated),
young Kent wanted to use the stolen correspondence between
Churchill and Roosevelt to show that the two were conspiring to
replace Chamberlain and bring America into the war. Even the full
correspondence between the two leaders, published in 1985, could
not support such a conspiracy theory. But anything could have
happened in 1940 with the public release of Kent's material. Britain
was desperately weak, torn between those who would appease Hitler
and those who would fight him. Europe was already overrun.
America was still overwhelmingly opposed to intervention, and
Roosevelt was seeking an unprecedented third term.

Kent had started taking documents almost immediately after his
arrival in London in October, 1939. He soon met Anna Volkov (*see
Sites 41 and 45*), a passionately pro-Hitler Russian émigrée; she took
two of the documents to a photographer and gave the photos to an
Italian diplomat to send to Berlin. Kent also met Captain Ramsay
(*see Site 39*), a vehemently pro-fascist MP; Ramsay planned to bring
Kent's material to the floor of the House of Commons.

But MI5, and particularly Maxwell Knight, had been interested in
Kent since his arrival in London (a suspected German agent was seen
visiting his hotel room). MI5 also kept an eye on Kent because of

his sexual liaison with a woman named Danischewsky, one of many Russian émigrés believed to be working for the NKVD and GRU. Only after the cool-headed Joan Miller managed to infiltrate Ramsay's Right Club, however, did Knight have what he needed for an arrest.

Ambassador Joseph P. Kennedy, presiding over the violated American Embassy, was furious at the British for their delay in apprehending Kent (and for their delay in informing him of the matter), but he waived Kent's diplomatic immunity and allowed the British to arrest Kent. Kennedy had not been informed because he himself was under suspicion − for his defeatism, his eagerness to 'do business with Hitler' and his activity in pressuring for a negotiated peace. (His 'every move' was 'monitored' by the British authorities, writes Andrew Lownie in an essay on Kent in the recent book *North American Spies*.) Kennedy resigned upon Roosevelt's re-election. Subsequent publicity about his hatred of Jews and of the British, and about his opposition to the war, destroyed any further political career he might have had.

Kent's trial was held *in camera* in October, 1940, thus keeping his activities secret from American voters a month before they would return Roosevelt to the White House. Pleading that he had merely wanted to give the documents to US senators in order to keep America neutral, Kent was nevertheless found guilty of giving documents to a 'foreign agent' (as Volkov was shown to be). The jury deliberated only 24 minutes. At his sentencing, Kent again protested his loyalty and patriotism. There was no felony, he said, because there was 'no felonious intent.' (His acts were felonious, of course, no matter what his intent.) He received a seven-year sentence and spent five years on the Isle of Wight before being deported to the US and released. He soon married an American divorcée 13 years his senior and spent the next four decades running through her considerable fortune (from Carter's Little Liver Pills) in pursuit of his two abiding hobbies: yachting and publishing diatribes against Jews, blacks and Franklin Roosevelt. He died in 1988, his last home a caravan park in Texas.

And here the story might end: the story of a man who, like Daniel Ellsberg years later, simply attempted to unseat a US president through the release of certain information. This was Kent's claim.

But Kent did more, making his information available to Nazi sympathizers. And very probably he did even more. Before the war ended, the FBI had tentatively reclassified Tyler Kent as a *Soviet* agent, and both CIA and MI5 made it official soon afterward. 'One of the factors involved in reaching that decision,' write Ray Bearse and Anthony Read in *Conspirator: The Untold Story of Tyler Kent*, was a CIA memo after the war analysing the documents stolen by Kent. Of almost two thousand documents, only six had originated in Moscow; Kent's material was overwhelmingly of value to the *Soviets*, not the Germans. In fact, Kent had sought a posting to *Berlin* in February, 1940. Of critical importance, the Hitler-Stalin Pact had been in force the whole time Kent was taking the documents. As Bearse and Read tell us in *Conspirator*, Kent had worked for the Soviets earlier. He had been a clerk in the first US Embassy in Moscow. Arriving in that inhospitable country in 1934, he was by 1935 keeping company with an attractive woman whose NKVD connection he understood fully. 'We used to lie abed mornings and laughingly discuss what she would tell her bosses that day,' Kent told Bearse and Read. With help from his NKVD girlfriend, Kent earned substantial sums for himself by smuggling furs and jewellery out of the USSR. Only two or three of the embassy staff in Moscow owned cars, *Conspirator* tells us. Kent was one of them. (Didn't anyone *notice?*)

Did the Soviets force Kent to work for them (through the several holds they had on him), or did he volunteer? I can see it either way. He was an exploiter all his life: 'a real rotter' as Tony Read described him to me. If Kent worked willingly for the Soviets both in London and Moscow, we need only reconcile his service to them with what Malcolm Muggeridge has called Kent's 'maniacally hostile attitude towards the Soviet régime.' This display could have been real – it apparently got him PNG'd from the Moscow Embassy and it persisted to the end of his life – or it could have been a façade. Alternatively, as Andrew Lownie suggests, Kent may have worked for the Soviets (in London at least) without being fully aware of it; their interests could simply have coincided with his. Some part of the Tyler Kent story remains untold.

Walk now in the opposite direction on Gloucester Place. (Benedict

Arnold, the American hero-turned-traitor − or traitor-turned-hero, as some readers may prefer to think of him − spent his last years at No. 18.) At Portman Square, the best surviving townhouse by Robert Adam is on your L at

Site 82: **the former Courtauld Institute of Art, 20 Portman Square.**
In 1946 Anthony Blunt came to work at the Courtauld Institute. We know from the way Soviet Intelligence operated that they wouldn't have let him leave MI5 unless they could count on his continued availability and unless they had other assets within MI5. Blunt's later explanation that he had resigned from service to the Soviets because he was 'no longer interested' must have amused the dour crew at Moscow Centre. Much later, of course, he agreed with the assumption made by Western Intelligence: that he hadn't left MI5 untended, as it were, when he left.

For almost three decades, Blunt occupied an elegant apartment overlooking Portman Square. He was a dynamic director; during his tenure (1947-74), the Courtauld became the pre-eminent institution of its type in Britain. He also did well for himself here. Free to pursue his chosen career, he gained fame, honours, deference. He became Surveyor of the King's Pictures in 1945 (Surveyor of the Queen's

Pictures in 1952), a Knight Commander of the Victorian Order in 1956, Adviser to the Queen's Pictures and Drawings in 1972. He gained material comfort as well. Discouraging the Courtauld staff from working late, he had this entire 80-room mansion to himself after hours. I find it grotesque that he was so lavishly rewarded by the nation and society he was working so hard to destroy.

Courtauld students were well aware that Blunt was 'a Russian spy,' according to Barrie Penrose and Simon Freeman in *Conspiracy of Silence*. For all his years here he was probably servicing dead-drops and acting as a cut-out. In 1954, for example, the Soviets used him to contact Philby. What happened was this: Yuri Modin, formerly Blunt's controller, approached Blunt after a lecture here and asked his scholarly opinion about a picture on a postcard. On the back of the postcard was Modin's familiar handwriting telling Blunt to go to a certain pub the next evening. There Modin gave Blunt the details of a meeting he wanted with Philby. Blunt contacted Philby. Thus Modin and Philby hadn't risked contact prior to their meeting, and long before reaching their rendezvous they would elude any surveillance. Neatly done.

MI5 interrogated Blunt immediately after his life-long friend, Guy Burgess, had fled to Moscow. Coolly and steadfastly Blunt told his interrogators nothing. They had no evidence and he knew it; only his own faltering or the testimony of his fellow-communists could damage him. He had a scare in 1959 when Burgess seemed eager to return to Britain to see his ageing mother. Blunt needn't have worried. The government was even less interested than he was in seeing Burgess return; lacking evidence to bring Burgess to trial, the government would have been seriously embarrassed by his presence. What kept Burgess from returning? Did the Soviets veto the trip, fearing that Burgess would want to stay in London and would eventually tell MI5 all he knew? Or did HM Government thoughtfully warn Burgess that he might not be altogether safe in London — hinting at some misadventure, perhaps, at the hands of an indignant patriot? Chapman Pincher, in *Their Trade Is Treachery*, writes that it was Hollis (*see Sites 52 and 54*) who was 'determined to dissuade Burgess from ever returning to Britain.' Here is Pincher's thinking: 'If Hollis was a spy' — and Pincher has little doubt that he was — and if Burgess had somehow learnt of this, perhaps from

Maclean, then Hollis would have gone to any lengths to spare Burgess an MI5 interrogation. And, adds Pincher, the Soviets would have gone to any lengths to spare Maclean the same, even putting Philby and Blunt at risk with Maclean's defection (*see Site 120*). Burgess never did return; he died in Moscow in 1963.

Just when Blunt could stop worrying over Burgess, another old comrade surfaced. Michael Straight, an American whom Blunt had recruited to Soviet Intelligence (*see Site 95*), wanted a prestigious appointment under President Kennedy. Worried that the customary FBI check would reveal his communist affiliations, Straight decided to confess. The FBI debriefed him and turned him over to MI5; in 1964 Straight told MI5 everything he knew about Blunt. And now Blunt confessed, calmly but unequivocally. Later in 1964 the two confronted each other here. Thirty years earlier, Blunt had been manipulative in the extreme, resorting to emotional blackmail against an unwilling Straight. Here at the Courtauld they supposedly discussed a painting.

MI5 began interrogating Blunt in April, 1964, in his living room overlooking the square. The interrogations continued for 12 years. How much useful information did Blunt impart? Your guess, gentle reader, is as good as mine – unless, gentle reader, you happen to have been with Moscow Centre. He revealed nothing about still-active spies; his excellent memory failed him whenever his debriefers asked about such persons.

The Soviets wanted Blunt to follow Burgess and Maclean to Moscow, but he refused to leave the pleasures of his London for the idiotic boredom of Moscow. Interestingly, the Soviets did not kidnap or murder him to silence him. Why not? Years earlier, a communist courier named Whittaker Chambers had faced a similar situation in America. He assembled some documents he was supposed to pass to the Soviets and he told his handlers that if anything happened to him the documents would become public (thereby exposing both his *apparat* and its government sources). These were the famous 'Pumpkin Papers' of the 1948 Alger Hiss trial. Maybe Blunt did the same. Supporting my hunch is Blunt's odd statement during his only press conference. He began, 'I suppose he [Burgess] thought that if the thing got critical, they [the Soviets] might simply take me out, not reckoning on the fact that...' and then he stopped. John Costello reports this slip and observes that Blunt quickly changed the subject. What Blunt narrowly avoided saying, I think, was that he had entrusted some documents to a friend, with instructions to make the documents public should Blunt die mysteriously or disappear. I have no evidence to support this theory, but it seems likely, doesn't it? It turns out that one of Blunt's case-officers did exactly the same thing Chambers did (*see Site 121*), and Blunt was certainly canny enough to replicate Orlov's still-secret scheme or to copy Chambers's well-publicized scheme.

You are now at the end of this walk. Go S to Oxford Street for the tube at Marble Arch. (Here for 600 years was Tyburn Tree, site of public executions and of much delight at the spectacle.) To continue with the next walk, go E along the N side of Portman Square to Manchester Square and Hinde Street. Along the way, stop at the Wallace Collection: outstanding European paintings and an important collection of arms and armour.

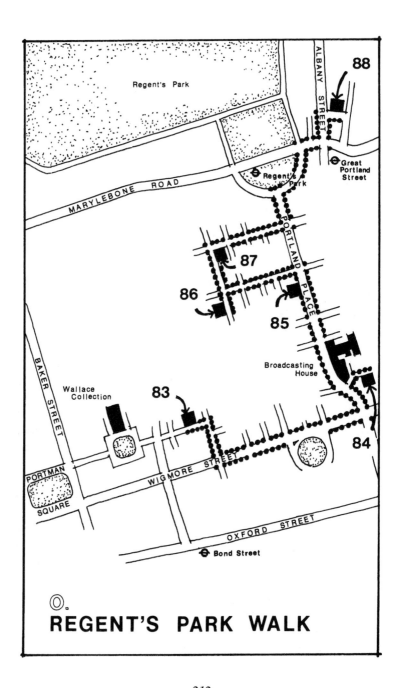

REGENT'S PARK WALK

O. REGENT'S PARK WALK

From Bond Street tube station, walk N on James Street into Mandeville Place. Turn R at Hinde Street, which leads into Bentinck Street. Edward Gibbon wrestled here with the Roman Empire. On your L is

Site 83: **5 Bentinck Street.** Victor Rothschild owned most of this building during WWII. When he turned the place over to friends, they sublet several floors to Anthony Blunt and Guy Burgess who, in turn, transformed it into what Penrose and Freeman in *Conspiracy of Silence* call 'a cross between a high-class male brothel and a debating club for off-duty intelligence men, senior military figures, politicians and journalists.'

The incomparable Malcolm Muggeridge has written superbly about this flat and about Burgess in it. 'Etonian mudlark and sick toast of a sick society,' Burgess seemed 'morally afflicted in some way. His very physical presence was, to me, malodorous and sinister; as though he had some consuming illness.' In this place with its distinguished group of 'notabilities' ('a whole revolutionary *Who's Who*,' writes Muggeridge), 'there was not so much a conspiracy gathered round him as just decay and dissolution. It was the end of a class, of a way of life; something that would be written about in history books, like Gibbon on Heliogabalus, with wonder and perhaps hilarity, but still tinged with sadness, as all endings are.'

The basement was the scene of frantic nightly parties; as the bombs fell, guests chewed on rubber bones thoughtfully provided by their hosts. The first floor (or, as Americans say, the *second* floor) contained a kitchen and sitting room. The next level had Blunt's bedroom and bathroom at one end, Burgess's at the other. Above them lived two young women (Rothschild's friends) whose home had been bombed out. A medical journal occupied the ground floor.

Burgess evidently used the house to advance his three passions in

Site 83: **5 Bentinck Street.**

life: drink, sodomy and intelligence-gathering for the Soviet Union. He was producing talk-shows at nearby Broadcasting House, having left the Joint Broadcasting Committee to rejoin the BBC in 1941. But he couldn't have been living within his salary since he was serving great quantities of hard-to-get (and therefore very expensive) whisky. The Soviets always got their money's worth from Burgess; a defector commented that the 'colossal' volume of material from Burgess sometimes 'almost fully employed' the embassy's cypher clerks; other urgent messages went to Moscow unencrypted in diplomatic bags.

In this house in 1940 Anthony Blunt was introduced to Guy Liddell (then head of counter-espionage at MI5), either through Victor Rothschild or Tomás Harris — opinions vary. At the end of a pleasant hour it was apparent that Blunt would soon be joining MI5. Before the year's end he was Liddell's personal assistant. Blunt did much to cultivate the easily flattered Liddell, even taking him on expeditions to buy artwork; Liddell was an avid collector. And Liddell, whose wife had scandalously run off to America with her half-brother, often relaxed here in the company of Blunt and Burgess and their odd collection of friends.

At the end of Bentinck Street turn R into Welbeck Street, then L into Wigmore Street to reach Langham Place at the top of Regent Street. (Perhaps detour south to Oxford Circus, where the top floor of the Peter Robinson department store was requisitioned in WWII for the Theatre Intelligence Organization — 'a constantly expanding group of scholars' who collected and catalogued a 'staggering' amount of material, from POW interrogation transcripts to aerial photos, from beach sand tests to refugee interviews, as an admiring OSS officer described it.) Across Langham Place you'll see the Church of All Souls: small, round, columned. Just beyond is All Souls' Place. Last building on the R is

Site 84: **5 All Souls' Place.** We know a bit about George Blake. We know that his promising career with MI6, which began in 1944, ended in 1961 when he was convicted of five violations of the Official Secrets Act. We know that in 1966 he escaped from Wormwood Scrubs Prison and an extraordinary 42-year sentence;

Site 84: **5 All Souls' Place.**

he surfaced in Moscow, where he is living still. And we know that in one of his brief periods in London, in 1954, he lived here.

But there is much we don't know about Blake, who was the only Soviet spy, other than Philby, ever found within SIS. What precisely did Blake do, for instance? After the trial, a government leak revealed that Blake had betrayed at least 40 British agents to the Soviets. Blake places the total 'nearer 400' – even '500 or 600.' Incredibly, in his 1990 autobiography, he challenges anybody 'to name one who has been executed.' He revealed their identities, he says, 'on the express understanding that they would not come to any harm.' If one's jaw has not already dropped in amazement at Blake's naiveté (or at his gall in passing off this fantasy about the KGB's *modus operandi*), he then reassures us that in any case they weren't British nationals.

Blake says that he gave the Soviets every important paper to cross his desk for a decade. There is no question but that he tipped off the Soviets about the Berlin Tunnel (*see Site 63*), 'before even the first spade had been put in the ground,' he writes. This was an immense coup for the Soviets. While they fed the West some genuine information in this operation, they sent much disinformation, and they swamped the West with so much material that the keenest analysts worked at little else and the planners sought no additional tunnels.

Finally, concerning Blake's treachery, he was very probably assigned by MI6 to pretend to be a double agent – to give disinformation to the Soviets and to find out what the Soviets wanted to get. It doesn't require much imagination to see the enormous potential here for Blake to aid the side he was really on. He *earned* his Order of Lenin.

We don't know when Blake became a Soviet agent. In his book he would have us believe that he was softened up by experiences in MI6 itself: the special course in Russian he took at Cambridge in 1947-8, and the Marxist literature he read before going to South Korea as an intelligence assistant in 1948. He claims that only when he was a prisoner of the North Koreans in 1951 did he offer his services to the Soviets – not to save his skin, mind you, but because he believed in their 'great' cause, their 'heroic' experiment. (In 1992, a former KGB general said it was tinned food and chocolate that had bought Blake's loyalty in Korea.) As a boy Blake had been close to a left-leaning cousin, later a co-founder of the Egyptian Communist Party, but he claims that the cousin's views didn't affect his thinking. (Most sources identify Henri Curiel as Blake's *uncle* but I think we can take Blake's word here, if not on much else.)

We will probably never know why the British failed to discover Blake. Were counter-intelligence procedures so poor? Or were they neutralized by some person or persons inside? Blake was caught because a Polish intelligence officer named Michal Goleniewski wanted to change sides and told the Americans about two unnamed Soviet agents in Britain, and because a German named Horst Eitner, arrested as a Soviet spy, named Blake precisely. Goleniewski's information had led to a list of ten people in MI6 as the source of a vital leak — Blake among them — but all ten were soon exonerated. Only later did suspicion settle on Blake, and after several days of interrogation he suddenly confessed. The government had no case without this confession, which came when his weary interrogator, according to Chapman Pincher, was making 'positively his last throw.' The interrogator stated his assumption that Blake had succumbed to the communists because of intimidation. No, Blake insisted emphatically, he had acted from idealism! Other people remember it differently, writes Nigel West in *Seven Spies Who Changed the World*. Blake had been under surveillance as he wandered alone through the West End for lunch and he broke down later when asked who he had almost telephoned. Whichever story is closer to the truth, Blake's interrogation was apparently no day at the beach.

In his book *No Other Choice*, Blake reminds me of some of the idealists whom I knew at college — simplistic, self-righteous, self-dramatizing. The noble experiment of communism has failed, Blake admits, because nowhere on earth have people reached the necessary 'moral stature.' But he is certain that 'mankind will return to this experiment, it will try again.' He asks himself about the 'untold human suffering this experiment has required' and he has a ready answer: 'Has there ever been a human endeavour of any magnitude which has not involved suffering and sacrifice?' (As Stalin said, 'you can't make an omelette without breaking eggs.') One gasps at Blake's moral certitude, the equal of any poorly-read undergraduate.

Blake's personality is undoubtedly more complex. A fellow inmate in Wormwood Scrubs described him as having three personalities: one charming and kind, the second pessimistic and defeatist, the third cruel and ruthless. 'When that third man bared his teeth (which he physically in fact did), a sensible person could see that he was an extremely dangerous customer.' This opinion was echoed by another inmate, the spirited Irishman Sean Bourke who helped Blake to escape and followed him to Moscow (where Bourke finally saw Blake as a born betrayer and a bit of a madman). Bourke preferred the possibility of incarceration in a British jail to the dismal certainty of life in the Soviet Union and he was allowed to leave the USSR – without the manuscript of his book, *The Springing of George Blake* which he simply rewrote. Bourke died in Ireland in 1982; his extradition to England had been denied because helping Blake was considered 'a political offence.'

Two other inmates of Wormwood Scrubs assisted in Blake's escape, and by 1989 they too had written a book admitting it. Michael Randle and Pat Pottle, who were both members of the Committee of 100 (a militant splinter of the Campaign for Nuclear Disarmament), came to trial in 1991 and in what lawyers call a 'perverse verdict' were acquitted. This, after Randle and Pottle pleaded *not* guilty, then *defended* their guilt on political and moral grounds, then finally asked jury members to use their 'common sense' and ignore the 'legal mumbo-jumbo.' (The jury surely ignored the judge, who had emphatically ruled out such a defence.) The trial featured a videotaped statement from Blake in Moscow, stating that Randle and Pottle had had no connection with the KGB. Naturally, no cross-examination of Blake was possible. A final note about these recent events: Blake claimed that he would willingly have returned to a British prison if Randle and Pottle had gone to jail; he said this, however, only upon their acquittal. Responding to rumours that Russia's new leadership might return him to Britain anyway, Blake hastily shifted his allegiance to Boris Yeltsin. With the collapse of communism in Russia, another rumour surfaced: that Blake might choose to live in North Korea. No, said Blake, he'd prefer Wormwood Scrubs.

Was Blake's escape in 1966 a deal between MI6 and the Soviets? MI6 would have been rid of this man whose perfidy had brought such embarrassment to Britain and such uneasiness to Britain's allies. And the KGB would have reminded its agents and potential agents, the world over, that the KGB looks after its own. Anything is possible. But I don't buy the idea of a deal, and not just because Philby was one of those on both sides of the Iron Curtain suggesting it.

Through it all in Moscow sits George Blake, now over 70, advising the KGB as long as it lasted and now working for the Foreign Intelligence Service. He has a Russian wife, a Russian son, a Russian dacha, and a cocker spaniel named Danny. He professes a certain religiosity. He natters on about his ideals. He is reported to be drinking heavily. But how proud he is that he never took money for spying. His autobiography is unsatisfying. The real man is hidden. The book might have been written by someone else, or about someone else. And how telling that it does not mention, as Nigel West does in *Seven Spies*, how Blake 'co-operated to the full' in Wormwood Scrubs, even identifying his three KGB case-officers!

This man who was a British subject by accident (his father came from Turkey, his mother from Holland) writes that four nations have imprisoned him: Germany and Spain during WWII, North Korea and Britain. Does he consider his time in the USSR a fifth imprisonment? We will probably never know. Blake's story is so full of unanswered questions and improbable explanations that one is sceptical even about the cocker spaniel named Danny. At least we are not told that he, too, is an idealist.

Back at Portland Place, past BBC's Broadcasting House (where Neville Chamberlain read his declaration of war against Germany), proceed N towards Regent's Park. On the L is

Site 85: **35 Portland Place.** Much of the SOE legend rests on its ingeniously-disguised explosive devices. There were exploding rats (real rat corpses stuffed with explosives) to be planted in coal-piles and shovelled into the enemy's train and ship boilers. There were exploding animal droppings (simulated road-apples with pressure-switched charges) to be planted on roads and tripped by the enemy's

Site 85: **35 Portland Place.**

trucks. The sub-section of SOE that developed such devices worked here until 1940 when a *Luftwaffe* bomb forced the research group into a large country house near Aylesbury.

Turn L at Weymouth Street and L into Wimpole Mews. On your R is

Site 86: **17 Wimpole Mews.** I've never found the bullet-marks (reported to exist) that catapulted the resident of this house onto Page One of all the tabloids in the early 1960s — and toppled a British government. This singular drama of sex and the secret world was described recently by *The Sunday Times* as 'Britain's worst cold war political scandal.' It received further attention when one of the latest tell-all (and invent-more) accounts emerged from Moscow in 1992. The following is what we know now, or can deduce, about the Ward-Keeler-Ivanov-Profumo case.

Stephen Ward, who lived here, was an osteopath with a glittery clientele of maharajahs, kings and leading figures of society and entertainment. He gained the friendship of some of his clients through his osteopathic skills; he kept their friendship by providing them with 'popsies.' Christine Keeler was one of the striking young women whom Ward took into his home (apparently not into his bed).

He taught these women how to manage in social situations – and, going beyond Professor Higgins, how to enhance the sexual pleasures of the jaded, the perverse, the uninhibited. Ward possessed a few fetishes of his own, not to mention an interest in all things kinky.

Ward met Yevgeny Ivanov, assistant naval attaché at the Soviet Embassy, through the good offices of a patient – Colin Coote, editor of *The Daily Telegraph*. (Coote had published Ward's drawings of the Eichmann trial; Ward now wanted to sketch each Politburo member, and Coote thought Ivanov might get Ward a visa.) Ivanov and Ward became friends. Ivanov argued politics with MPs at Ward's flat, played bridge with Ward's aristocratic friends in their homes, and stayed at Ward's weekend cottage on the estate of Lord Astor. And he knew Ward's young women.

Suddenly in May, 1961, Ivanov was identified to MI5 as an important GRU officer. (Oleg Penkovsky had been identifying all Soviet intelligence officers in Britain to prove his *bona fides*.) MI5 already knew of Ivanov's pleasures in London. He seemed ripe for a 'honeytrap.' If all went well, he might be blackmailed into becoming an agent-in-place. Failing that, he might still be blackmailed into defecting. MI5 asked Ward's help in springing the honeytrap. Ward agreed.

Then, as often happens, the unexpected happened. The Secretary of State for War, John Profumo, met Christine Keeler at Lord Astor's swimming pool and began a liaison with her – while she was keeping some sort of company with Ivanov (among others). When one of her West Indian lovers appeared outside the Wimpole Mews flat with a gun, late in 1962, firing at the building to emphasize his eagerness to see her, the press took notice. A 'freelance model' in the home of a society osteopath? And a violent black man threatening to storm the place? Soon enough the press gave people the story they really wanted – true or not – about Keeler's simultaneous relationships with a Soviet diplomat and a British Cabinet Minister, and about her efforts to wheedle state secrets from the latter to give to the former. Profumo lied to a crowded House of Commons, claiming 'no impropriety whatsoever' in his 'acquaintanceship' with Keeler. Ivanov meanwhile had been hustled back to Moscow at the first whiff of scandal.

The idea of pursuing Profumo soon subsided. He had his enemies but was part of the Establishment. Ward was not. In July, 1963, four months after Profumo's denial of wrongdoing and two months after Profumo's resignation from the Cabinet anyway (after it was clear that he had lied), Ward was brought to trial. The most prominent of the absurd charges against him was 'living on immoral earnings.' If anything, the young women were living on *his* earnings.

The trial was unquestionably a travesty of justice. Ward's girls later recanted testimony coerced from them by police. The jury knew nothing of Keeler's prior conviction for perjury. The judge, in a shocking display of partiality, suggested that Ward's wealthy friends had deserted him because he was guilty. (They deserted him because he didn't matter to them. And perhaps MI5 wouldn't have abandoned him so readily if he had been of a different class.) The jury brought a verdict of guilty later on the same day that Ward was rushed to hospital. He had taken an overdose of Nembutal — 'to disappoint the vultures', he wrote in a farewell letter. He died three days later, unaware of the verdict that could have imprisoned him for 14 years at a time when pimps were customarily only fined. But he already knew that he had lost his practice, his friends, even his status as an artist, the BBC having savaged his show of drawings earlier that week.

Ward's trial turned the public's attention from worries about national security to jokes about flagellation. But governments are not inclined to be grateful when they have their own troubles (as the Macmillan government did, largely over this case; the Prime Minister resigned later in 1963). And the secret services are not inclined to make statements of sympathy on behalf of individuals in their employ; MI5 had cut Ward adrift, his case-officer only later confessing that they felt 'very sorry' for Ward and were 'very cut up' at what happened. The honeytrap operation remained secret until the early 1980s when Nigel West broke the story in *The Circus: MI5 Operations 1945-1972* and when *The Sunday Times* found and interviewed the MI5 officer who had recruited Ward.

The above account cannot begin to include all the events and characters in the drama. The so-called 'American connection' which linked several of Ward's girls to President Kennedy. Or Ward's part (with Ivanov) in back-channel communications between Britain and the USSR during the Cuban missile crisis. Or the official inquiry by

Lord Denning (senior judge of the Court of Appeal), who seemed determined to ignore any possible connection between MI5 and the evil Ward, and to cover up any possible damage to national security from the whole business. The twists and turns of plot are presented in detail and with relish in *Honeytrap: The Secret Worlds of Stephen Ward* (1987) by Anthony Summers and Stephen Dorril, and *An Affair of State: The Profumo Case and the Framing of Stephen Ward* (1987) by Phillip Knightley and Caroline Kennedy (no, not *that* Caroline Kennedy).

For a wholly different interpretation of the Profumo affair see Chapman Pincher's *Too Secret Too Long* (1984). Pincher holds that Ward was never recruited as an agent by MI5 but promised only to keep MI5 informed of anything interesting concerning Ivanov. Ward may well have served as an agent for *Ivanov*, says Pincher (Keeler thought so), even organizing the Ivanov-Keeler liaison in order to entrap Profumo. Ward was so sympathetic to communism, notes Pincher, that some of his patients 'appear to have reported him to MI5 as an agent of influence.' The real villain, for Pincher, however, is Sir Roger Hollis (*see Sites 52 and 54*). Hollis continually minimized the security aspects of the matter: failing to inform Macmillan at the time, considering the matter closed when Ivanov departed, and misleading Lord Denning afterward even as to the information that Keeler was instructed to get from Profumo (it was nothing so complicated as 'atomic secrets' says Pincher, but was simply the date of delivery of nuclear warheads to West Germany, information she would surely have been able to request and Profumo would probably have been able to supply).

For 30 years, until 1992, nothing was heard from Ivanov until *The Naked Spy* appeared, written for a British publisher ostensibly by Ivanov, now 65 years old and (I am told) drinking heavily in Moscow. Ivanov tells us that he was ready to blackmail Profumo about Profumo's affair with Keeler, until Keeler sold the gaudy story to the tabloids and ruined everything. Ivanov claims to have obtained ample secret information on his own, photographing or stealing important papers from the homes of Lord Astor, Profumo and Churchill. Is *The Naked Spy* the unclad truth? The book caused the nonagenarian Lord Denning to declare Ivanov 'a much more effective spy than I ever believed.' But Mrs Profumo insisted that Ivanov never visited the Profumo home and couldn't have obtained secret documents there. She received a public apology in the High Court: Ivanov's claims were proclaimed 'false in every material respect' and the publisher agreed to pulp undistributed copies of the book.

I don't think that Ivanov gleaned secrets from pillow-talk; I doubt whether Keeler could have interrogated Profumo about nuclear weapons for Germany, no matter who might have prompted her (Ward? Ivanov?) to ask. But did *Ward* give information to Ivanov, as Ivanov claims? Why? And how would Ward have got it? And how can Ivanov be so certain that Ward *didn't* work for MI5? Because Ward *told* him so? It's a seller's market in spy memoirs these days in the former Soviet Union.

My own view of Ward is that he was a naif, a social climber who got in over his head. He saw himself as an arranger — with his society friends, his MI5 contacts, even with Ivanov — never imagining that *he* was the one being used. He made some powerful friends and some powerful enemies; unfortunately for him, his enemies proved more steadfast than his friends. And then, of course, there was the political opposition to the Conservative Party, delighted by an orgy-filled scandal among the upper classes. Knowing what I know about politics, and about life, I suspect that the opposition would be as uncomfortable in a monastery as the Tories would be. Maybe it was just the Tories' turn to get caught. It usually is.

Retracing your steps to Weymouth Street, cross into

Site 87: **Devonshire Mews South.** Vera Atkins, 'the mainspring of F Section', tells me that SOE debriefed its 'Jeds' somewhere in Devonshire Mews. The WWII Jedburgh teams weren't trained near the Scottish town but were named for the guerrilla warfare there during the border disputes between England and Scotland in the 12th century.

Jedburgh teams consisted of an Englishman, an American, and a Frenchman (the order is M. R. D. Foot's). At de Gaulle's insistence, each team had a French officer. The second team member was either an American or British officer; the third was an NCO wireless operator. All were trained in guerrilla tactics and demolition. 'Their objects,' writes Foot, 'were to provide a general staff for the local resistance wherever they landed, to co-ordinate the local efforts in the best interests of allied strategy, and where possible to arrange further supplies of arms.'

Site 87: **Devonshire Mews South.**

As Foot observes, policy makers were 'probably over-cautious' in delaying Jedburgh operations until June of 1944. But Foot is cautious in his judgment. 'It would certainly have helped to heighten the enemy's sense of insecurity if uniformed as well as armed parties of allied subversive agents had begun to operate in the interior of France in appreciable numbers for some months before D-Day; but the risks in this particular case were large, and only the impetuous will wish to blame the allied command for not taking them.'

Uniformed agents? Yes. The 93 teams of Jeds dropped and worked *in uniform*, bringing immeasurable encouragement to people who had seen only Nazi uniforms for four long years.

Exiting from Devonshire Mews South at its N end, and looking straight ahead into Devonshire Mews West, do not be so churlish as to seek accurate names for such charming streets. Take Devonshire Street to Portland Place and turn L. Follow Park Crescent into

Marylebone Road and turn R. Almost immediately turn L into Albany Street. Behind the church, facing Osnaburgh Terrace, is

Site 88: **the White House, Albany Street.** Chapman Pincher in *Traitors: The Labyrinths of Treason* defines a spymaster as an experienced case-officer who runs a ring of several agents. He gives two examples: the American Julius Rosenberg and the Russian Konon Molody, a/k/a 'Gordon Lonsdale.' Here in Room 634 of the White House, high above neighbouring rooftops for good wireless reception, Lonsdale had a tiny serviced flat in January, 1961, when MI5 concluded an extensive surveillance on him (partially from the adjacent flat) and arrested him and as much of his ring as they knew about. Arrested with him were the 'Krogers' (*see Site 94*), Harry Houghton, and Ethel Gee.

With good reason, Oleg Gordievsky has described Lonsdale as 'one of the most gifted of all KGB residents.' Lonsdale was good at his job. He gave Moscow invaluable data on Britain's latest underwater defences – on submarine-detection systems, homing torpedoes, sonar buoys. And he was good at evading detection. He would probably never have been caught if a Polish double agent, Michal Goleniewski, hadn't told the CIA that a British clerk named

Houghton was taking material from the Admiralty Underwater Weapons Establishment at Portland; MI5's surveillance of Houghton led straight to Lonsdale.

Perhaps none of this, though, would have earned Konon Molody his exalted position in the KGB's secret Memory Room. Perhaps his most valuable service was in getting arrested when and where he did. He had left the country briefly during MI5's surveillance, and Peter Wright argues that the Soviets 'must have known from the beginning that we were onto Lonsdale'; only a leak at 'the very summit' of MI5 could explain all the inconsistencies of the case. 'The only way of forestalling the hunt inside MI5,' Wright believes, 'was to send Lonsdale back.'

And so Lonsdale may have been sacrificed for someone more important. But for whom? Take your pick. An East German defector told the CIA that two East Germans running the Krogers had left England when the Krogers were arrested. Were there others who stayed? We may never know the magnitude of the KGB operation that survived because of Lonsdale's arrest. For that matter, we may never know the magnitude of his operation *before* his arrest.

The eight-day trial of 'the Portland ring' was exciting stuff: techniques of spying and counter-spying, protestations of innocence, admissions of guilt, and confessions of a spy's loneliness. Dame Rebecca West, in *The New Meaning of Treason*, observes that Lonsdale's letter to his wife was very similar to letters in the Abel spy case. Were they all written, she wonders, to convince jury members that a spy is just 'a man like themselves'?

Lonsdale was easily found guilty. Subminiature cameras, secret writing, microdots, transmitter, code pads, hidden compartments in talcum-powder tins — he was caught red-handed, as it were. The other four were found guilty too, their sentences considered severe even by the appeals court that upheld them. Of his 25-year sentence, Lonsdale served only three years before being exchanged for Greville Wynne (*see Site 34*).

Back in the USSR in 1964, Lonsdale immediately wrote his memoirs, with Philby's help. The book is absurd. True, it is titled *Spy: Twenty Years in Soviet Secret Service*, but the truth may end there. Molody continues to portray himself as a Canadian named Lonsdale (no matter that the real Lonsdale, long dead, was known to have been circumcised while Molody was uncircumcised). He continues to proclaim the innocence of the kindly Krogers who were merely his friends. The book stops at nothing: Lonsdale says he was successful in Britain in preventing the biological warfare that was planned by a Nazi war criminal — as he was also helpful in preventing a nuclear holocaust. World peace was his only desire. How they must have chuckled as they constructed this manuscript, Philby and all those sombre 'active measures' specialists in Moscow. The first sentence alone is a flat-out lie: 'I come from what social workers nowadays call a broken home.'

Nowhere in the book does he mention his women and free-spending entertainments while in London. His cover was the bubble-gum and vending-machine business, and he worked very hard at that too. Rebecca West notes his 'great gift' for 'the minor social festivities' and she dismisses him crisply: 'He would have been the life and soul of a gala night at any Thames Valley hotel.'

He was not dismissed back in Moscow. He became a lecturer at the KGB's training school and enjoyed a fame that caused some envy among other KGB 'illegals.' But he didn't enjoy it for long. He died in 1970 at the age of 48, Gordievsky tells us, 'after a prolonged drinking bout at a picnic on a hot summer's day.'

Two further notes about Konon Molody. He wasn't even remotely Canadian (his father was a noted Moscow science writer). But he did spend five years in California, staying with an aunt. He argued that his kindergarten photograph, taken in San Francisco, would prove he was Lonsdale. (When the FBI located the school's headmistress she did indeed choose the correct lad in the photograph but identified him as *Konon Molody*!) During those years in America, young Molody was able to master Western ways. 'His story is one of a number,' writes Rebecca West, 'which suggests that clever children are dedicated by their parents to service in the Soviet Intelligence long before they can make such a decision for themselves.'

He worked as an 'illegal' — that is, without diplomatic immunity. If caught, he would be tried. What were the odds of getting caught? Here is Nigel West, in *Games of Intelligence*: 'Having accepted that illegals are regarded by the KGB and GRU as essential, and knowing that greater emphasis was placed on their development as early as 1952, it is odd that the British authorities failed to uncover a single case of an illegal until the Portland spy ring was wound up in January, 1961.' And between 1961 and 1985, continues West, 'no illegals were caught in England.' How many were not caught? Estimates of the number of Soviet illegals operating in the West in the late 1960s ranged from several hundred to a thousand, according to Harry Rositzke's *The KGB: The Eyes of Russia*. (These estimates were based on the testimony of defectors, the size of training classes for illegals in Moscow, and the confessions of arrested illegals.)

In all probability, then, Lonsdale was the barely visible tip of an iceberg. This iceberg thawed not at all during the years of warming relations between the declining Soviet Union and the West, and we can assume it hasn't fully melted yet. But we are at least getting a clearer view of it. In 1990 the Soviet government issued five postage stamps honouring Soviet spies. Along with Kim Philby, Rudolf Abel, and two partisans operating behind German lines in WWII, we see a dignified portrait not of 'Gordon Lonsdale' but of 'K. T. Molody.'

This walk ends at the White House. You have a choice of tube stations from here (Regent's Park or Great Portland Street). If you're up to the next walk, perhaps after an elegant repast at the White House, make your way to heavily travelled Euston Road and head E.

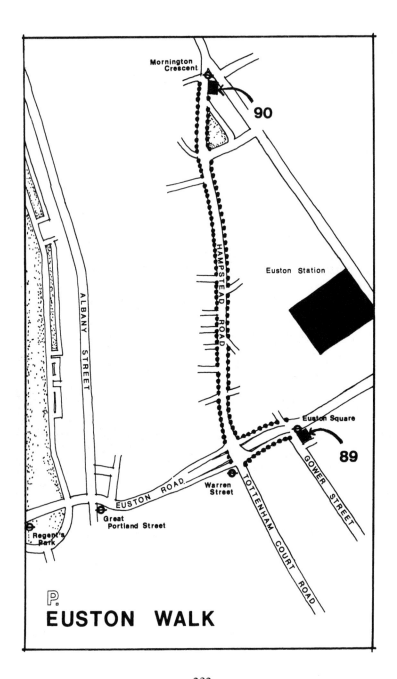

90

Mornington
Crescent

Euston Station

Euston Square

89

ALBANY STREET

HAMPSTEAD ROAD

GOWER STREET

TOTTENHAM COURT ROAD

EUSTON ROAD

Warren
Street

Great
Portland Street

Regent's
Park

P.
EUSTON WALK

P. EUSTON WALK

If you're walking E on Euston Road — not the most pleasant stroll — you'll find this next site at Gower Street above the tube station. The more scenic approach is on the underground. Get out at Euston Square for

Site 89: **140 Gower Street.** 'You don't actually see it,' exults a commentator on the BBC's recent exploration of 'secret architecture' as he points to this MI5 headquarters. 'Almost an invisible building', it is deemed more suitable to rebuilt Dresden or to anywhere in Poland.

This building is one of the many modern structures that sprang up in the 1950s in London, trying to stand out and fit in at the same time. Recently, it has been one of the rather few (mostly anonymous-looking) MI5 properties spread out across London. *The Times* numbers them at 'about eight', serving various purposes: human, technical, vehicular. Like other of these 'secret' buildings, Gower Street hasn't been secret for quite a while. Among those who have talked openly about this headquarters, *The Tatler* naughtily revealed a decade ago that MI5 candidates came here (sworn to secrecy) for their positive vetting.

Anyone who doesn't have the run of the building might like to know about the flat on the top floor; Peter Wright stayed in it on his last night with MI5. Presumably there are other unexpected amenities behind these bland-looking windows.

With the publicized move of some 2,300 MI5 personnel to the expanded Thames House (*see Site 10*), fewer and fewer secrets remain. Newspaper readers learnt in 1991 not only the name of MI5's new director-general (Mrs Stella Rimington) but also her prior place of work ('the fifth floor of MI5's headquarters in Gower Street, north London'). I can't imagine which of these revelations would most have amazed Sir Vernon Kell who launched the service 80-odd years ago.

Walk one block W on Euston Road. You can't miss Euston Tower on the NW corner of Euston Road and Hampstead Road. Here, until recently, one of MI5's main computers kept track of the Watchers. And now walk N on Hampstead Road for a jaunt through the kind of London that only Londoners know. For the next eight or so blocks you'll see a microcosm of British commercial and institutional life: a government surplus store, an overseas airways office, a 'gents hairdressing', a printer, a café, a convent school, a retail butcher, a hardware store named 'Things-U-Need', a temperance hospital, a bookmaker. You'll pass high-rise housing on mean little patches of lawn, and you'll cross the tracks leading to Euston Station. It is an interesting few blocks, culminating in the more conventional shopping area surrounding

Site 90: **Mornington Crescent underground station.** Klaus Fuchs was imprisoned by the British in 1950 for having given vital atomic secrets to the Soviets between 1942 and 1949. But he had occupied the most sensitive positions in atomic weapons research because someone in MI5 either had neglected to subject him to scrutiny or had shielded him from scrutiny. Fuchs, a known communist, was somehow able to work on the Manhattan Project (in the US) and at Harwell (in the UK), both of which were closed communities of the most trusted physicists the West could assemble. On his return from Los Alamos in 1946, Fuchs was to meet his new Soviet controller outside this tube station. The contact would carry a bundle of five books in one hand and a book by Bennett Cerf in the other. Fuchs would carry a copy of *Life*. Fuchs never appeared, later claiming he was suffering 'doubts about Russian policy' in the postwar period. But he delivered atomic secrets to the Russians until 1949, using a pub in Putney and the Kew Gardens tube station as his London meeting places.

Site 90: **Mornington Crescent underground station.**

Soviet case-officers favoured tube stations as meeting places. John Vassall (*see Site 12*) met his controller at Finchley Road station; Blake (*see Site 84*) used Belsize Park station; Yuri Modin preferred Turnham Green and Ealing Common when Burgess hadn't insisted on meeting in a Soho pub; Oleg Penkovsky (*see Site 76*) told his debriefers that Washington was a difficult city for agents because it lacked a subway system. With all the comings and goings at a station, anyone tailing either party would be noticed. Elaborate recognition signals would keep sensitive material from being pressed into the hands of some bloke simply waiting for his train. The signals were comical – who would stand in a public place holding a *tennis ball*, or a leather belt and an *orange*? But the work was hardly comical. Fuchs, for example, damaged the West far more than the Rosenbergs did, and Soviet possession of nuclear weapons by 1949 may well have encouraged North Korea to invade South Korea in 1950.

Where did security fail in the Fuchs case? The British opened a file on him as early as 1933, according to Robert Chadwell Williams, author of *Klaus Fuchs, Atom Spy*; young Fuchs then belonged to the German communist party. Fuchs fled Germany immediately after the Reichstag fire and reached England later in 1933. He made no secret of his communist loyalties when he entered the University of Bristol, or later when he was interned briefly as an enemy alien, or later still when he wanted to emphasize his anti-Nazism before an aliens' hearing board. Only after he began research on nuclear weapons did he encourage people to perceive him as apolitical.

By then, Fuchs had acquired impeccable credentials and important friends. He had done research in Edinburgh with Max Born. He had met Rudolf Peierls who (with Otto Frisch) was the first to calculate that an atomic bomb could be built; when Peierls began working on nuclear fission in 1941, MI5 approved his choice of Fuchs as his assistant. And in 1943 when Peierls asked Fuchs to go with him to the Manhattan Project, MI5 told the FBI incorrectly that Fuchs had been fully investigated.

When Fuchs returned to England in 1946 to head the theoretical physics division at the Atomic Energy Research Establishment at Harwell, again MI5 seemed incurious. Nigel West tells us in an article in *Intelligence Quarterly* that an immediate investigation of Fuchs was recommended in 1947 after a routine review of his file. 'For reasons that have never been properly explained,' writes West, MI5 'overlooked the matter'. West concedes that Roger Hollis was 'economical with the truth' concerning this lapse. Chapman Pincher goes further, charging in *Too Secret Too Long* that 'the person most responsible for [Fuchs's] successive security clearances was Roger Hollis'.

Serious suspicion fell on Fuchs in 1949 when the FBI deciphered some wartime messages between Moscow and its US diplomatic missions; one message pointed to a British scientist as having supplied information on the atomic bomb project. At this discovery, the security officer at Harwell and a skilled interrogator from MI5 began quiet discussions with Fuchs. Within the month, a strangely calm Fuchs confessed to even greater transgressions than his interrogators had suspected. For four violations of the Official Secrets Act, he received the maximum sentence: 14 years. (Had Britain been at war with the USSR, he could have been hanged.) Kept secret at the one-day trial was the fact that Fuchs was working at Harwell on Britain's atomic bomb – a project hidden equally from the British public and the American government. John Costello thinks it 'plausible' that the authorities knew of Fuchs's spying but accepted it because of his contribution to Britain's nuclear effort. Were the British so desperate to join the nuclear club that they didn't mind carrying the Soviets along with them?

Fuchs left prison after ten years. He could have stayed in Britain (even with his naturalization revoked) but he went instead to East Germany and became deputy director of that country's Institute for Nuclear Research. The institute's director later defected and testified to the immense assistance Fuchs had given the Soviets: in April, 1942, Fuchs supplied the crucial early news of Western efforts that prompted the Soviets to start their own atomic-fission laboratory; he later supplied the details that enabled the Soviets to produce their own weapons; he even calculated America's production of atomic bombs immediately after the war.

After his release from prison and until his death 39 years later, this man who had said in his confession that he eventually 'disapproved of a great many actions of the Russian Government and of the Communist Party' gave his working mind completely to the Soviets and became a mouthpiece for all their nuclear propaganda. He never travelled outside the Soviet bloc, presumably because he wasn't trusted. I'm not surprised. Fuchs, unforgivably, had made possible the capture of David Greenglass and the Rosenbergs when he co-operated with the FBI and identified the courier Harry Gold. (The Soviets, of course, had slipped up by using the same cut-out for Fuchs and Greenglass.)

Fuchs was, I think, a distorted and stunted personality. Three family members had committed suicide (his maternal grandmother, his mother, a sister). His father, a Lutheran clergyman, had become a Quaker and vehement pacifist. Fuchs himself exhibited a belief in the correctness of Marxism that was not very different from his father's religious fanaticism: a belief that The Truth had been uniquely revealed to him and that it justified any kind of behaviour from him. Klaus Fuchs's faith in communism may have wavered, over the years, even when he was serving his religion most obediently, but he seems to have suffered no lasting doubts from either the Hitler-Stalin Pact (which he accepted as a necessary expedient) or the Khrushchev revelations of 1956 (which he ignored in moving to East Germany). Was he a 'selfless' man, 'driven by a moral passion to do what is right' as Norman Moss describes him in *Klaus Fuchs: The Man Who Stole the Atom Bomb*? I think not. Anyone who remained committed to the communists after 1956 could hardly claim the moral high ground. But Fuchs was not living in the real world. On his release from prison he said he bore the British no bitterness. By any sane reckoning, however, he had seriously harmed the British and grievously betrayed their trust and hospitality. This man was untroubled by sane reckoning.

It is popular to regard the American concern with Soviet espionage, especially in the early days of the Cold War, as a 'witch hunt', suggesting that America was obsessed by a figment of an imagination gone hysterical. There were no witches, of course. But there *were* Soviet agents, and in his time and in his trusted place Klaus Fuchs did much to serve the Soviet system, a system that despised its own subjects and sought by every means to extend its tyranny everywhere.

The hardy may wish to take the underground from here to Goodge Street, to visit the British Museum. If so, enter the museum by Great Russell Street; here, near Museum Street, the later-convicted atom spy Alan Nunn May was told to meet his new controller. (The two would approach from opposite directions. Recognizing each other by the publications carried in their left arms, the two would exchange recognition signals within a tightly scripted conversation about the distance to the Strand.) The fact that Marx and Lenin each studied at the British Museum − Marx when he reached England in 1849 and Lenin for the year beginning in April, 1902 − should be of some comfort: both Marxism and Leninism have more of a past than a future, while the British Museum will probably exist for ever. For the next walk, take the tube from Mornington Crescent to Camden Town and change for the short trip to Bank station.

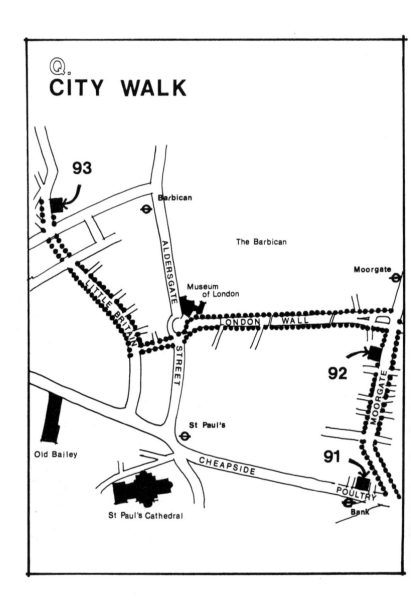

Q. CITY WALK

Q. CITY WALK

Starting point of this walk is the Bank of England. If you have time, take the bus; the changing glimpses of St Paul's Cathedral will remain with you long afterwards. At the Bank of England, look W for the street named Poultry (where poultry was sold in medieval times). In the 1920s the Midland Bank asked the eminent architect Sir Edwin Lutyens to design the bank's head office here at

Site 91: **27-32 Poultry.** In June, 1983, the Midland Bank received word that Dennis Skinner, its resident manager in Moscow, had fallen to his death from his flat high above Leninsky Prospekt. Two

days earlier he had sent an urgent message to the British authorities indicating knowledge of 'a Soviet spy' in the British Embassy.

Naturally there was no evidence to support a verdict of 'unlawful death' but a coroner's jury in London brought exactly this verdict, differing sharply from the Soviet view that no crime had occurred. Naturally too, the Foreign Office took the position that the case had no implications for national security, and at the coroner's inquest in London a British diplomat mentioned Skinner's 'exaggerated' fears. A bit unnaturally, the Labour Party sided *against* the Soviet Union − more precisely, against the Conservative Party − in suggesting that HM Government knew more than it was saying about the whole thing. Undoubtedly so. For decades, both the American and British intelligence services (and others, no doubt) have arranged cover for their operatives as employees of the larger international banks.

According to Corson and Crowley in *The New KGB*, Skinner was 'murdered in circumstances resembling the classical "artistic suicide" so long favored by the organs.' Undoubtedly so. The incident marked a return to the tried-and-true technique of defenestration that had enjoyed some currency after WWII. The death of Jan Masaryk, Foreign Minister of Czechoslovakia, was the best known of these 'suicides', several of which were connected with the Alger Hiss case in the US.

The only real mystery about Skinner's death, to my mind, concerns what he knew that caused him to be thrown to his death by KGB thugs.

From the Bank of England, walk N into Princes Street to reach Moorgate. The Moor Gate was for centuries the northern entrance to the City; in the 17th century it was a main exit for Londoners escaping the Great Plague. On the L, past Great Swan Alley, a new office building at No. 51 has replaced

Site 92: **49 Moorgate.** A singular event took place here on the afternoon of 12 May, 1927. The All-Russian Co-operative Society (Arcos) − ostensibly a company to increase trade between Britain and the Soviet Union but virtually a command centre for Soviet subversion − was raided by the Special Branch of the Metropolitan Police. Fifty plainclothes detectives came by underground to join the uniformed policemen for the operation. As the raid began, some of the 'managing directors' of Arcos (who were mostly GRU officers) ran to the basement to seal an immense steel door; others were already burning documents throughout the building. Police breached the basement vault the next day and among other things found crates of rifles (Arcos called them manufacturers' samples). Two truckloads of material — 250,000 documents — went off to Scotland Yard. The British learnt much from the event. So did the Soviets.

Site 92: **49 Moorgate.**

First, some history. In 1921 the two powers signed the Anglo-Soviet Trade Agreement, despite Britain's knowledge (from decrypted cables) that subversion would be a big part of the Soviet 'trade' effort. The impoverished Soviets immediately invested over £300,000 'in one of the City of London's most expensive office buildings,' writes John Costello in *Mask of Treachery*, and made Moorgate their London base until permission was granted for an embassy.

Smaller and less sophisticated firms were eager to do business with the Soviets, as Corson and Crowley report in *The New KGB*. These firms sent product samples, drawings, even spare parts, to Moscow.

But genuine trade was rare. 'Once the goods were shipped, Arcos lost interest in the company,' Corson and Crowley write. The real game of the several hundred GRU and GPU officers attached to Arcos was espionage and subversion.

In 1927 the British saw their chance to end the game without revealing that they had been reading Moscow's codes for a decade. A Briton named George Monckland had been approached early in 1927 by a British communist, Wilfred Macartney, for information on arms shipments. Monckland produced some information for Macartney and then told the authorities. When Monckland was again asked for information, the government gave him an outdated RAF manual to hand over. MI5 understood from an informant inside Arcos that the manual was being copied at 49 Moorgate.

The Arcos raid netted a list of Comintern agents world-wide: proof that the Soviets were conducting espionage and subversion on a vast scale. MI5 now clearly saw what John Costello sums up as 'the interrelation between the GRU's foreign industrial espionage, the GPU's undercover operations and the Comintern-directed CPGB' — here was an 'interlocking network of Moscow-directed Communist cells' linked to Arcos, the primary cell. Writes Costello: 'Contrary to later official British assertions, MI5 had unravelled the "genetic code" of the Soviet virus by 1927' and fully understood by then the Soviet attack on Britain's 'political system, trade unions, armaments factories, and intellectual elite.'

The RAF manual was never found. Also, writes Richard Deacon in *The Greatest Treason*, 'what the British fatally failed to find was the names of the chief Soviet agents and recruiters in Britain, or, more importantly,...any evidence of the infiltration of the British Foreign Office and the Security Services.' Why? Because Arcos *expected* the raid. Ten years later, the defector Walter Krivitsky pointed to 'someone in Scotland Yard' as the source of the GRU's prior knowledge of the raid. Speculation runs high that this was Guy Liddell. In 1927 Liddell was with Scotland Yard supposedly fighting communist subversion; later he was MI5's second highest officer; today he is strongly suspected of having been a communist mole (*see Site 32*).

Immediately after the raid the Labour Party joined Moscow in protesting about it. And now the Prime Minister made a serious error. Unable to produce the RAF manual, Stanley Baldwin read to the House of Commons the verbatim text of seven secret Soviet messages! He thereby justified the government's raid but threw away the government's advantage (its ability to read the Soviet codes). Predictably, from then on, the Soviets would use unbreakable one-time pads. Predictably, too, they would place their espionage and subversion largely in the hands of 'illegals' who couldn't endanger diplomatic relations.

Within two weeks of the Arcos raid, the British had severed relations with the USSR. The top Soviets left London. The ordinary employees requested asylum and told the British everything they knew. And this led, also quite predictably, to tightened Soviet control of their people abroad; wives and children would henceforth be held hostage at home even after the most careful state scrutiny of individuals working abroad.

Perhaps the only surprising aftermath of the Arcos raid was the persistent effort by leftists to deny the truth revealed by the raid — that the anti-communists so hated by the leftists were absolutely correct in saying that the Soviet Union's dedication to subverting Western society made it a state like no other.

At the corner of Moorgate and London Wall, turn W into a surreal landscape of modern towers and elevated walkways. (Detour through Fore Street to see a section of the ancient Roman wall.) At the W end of London Wall, cross Aldersgate Street to the small alleyway called Little Britain. Turn R into the broader street called Little Britain. On your L is the oldest hospital in London; enter Bart's to see the Hogarth murals. On the R is the oldest parish church in London; enter St Bartholomew the Great to see the impressive Norman interior. You'll exit from Little Britain at the vast Smithfield Market. Just N of the market is St John Street, on which cattle were herded into 'smooth field' when this was a live market. On your R, the pretty little building with barred windows is

Site 93: **16 St John Street.** From 1980 until just after the dust-binning of Gorbachev *and* the CPSU *and* the entire Soviet Union in 1991, this was the home of the Communist Party of Great Britain (now disbanded). Membership was below 16,000 by 1983 and below 7,000

Site 93: **16 St John Street.**

by 1990, each of which was the lowest figure since WWII – and only half of *these* paid their dues.

The CPGB had turned reformist with the collapse of communism throughout Europe in the late 1980s. Hard-line Stalinists departed to form competing organizations. But little could be salvaged by any of them; the entire communist movement in Britain was seriously discredited and was in acute financial difficulty well before 1991. The CPGB, without fanfare, simply went out of existence. While it might have survived the evaporation of membership (it had done so in the past), it couldn't survive the evaporation of massive secret subsidies from the Soviet government.

Throughout the long history of the CPGB, now so surprisingly at an end, we regularly heard that the CPGB was just another political party. (No matter that it hadn't had an elected member of the House of Commons since 1950 – elected as a CP member, that is – and hadn't garnered more than a feeble total of 6,078 votes in the 1987 general election.) During the 1980s the CPGB was forced to be content with representation on the executive councils of only the most confrontational unions and with influence on only the most compliant Members of Parliament. Party members, to be sure, worked their way into positions of power in various umbrella organizations, where they advocated unilateral nuclear disarmament and opposed US nuclear submarines and strategic bombers on British territory. But espionage? We regularly heard, in the most righteous tones, that this was not the intention of the CPGB. In truth, MI5 long ago rendered the CPGB irrelevant as a recruiting pool for Soviet espionage efforts. But the odd bit of espionage, volunteered by the odd CPGB member? I wouldn't rule it out. (Arrested in 1992, in fact, was a former member of the Party who seems to have been supplying the USSR with Britain's most sensitive weapons secrets for years. What finally nailed him was the word of his one-time KGB case-officer who defected to the West in 1992.) I don't wish to quibble, however. The CPGB has denied, over the years, any connection with the intelligence efforts of any other country. Let me respond, with similar forthrightness, that I'm including this site in a book about intelligence and subversion because of the building's exemplary architecture.

If you have several hours and want to get in out of the rain, catch a trial at the Old Bailey. (There are still spy trials here; in 1993, Gordievsky became the first defector to testify in a British court about the KGB.) Or explore St Paul's Cathedral. Or walk N of Clerkenwell Road to No. 37A Clerkenwell Green, where Lenin printed his journal Iskra (The Spark) *for clandestine distribution in Tsarist Russia and where you can visit the Karl Marx Memorial Library. For the next walk instead, take the tube from Barbican to Temple (nine stops, no changes).*

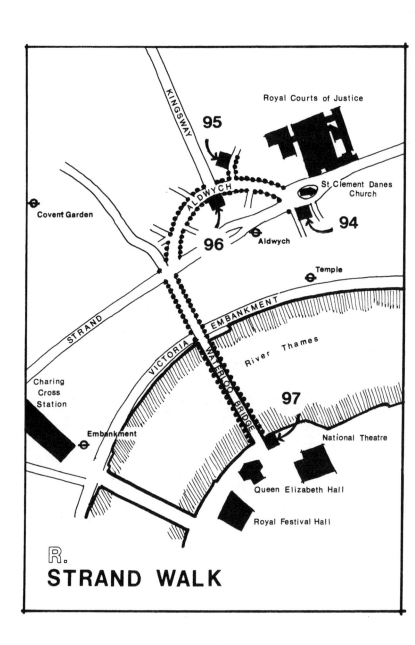

STRAND WALK

R. STRAND WALK

The Strand dates from pre-Roman times when it was literally on the strand (or shore) of the Thames. Starting point for this walk is either Temple station of the underground, by the river, or Aldwych station, a block inland. At the SE corner of Arundel Street and the Strand, opposite the forecourt of St Clement Danes, is a new building on the site of

Site 94: **190 Strand.** For a brief time in the mid-fifties, for £9 a week (Moscow Centre providing the money), 'Peter Kroger' rented a back room here over a tobacconist's shop to establish his cover as an antiquarian bookseller. He soon moved his business to the suburbs. It would be five busy years before he, his wife, two British accomplices, and a Soviet national would be caught sending

top-secret material to Moscow. To this day the 'naval secrets' (or Portland) case remains compelling not only for information it gave about how the Soviets operated their 'illegals', but also for questions it left unanswered about some of the best-known spies of that era.

Peter Kroger was an American, born Morris Cohen in 1911. A communist by his early twenties, Cohen went to Spain in 1937 to serve with the communist-led Lincoln Brigade; in 1938 he was sent to Barcelona to the first of the NKVD's secret spy schools outside Soviet territory. He returned to the US under another name (his original US passport probably re-cobbled for use by a Comintern agent), and worked for the Soviet pavilion at the New York World's Fair and for Amtorg, a *Cheka* front that was supposedly a Soviet-US 'trading company.' He was drafted into the US Army in 1942 and because his new wife Lona (also a communist) worked in a munitions factory, the two were fingerprinted; these prints would be significant 20 years later.

A schoolteacher in New York City after the war, Cohen disappeared overnight in 1950. He and his wife left a fully furnished flat, the rent for which was being paid (Arthur Tietjen tells us in *Soviet Spy Ring*) by atom spies Julius and Ethel Rosenberg. Upon the arrest of the Rosenbergs in 1950, the Cohens' furniture storage was paid by master spy Rudolf Abel until *his* arrest in 1957.

The Cohens probably spent the next four years in the USSR, being trained. In 1954 they surfaced in London on New Zealand passports as Peter and Helen Kroger, bookseller and housewife. Peter soon earned the respect of fellow antiquarians. He built up a good collection of Victoriana and 19th-century Americana (and he advertised further book specialities in handcuffs, leg-irons, fetters, and tortures). The book business was a superb cover for his spy work; overseas 'customers' received microdots in their books, and overseas 'booksellers' regularly visited the Krogers. Helen's 'hobby' as a photographer explained the blacked-out windows that made a darkroom of their bathroom.

The Krogers were typical of the 'illegals' used by Moscow Centre between the 1920s and 1950s. Capable, self-disciplined, intelligent, the Krogers could have made a success of any profession they might have chosen. Peter was the pleasant introvert, tending mainly to business and never talking politics. Helen was the busy extrovert:

'Auntie Helen' to neighbourhood children. They would probably never have been caught if not for the Polish defector Goleniewski, who pointed to another member of their ring and led MI5 to a surveillance that resulted in the arrest of the five in 1961. The Krogers put up a spirited resistance to being fingerprinted ('we're not criminals'), but lost. From their prints, the two were immediately identified as the Cohens, wanted by the FBI and Interpol for a decade.

In the Kroger bungalow in suburban Ruislip, the British found an enormous store of espionage gadgetry – the equipment to make microdots, a transmitter capable of reaching Moscow, a lot of signalling and coding materials (hidden in such common items as a Ronson table lighter and a tin of Three Flowers powder), the one-time pads for encyphering, and more. Also found was enough currency to suggest to John Frayn Turner, author of *The Good Spy Guide*, that here was 'the hub of a spy ring and...the bank of a spy ring as well'. (Subsequent owners of the house dug up another transmitter in the garden in 1980!) At the time of her arrest, Helen Kroger tried to dispose of several things, professing a wish to stoke the furnace before being carted off. In the ensuing struggle, police wrested her handbag from her and found it in a six-page letter in Russian, a page of cypher, and three microdots. She expressed no further interest in the furnace.

Throughout the trial of the five, the Krogers' innocence was loudly proclaimed by the Krogers themselves and by one of their co-defendants, the Russian national 'Gordon Lonsdale' (*see Site 88*). Lonsdale claimed to have been merely a friend who had brought in the spy equipment without their knowledge. He alone was guilty of spying, he said, and of abusing the friendship of these good and kind people. It was he, he said, who had obtained for the Krogers the pair of phoney passports found in their house; he did it because he knew that the Krogers would be in trouble if he were caught. The judge wondered how such passports would be useful to the Krogers if, as they claimed, they didn't know that the passports existed. Much of the testimony was similarly ludicrous, and the jury took less than two hours to find all five guilty – Lonsdale, the Krogers, and the two Britons (Harry Houghton and Ethel Gee) who had obtained these secrets on Britain's latest anti-submarine detection. Sentences were heavy: 25 years for Lonsdale, 20 each for the Krogers, 15 each for Houghton and Gee. By 1969 the Krogers were free, exchanged for a British college instructor who had been arrested within a year to serve as hostage. Gerald Brooke had been charged with distributing anti-Soviet leaflets in Red Square; thus, Moscow seemed to be saying, this amateur spy was being exchanged for the two Krogers who weren't spies at all. After the exchange, however, the relieved Brooke returned to Britain, while the 'innocent' Krogers went to live in Warsaw.

Without question, the Krogers were Soviet spies. Soviet newspapers admitted as much by 1991. But other questions persist. About Lonsdale, surely, and why he was virtually *given* to the British by the Soviets when he could easily have been moved out of harm's way. About Houghton, and why he was working at the Underwater Weapons Research Establishment at Portland after he had been declared a security risk and removed from his job at the Warsaw Embassy. Questions, too, about the Krogers and the extent of their activities in Britain. Houghton makes it clear in his memoirs that he and Gee were part of a much larger network serviced by the Krogers and run by Lonsdale. In fact, the Krogers and Lonsdale were in Britain for *three and a half years* before recruiting Houghton and Gee. What *additional* mischief did this larger ring do with the Krogers – and later without them? And who took over from the Krogers and Lonsdale?

The work of the Cohen-Krogers in America is another mystery. They vanished from New York City just before the Rosenbergs were arrested, and photos of the Cohens were found among Colonel Abel's things when *he* was arrested – along with false names to go with the images, and a cryptic phrase ('who are Joan's murderers?'), which was undoubtedly a *parol*, or password, for Abel's successor. Robert J. Lamphere writes in *The FBI-KGB War* that the Cohens were probably 'cut-outs' between the Rosenbergs and their Soviet control, who was probably Abel. Since the Rosenbergs and Abel wouldn't have had direct contact, the Rosenbergs couldn't burn Abel. Only the Cohens could. The Cohens therefore must be extricated (and they were) so that Abel could stay on safely. Alerted by their controller as soon as Fuchs was arrested, they were off to Moscow within hours via Mexico.

Morris had apparently been a masterspy, recruiting a still-unidentified 'Percy' to the Los Alamos spy ring, according to a Walberry Productions film seen on British television in 1991. If we are to believe all the revelations coming from former KGB officers these days, 'Percy' played a more important role than Fuchs himself in helping the Soviets to build their bomb so quickly. Furthermore, of the ten agents that the Soviets say they used in the Los Alamos operation (five sources and five couriers), only seven have been known to the Americans for all these years. One of the unknowns was apparently the courier Lona Cohen, who carried a doctor's statement saying she needed to be in the desert for her health. Is this *braggadocio*? Hard to tell. The Soviets typically had multiple, parallel, *apparati*, any number of which could have been unknown to the other networks and undetected by the target country.

But we had an indication of the importance of the Cohen-Krogers in 1967 when they were still imprisoned in Britain. Kim Philby, interviewed in Moscow for *The Sunday Times*, made the bizarre suggestion that he would forego publication of his book (and thereby spare the British great embarrassment) if the Krogers were released. They were innocent, Philby explained; this was the sole reason behind his offer. If anything, his offer suggests that the Cohen-Krogers were *not* innocent of anything the West knew about (and were probably guilty of things the West *didn't* know about), and that Moscow Centre feared they might crack in prison and tell all.

There is another postscript to the case of the Krogers. A recent play by Hugh Whitemore, *Pack of Lies*, tells of the surveillance on the Krogers from a neighbouring house. Whitemore takes the position that since *everyone* hides the truth, on *some* level with *some* people, then all dissembling is equal — the neighbour's daughter sneaking off on her boyfriend's motorbike, the neighbour's wife keeping silent about MI5's surveillance, the Krogers concealing major aspects of their lives. *Pack of Lies* is an affecting human drama but it begs the larger question of the overarching betrayal by the Krogers of everything and everyone around them.

Walk into the Aldwych. On the N side of the curve, in Houghton Street, is the main entrance to

Site 95: **The London School of Economics.** Tangentially connected to the LSE are two people whose stories I am eager to tell and for whom I can find no other sites in London. My apologies to all the decent people at the LSE (even the seriously deluded ones) who did *not* serve Soviet Intelligence.

Michael Whitney Straight, son of an American heiress, studied for a year here before he went up to Cambridge in 1934 and was recruited to the Soviet cause by Anthony Blunt. Almost three decades later, Straight would implicate Blunt: the first to do so. He was 'one of Blunt's recruiting failures,' writes Knightley – and a costly failure it was for Blunt, despite the immunity given him.

Straight suffered too, as he tells us in his book *After Long Silence* (1983). At first he pleaded with Blunt about the orders relayed to him by Blunt: to return to the US, work in Wall Street, and begin feeding information to the Comintern; Straight wanted to become a British subject and stand for Parliament. 'I even offered to turn over all the wealth that I had if I were released,' writes Straight. He was not released. He wouldn't have been, of course, but we have only his own word that he even made the request. In the US in 1938 and 1939, working in the State Department, then in the Interior Department, then as a speechwriter, he gave the Soviets various documents and reports, including some he had written. These were not very secret and probably not very useful. But his return to the State Department late in 1940 inspired renewed interest from his contact. This in turn inspired Straight to leave government altogether, as he tells it. In 1941 he joined *The New Republic*, a magazine founded by his parents. In 1942 he joined the US Army Air Force. He claims not to have seen his Soviet contact after 1942. In fact, the man disappeared: a victim of Stalin's paranoia.

Whether or not Straight gave the Soviets further information after the war, he dutifully rendered other services. Late in 1945, he was the organizer of a protest in Washington by pro-Soviet scientists; in 1948, he was an important backer of Henry Wallace's presidential bid; in the 1950s, as editor of *The New Republic*, he was a leader of the media pack in full cry against Senator Joseph McCarthy and his 'ism.' One can reasonably say many bad things about the late Senator: he was irresponsible, a bully, arguably a psychopath. But the main theme of the anti-McCarthyites was that he was lying about communist infiltration of the US government. When Michael Straight published all those words ridiculing McCarthy's crusade against 'reds under the bed', implying that there *were* none, it was Straight who was lying. He knew better. He had *been* one.

But it's not so much what he did as what he failed to do. He didn't tell about Blunt, and then Burgess, even after telling them that he was no longer with them. Nor did he tell about Burgess, even after Burgess escaped to Moscow. Straight claims that he threatened Burgess with exposure earlier in 1951 when they met by chance in Washington. But once Burgess had gone, and for another 12 years, Straight kept silent − about Blunt, Burgess, and others.

Finally, in 1963, when Straight was asked to chair the new National Endowment for the Arts, he decided to rid himself of his 'burden' before the required FBI check might discover it. He hoped that by telling the story himself he could still become chairman. (He later served as *deputy chairman* appointed by − of all people − Nixon.) I have seen Straight's gesture called 'an act of personal honesty' but I cannot forget that he acted only when there was something in it for *him*. He didn't care about the damage that Blunt and the others had done to the West; he cared only about the damage that his own connection with them might do to *him*.

Was Straight the vacillating and troubled soul, the moral weakling, that his book would have us believe? Hard to know. He tells us that he didn't deliver anything of real value to the Soviets. But he also didn't deliver his Soviet case-officer to the FBI. Straight comes across as a clear-headed pragmatist, co-operating knowingly with a Soviet intelligence officer and maintaining security like the most tough-minded agent.

A writer of fiction in addition to his book *After Long Silence* (and possibly *including* that book), Straight tells us that when he saw Blunt for the first time after Straight's confession, the response
from Blunt was − *relief!* Although Straight's book should cure me of reading spy memoirs, it probably won't. At least I didn't pay good money for this one. I found it at my library's annual rummage sale, where it had been donated by someone else who has had enough of Michael Straight.

Sonya's Report, the memoir of long-term Soviet agent Ruth Kuczynski, is also outrageous: for her fantastic rationalizations of Stalin's crimes and her grotesque defence of herself. (Was she 'anti-fascist' before Hitler even came to power? during the Pact? after the war when she worked against Labour-governed Britain?). Even in a book written as an *apologia pro sua vita*, she comes across as the quintessential Leninist − cold-blooded, ruthless, willing to sacrifice anything and anyone to her work.

Unlike Michael Straight, 'Sonya' was enormously helpful to her chosen side, she was well trained, she probably had the protection of a person or persons inside MI5, and she had no regrets whatsoever (even Straight allowed himself some arguments as to the nature of Soviet power). Unlike Straight, she never attended the LSE. Her father, a Soviet sympathizer, taught here as a pioneer in the field of demography; her brother, a Soviet agent, did graduate studies here in economics. Both Robert and Jürgen Kuczynski knew that Ursula Ruth Kuczynski Hamburger Beurton was a GRU agent.

Ruth Kuczynski came early to her service to the Soviets. Born in Germany in 1907, she was an agitprop leader for the KPD by the age of 19. She met her first husband on a trip to the US; when they went to live in China in 1930 she worked for Soviet Intelligence as protégée and lover of the legendary Richard Sorge.

Next came a six-month stay in the USSR learning tradecraft. Then Manchuria (during the Japanese occupation), Poland, Switzerland, and (in 1941) England.

Now she had two children and a second husband, Len Beurton, a British veteran of the Spanish Civil War. (In Switzerland she had been ordered by Moscow Centre to marry someone British in order to gain entry to the UK, and she was rejected by the only other possibility, Allan Foote.) In England she went immediately to Oxford to live, journeying twice a month to London to gather information from her father and brother. In Oxford itself she made other contacts and served as Klaus Fuchs's case-officer (her brother had sent Fuchs to her in 1942). That's according to her own story. According to others she ran 'a bevy' of Soviet agents, including Roger Hollis (*see Sites 52 and 54*) who worked at nearby Blenheim Palace with the rest of MI5 and was acting head of the section in MI5 responsible for overseeing Soviet and pro-Soviet activities in the UK.

The 'probability' that her target in Oxford was someone important in MI5 'seems overwhelming', writes Chapman Pincher in *Too Secret Too Long*. Certainly she was not sent there to assist Fuchs, who required servicing only *after* her arrival. And her residence a mile from Hollis's home is 'rather difficult to accept as sheer coincidence,' continues Pincher. Hollis denied their having met – in China, Switzerland, or Oxford. Her book doesn't even include Hollis in the index, although a one-sentence mention of him denies that she 'ever had anything to do' with him.

MI5's approach to Ruth Kuczynski was 'criminally soft', writes Pincher in *Their Trade Is Treachery*. The fact that she was never under surveillance, either during or after the war (even after Fuchs named her as his controller), the fact that her transmissions from Oxford continued until at least 1947, the fact that she was allowed simply to leave Britain for East Germany in 1950, all suggest to Pincher (among others) 'the existence of a powerful protective hand inside MI5.' It is certainly curious that the government became interested in her only after Foote's defection in 1947 (*see Site 58*). According to Foote, she had ceased spying when she left Switzerland. Did Foote really believe this, Pincher wonders, or did MI5 'exaggerate' it when ghost-writing his memoirs, to excuse their own negligence?

Interviewed too cordially on American television a few years ago, the grandmotherly 'Sonya' remains a clever manipulator. She is still a communist, hoping only that a better communism will take over the world, and she is still unrepentant about the excesses of Leninism and Stalinism. Even Rosa Luxemburg, greatly admired by her, stood up to Lenin. Ruth Kuczynski never protested; the wish to maintain her privileges in East Germany kept her silent.

Ruth's older brother Jürgen − like her, an émigré from Germany − was equally ruthless. He was head of the underground section of the German Communist Party in Britain and was an active GRU agent throughout WWII; he left for East Germany within months of the war's end. He never seems to have been questioned about his own activities or his sister's, writes Chapman Pincher; indeed, after a three-month internment in 1940, he 'never seems to have been subject to any interference by MI5.'

Jürgen had joined the US Army Air Force in Britain, and one of his wartime jobs was to help produce a fortnightly report on damage to the German economy from Allied bombing; this top-secret report, distributed only to about 15 people (reports Knightley), went secretly to the Soviets too. Certainly Jürgen made sure that all OSS agents dropped into Germany near the end of the war were inclined towards the Soviet Union (he was in charge of selecting these agents from German refugees in Britain). And it is more than likely that he betrayed to the Soviets the OSS project to photograph all of Central and Western Europe from the air in early 1945; the Soviets responded by shooting down several of the British and American planes.

At Kingsway, you have a direct view of the grand edifice containing the external services of the British Broadcasting Corporation. Named for an American businessman, Irving T. Bush, and featuring heroic 1930s statuary dedicated to 'the Friendship of the English-Speaking Peoples', this building is known as

Site 96: **Bush House.** On the eighth floor of the north-west wing of this large office block, C. E. M. Dansey's small and secret Z Organization had its small and secret headquarters. Rented under the name of C. E. Moore, these rooms had a hidden back entrance through the office of a barrister friend who worked, on the side, for Dansey. The Z office was ostensibly the export department of a diamond company, courtesy of another friend in the building.

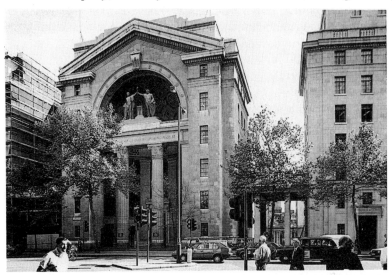

Site 96: **Bush House.**

If there are various ways of looking at Claude Edward Marjoribanks Dansey (*see Sites 46 and 117*), there are various ways of looking at the origins of his Z Organization. In 1936, writes Nigel West in *MI6*, Dansey 'pointed out the dangers of relying on the overt, fixed Station system and offered to build a more flexible parallel ring which would operate under commercial cover.' Admiral Sinclair, then chief of MI6, 'grasped at the idea,' writes West. That's one scenario. But Anthony Cave Brown writes in *'C'* that Sinclair, 'believing that SIS might have been penetrated by the Germans', established Z and recalled Dansey from Rome to be in charge of it. And here's a third scenario, from Read and Fisher, authors of the Dansey biography *Colonel Z*: Dansey's apparent banishment from SIS in 1936 (for some financial impropriety, it was rumoured) was 'part of a startling proposal he put to Sinclair' − that his dismissal be used as a cover for his creating an alternative intelligence service in Europe, this service to replace the SIS completely if either Britain or SIS were incapacitated. Sinclair was 'joint author of the scheme with Dansey,' write Read and Fisher. And then we have various combinations and permutations of these explanations. Phillip Knightley in *The Second Oldest Profession* can barely disguise his dislike of Dansey. Believing Dansey to have earned his banishment from SIS, Knightley writes that 'Sinclair, unable to stand Dansey in the office, got rid of him by allowing him to create his "Z" network of amateur spies, mostly businessmen and journalists'. Still another theory, advanced by a senior SIS man and passed along by Read and Fisher in *Operation Lucy*, has it that after Dansey was banished by Sinclair he established 'his own private network of agents with SIS funds but without official approval, sensing the opportunity of building himself a personal power base for the future'.

Whatever its origins, the Z Organization was well developed by 1938, with agents active throughout Europe, even in Germany. Many agents pretended to be representatives of Alexander Korda's rapidly expanding London Film Productions. No one was attached in any way to SIS — indeed, no mention of the Z Organization was permitted in SIS files — and agents did not use British embassies or consulates in any way. Communication was by mail or courier, never by diplomatic pouch or radio.

Despite these precautions, the Z Organization suffered a major disaster early in the war. Menzies had instructed Z's chief agent in Holland, Sigismund Payne Best, to make contact with several men who seemed to represent a group inside Germany seeking Hitler's overthrow. Together with a Major Stevens from SIS in The Hague, Best was soon negotiating with these men, carrying messages to and from Neville Chamberlain. The men were actually agents of the *Sicherheitsdienst*; in November, 1939, they kidnapped Best and Stevens at the German border near Venlo and proceeded to roll up the Z and SIS networks in Holland with information extracted from the two captives (*see Site 116*).

Read and Fisher write that 'Dansey's intervention almost certainly prevented a greater disaster' — the kidnapping of additional, more senior members of the intelligence services. 'Thanks also to Dansey,' continue Read and Fisher, 'Menzies survived to fight another day, with his reputation more or less intact.' Dansey alone (not counting Stevens and Best who were in a German concentration camp) knew the errors committed by Menzies, and Dansey became assistant chief of SIS (at the request of Menzies) ostensibly to help Menzies, now chief, make better decisions. Credible? Yes. But opinions differ on this question too. Anthony Cave Brown, the biographer of Menzies, minimizes both the errors of Menzies and the rescue efforts of Dansey.

After the Venlo Incident, the Z Organization as a separate entity was 'impossible to sustain' Read and Fisher write; Dansey incorporated the main body of Z 'into the official service as its Swiss section, absorbing the existing office in Geneva, answerable only to himself'. Some of Z's agents would remain 'known to no one else in the SIS'.

I understand that a liaison between British and Soviet Intelligence was also headquartered here in Bush House during WWII. This 'liaison' was primarily a one-way affair. The Soviets' man in Tokyo, for instance, advised Stalin in late 1941 that the Japanese planned to move south and east against the British and American presence in the Pacific, rather than north and west against the USSR. With this information, Stalin was able to withdraw substantial forces from his eastern provinces and throw them against the German onslaught on his western front. Significantly, he did *not* share the information with London or Washington. He *wanted* the Japanese to engage the British and Americans – not only to reinforce the new Anglo-American commitment as his co-belligerents but also to guarantee a continuation of his amicable arrangement with the Japanese.

A far more productive organization operating out of Bush House – and out of Woburn Abbey outside London – was the Political Warfare Executive, originally part of SOE (*see Site 69*). The PWE ran all of Britain's propaganda during WWII. Its 'black propaganda' was so damaging to German morale, civilian and military, as to earn explicit praise from Hitler's propaganda minister Goebbels. Its effectiveness was further acknowledged implicitly when the Nazis imposed Draconian penalties on anyone caught listening to British broadcasts.

Continuing round to the Strand again, take Lancaster Place on to Waterloo Bridge. Ahead of you on the far shore you'll see the Royal

Festival Hall and National Theatre; on your L, just where the bridge comes down over the South Bank, is

Site 97: **the bus stop, Waterloo Bridge.** On the evening of 7 September, 1978, Georgi Markov, a Bulgarian intellectual who had taken refuge in the West in 1969, was waiting for a bus here when a stranger jabbed him in the right thigh with an ordinary-looking umbrella and disappeared into a passing taxi. At 2 am Markov's body temperature was 104°F and his wife called an ambulance.

Four days later Markov was dead. But he had told his wife about the incident at the bus stop. A close examination of Markov's thigh yielded a tiny metal ball, 1.7 mm in diameter, of a platinum-iridium alloy that would not cause rejection in the victim's body. The ball had two microscopic holes filled with the exotic poison ricin. More deadly than cobra venom, ricin has no known antidote.

Who was responsible for the murder of Georgi Markov? Substances like ricin had been the subject of extensive research in the 1970s by Soviet bloc scientists; some of this research, surprisingly, was published. But the fingerprints are even clearer. Two weeks earlier in Paris another exiled Bulgarian intellectual, Vladimir Kostov, had been hit in the lower back with an identical pellet, probably fired from an air pistol. This attempt was less successful; the pellet did not disintegrate and Kostov survived.

Both Markov and Kostov had been writing for Bulgarian dissident journals and attracting the attention of the *Durzhavna Sigurnost*, Bulgaria's KGB-controlled secret police. Markov had also been broadcasting in his native language over BBC, Radio Free Europe and *Deutsche Welle*, telling his countrymen the truth about the Bulgarian communist dictatorship; he had been reading chapters of his memoirs, not so much attacking the dictator Todor Zhivkov as ridiculing him. Kostov reports in his book *The Bulgarian Umbrella* that Markov had been warned to stop his broadcasts or he would be killed. Kostov believes that the chief of DS, General Dimitar Stoyanov, decided to synchronize the killing of both troublesome defectors with Zhivkov's birthday.

By early 1991 Zhivkov was on trial in his own country — merely for fraud and embezzlement, but it was a start (and he was, in time, convicted) — and the new President was promising trials connected with Markov's murder. By the end of 1991 the Bulgarian government was admitting the involvement of its own secret police in Markov's murder. Andrew and Gordievsky had already revealed in 1990 in *KGB: The Inside Story* that the pellet came from a KGB laboratory and that the KGB created the weapon from an American-bought umbrella. By early 1993 a former KGB general had revealed that the KGB did indeed supply the poison, at Stoyanov's request; later in 1993 this general, Oleg Kalugin, was arrested at Heathrow Airport, questioned briefly, and released. The Russians still officially deny any responsibility and Bulgarian files have (of course) been destroyed, but I suspect that it isn't a matter of doubt in anyone's mind at this point — as it wasn't, in fact, to many people when it happened.

Back in the thirties and forties the Soviets murdered enemies like Leon Trotsky, Ignace Reiss and Jan Masaryk in rather an unsubtle manner. But by the fifties they were beginning to bring to their *mokrie dyela* (wet or messy doings) the subtlety that characterized their other covert ops. This new sophistication can be seen in their false-flag recruitment of assassins like Mehmet Ali Agca and Lee Harvey Oswald and in their use of hard-to-detect poisons like ricin. One of their hit-men, Nikolai Chochlov, defected in 1954 rather than carry out his assignment to murder the leader of an anti-Soviet émigré group in West Germany. He not only confessed to West Germany's BND but also turned over the murder weapon – a 'cigarette case' firing bullets coated with potassium cyanide. Chochlov did a lot of talking about *mokrie dyela* and related matters, especially to the media. He then suffered strange and irremediable symptoms: hideous blotches, black-and-blue swellings, bleeding skin, hair loss, internal cramps. His bones decayed and his blood turned to plasma. When the West German doctors gave up on him, US military doctors stepped in, persuaded to do so by the émigré leader whose life Chochlov had spared. Miraculously, Chochlov survived. He had been poisoned with the toxic metal thallium, which had been exposed to intense nuclear radiation to destroy his white cells.

A similar attempt on Aleksandr Solzhenitsyn's life took place in 1971 at a delicatessen counter in Novocherkassk. He developed dreadful blisters over much of his body from the same poison later used on Markov and Kostov; the unexplained 'allergy' didn't leave him for several months. The story only came to light in 1992 with the eyewitness account of a retired KGB colonel (the details were then supported by the suddenly enlightened Solzhenitsyn). The KGB's successors denied it. Here is their poker-faced explanation for why the story is 'absurd': 'If Yuri Andropov, then KGB chief, had ever dared to undertake such an action it would have inevitably caused a thunderstorm of public indignation all over the world.' The Russian journalist who broke the story in a Moscow newspaper says that he has a document from 1990 ordering the burning of 105 volumes of papers on Solzhenitsyn. Undoubtedly the order was carried out. The KGB wouldn't have considered such an action 'absurd'.

The mysterious death of Hugh Gaitskell, leader of the British Labour Party, may have been another *mokrie dyela* op. Gaitskell had led the fight to prevent extreme leftists from taking over the Labour Party. He died in 1963 of heart and kidney failure apparently caused by a form of lupus rarely seen in men over 40; he was 56. With Gaitskell gone, the Marxists were able to swing the Labour Party far to the left. MI5 became suspicious about Gaitskell's death when Soviet defector Anatoli Golitsyn told Western Intelligence of plans to kill an opposition party leader in Europe. In the ensuing investigation, MI5 learnt that shortly before Gaitskell died he had taken coffee and biscuits at the Soviet consulate. And from Angleton of CIA, MI5 learnt that the Soviets had published medical papers on successful experiments with a drug able to induce heart and kidney failure.

Was Gaitskell another victim of *mokrie dyela*? It was a GRU officer who said, 'Anyone can commit a murder, but it takes a real artist to commit a good natural death.'

Retrace your steps on Waterloo Bridge, enjoying a postcard view of London: the Houses of Parliament on your L, the dome of St Paul's Cathedral on your R. Several underground lines are nearby − at Embankment, Aldwych, and Temple stations. To start the next walk instead, descend the easy stone stairway from Waterloo Bridge to Victoria Embankment.

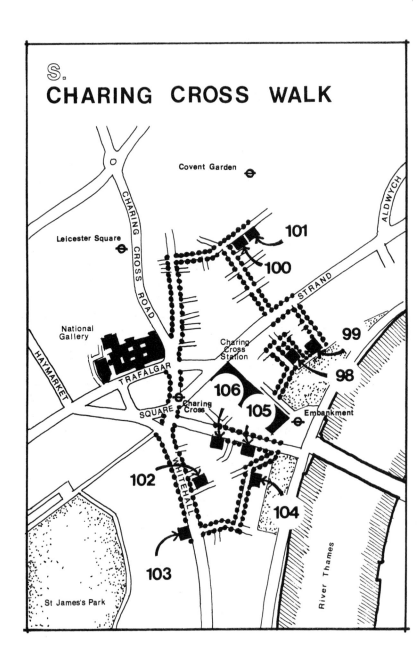

S. CHARING CROSS WALK

Covent Garden

Leicester Square

CHARING CROSS ROAD

ALDWYCH

101

100

STRAND

National Gallery

HAYMARKET

TRAFALGAR

Charing Cross Station

99

98

SQUARE

Charing Cross

106

105

Embankment

102

WHITEHALL

104

103

St James's Park

River Thames

S. CHARING CROSS WALK

Choose Embankment or Charing Cross tube station to start this walk. Villiers Street, accessible from either, leads to Watergate Walk at the rear of Victoria Embankment Gardens. The bank of the Thames was here, before the development of a modern sewage system. At the end of Watergate Walk is York Buildings. Cross this street for

Site 98: **Watergate House, 13-15 York Buildings.** Captain Mansfield Smith-Cumming (in Knightley's words, 'a genuine eccentric, even by the standards of the Royal Navy') worked in these comparatively staid premises when he was first chief of MI6. He also worked in Whitehall Court (*see Site 104*), in quarters fully as eccentric as the man himself. I have been told that SIS was near the Strand, then the centre of London's theatres and music halls, because of Smith-Cumming's interest in − some would say his obsession with − disguises, costumes, and the other deceptions of theatre. The very essence of the man was misdirection, and he enjoyed moving among professionals who did for a living something similar to what the professionals of his own calling did. Incredibly, as I write, one of the security secrets still withheld from the public is the name of the theatrical costumier to whom Smith-Cumming went for his disguises.

Also located here (briefly), after its founding in 1919, was the Government Code and Cypher School. The GC&CS was a 'section' not a school, despite its academic aura and its later recruitment largely from the universities. Before the heavy use of wireless transmission, this outfit was greatly aided by its access to all diplomatic and commercial messages between Europe and North America. Cable companies operating in the UK were required to make this traffic available to the GC&CS − the Official Secrets Act of 1920 permitted the government to read it − and the stuff arrived here in sackloads.

Site 98: **Watergate House, 13-15 York Buildings.**

The British make a distinction between codes and cyphers, a code being based on word substitution and a cypher being based on letter substitution. When Malcolm Muggeridge was chief of station in Portuguese East Africa during WWII, he was astonished to discover a word for 'eunuch' in his SIS code book. He couldn't imagine the circumstances under which an SIS officer would need to discuss such matters in an official communication. The resourceful Muggeridge found and seized his opportunity when SIS Alexandria invited him to a Christmas festivity. Muggeridge sent his regrets – in code of course (this was, after all, wartime) – explaining that 'like the eunuch, I cannot come.'

Walk N on York Buildings, turn E into John Adam Street and S into Robert Street. Here, facing the river, the Adam brothers built the Adelphi, an elaborate embankment arcade supporting a terrace of 11 houses. Popular with literary notables throughout the 19th century, the Adelphi was mostly demolished (for 'improvements') in the 1930s. Imagine, here,

Site 99: **9 Adelphi Terrace.** While Britain's intelligence organizations can be said to date from the time of William the Conqueror, the first

permanent overseas spy network dates only from the reign of Elizabeth I (when intelligence efforts led to the discovery and defeat of the Spanish Armada). The secret services have had their ups and downs since then, with the 19th century clearly a low point. The Depot of Military Knowledge, so bravely launched in 1803, fell into disrepute when its patron, the Duke of York, suffered a personal scandal. By mid-century, the government considered spying utterly distasteful. Let those on the Continent indulge in the indecent pursuit. Britain would not – except, of course, to keep tabs on the Irish.

And then came the Crimean War. 'Most of the catastrophes of that campaign were due to an almost total lack of information about the enemy,' writes Richard Deacon in *A History of the British Secret Service*. Warnings had been sounded for a decade by Major Thomas Best Jervis, a cartographer for 30 years with the Bombay Engineer Corps. 'Great Britain,' he argued, 'is the only country of note which has no *geographer* attached to the government and no national depot of geographical maps and plans.' He pleaded in vain for a topographical department in the Foreign Office. In 1854, at the start of the Crimean War, when he obtained two rare military maps while on holiday on the Continent and these proved of immediate value, the War Office set up a Topographical and Statistical Department under him in 1855. He had facilities here in a converted stables and coach house, according to Thomas G. Fergusson's *British Military Intelligence, 1870-1914*. Larger quarters were needed within a year.

The emphasis at the T&S Department was on making maps more than on gathering or analysing statistics; 26 of the 28 men under Jervis were civilian lithographers. But the Department fell on hard times in 1857 when Jervis died, and by the mid-1860s even the once-strong topographical mission was reduced. By 1869 the Department had only two officers, one of them its head, and in 1873 it was absorbed into the new Intelligence Branch.

'Much has been made of the creation of the T&S Department,' writes Fergusson. He is more cautious, pointing out that the T&S Department didn't accomplish much outside of cartography, had no real ability to process its meagre statistics, and had little or no access to the Secretary of State for War. Undoubtedly the former coach house and stables here saw the beginning of a modern intelligence capacity but, as Deacon observes, it was 'a very modest beginning.'

Leave this terrace via Adam Street (look for No. 7 with its original Adam decoration) and walk N to the Strand. Turn L. Turn R at Bedford Street. At the near corner of Bedford and King Streets is

Site 100: **16 King Street.** Until 1980 this building was the headquarters of the Communist Party of Great Britain. Peter Wright, MI5's resident gadgeteer before he was a molehunter, tells an amusing story about the place. Hoping for a foolproof technical surveillance here in the late 1950s, Wright devised a false door (with microphone attached) to fit over the real door of the coal chute. But how to affix it within full view of the building's occupants? Hugh Winterborn of MI5 devised the plan. Two groups of MI5 officers and their wives, 'pretending to be much the worse for drink,' Wright recalls,

converged here late one Saturday when the street was full of theatregoers. Winterborn dropped to his knees behind the group and with 'nerves of steel' he drilled the necessary holes in the chute (catching the brick dust in his handkerchief), then 'slipped the false door out from under his coat and clipped it into place.' (Presumably, then, the MI5 crew went off to have a real drink.) The device performed satisfactorily 'for some months', says Wright, until someone inside tuned to the same frequency and learnt of the bug. When Winterborn heard the top-to-bottom search of the building he went round immediately, 'unclipped the false door, and brought it back to the office like a trophy of war.'

For this *was* a war. The CPGB had been subsidized by 'Moscow gold' from the outset, although Moscow wouldn't admit it until the Gorbachev years, and members of the defunct CPGB claimed to be 'shocked' (shocked!) in 1991 when ledgers of the defunct CPSU revealed some of the details. The total given to the CPGB in 1920-1 alone, reports *The Observer*, was £55,000 — which approaches, so the newspaper said, in today's currency, a truly shocking £100 million.

The CPGB was firmly under Soviet direction from almost the outset. The road was never smooth, I'm happy to say. The 'Zinoviev letter', which the British released to the press in 1924, caused a furore. The letter purported to be a Soviet plan for CPGB infiltration of British trade unions and armed forces. It may well have been a forgery, as Moscow and others claimed, but Gordievsky reminds us that the Comintern soon frantically sanitized its archives before the arrival of a British Trades Union Council delegation whose members had portentously and naively journeyed to Moscow in search of The Truth.

Nor were things any better for the CPGB throughout the 1920s. A raid on this building in 1925 led to prison sentences for a dozen (mostly high-ranking) Party members on charges of seditious conspiracy and incitement to mutiny. Two years later the Arcos raid showed the firm connection between Moscow and the CPGB and caused an immediate rupture in diplomatic relations (*see Site 92*).

'Soviet "illegal" activity in Britain began in earnest after the diplomatic break of 1927' and only continued after relations resumed in 1929, writes Peter Shipley in *Hostile Action: The KGB and Secret Soviet Operations in Britain*. The 'illegals' didn't recruit from the

CPGB, which was already watched. But Party members were increasingly going underground in any case. The game was getting more complicated.

Percy Glading, one of the Party's leaders, was convicted in 1938 of violating the Official Secrets Act; Douglas Springhall, another key figure, was similarly convicted in 1943 (*see Sites 51 and 101*). These two were part of a substantial espionage effort by the CPGB in the years during and surrounding WWII. Average Party members did much of the work, at great risk and for no payment, according to Douglas Hyde, former editor of *The Daily Worker*. Moscow had been wary of recruiting CPGB members for espionage, for fear of destroying the Party's patriotic image, but that didn't stop CPs throughout the world from using their members for 'odd jobs.' These willing workers have included teachers, businessmen, clerks and otherwise ordinary people who might pick up or deliver an envelope or package, obtain a birth certificate or passport, or do a bit of uncomplicated research. People like Maclean and Fuchs have not been Moscow's only assets in the West.

By the mid-fifties the CPGB had been 'thoroughly penetrated at almost every level by technical surveillance or informants,' observes Peter Wright in *Spycatcher*. And because of a dazzling coup in 1955, 'the CPGB was never again in a position to seriously threaten the safety of the realm'; MI5 had obtained the Party's complete membership files, both overt and covert, and could henceforth bar these people from access to classified material. The files had been stored in the Mayfair flat of a wealthy member. When the occupants were away one weekend, MI5 removed 55,000 files to nearby Leconfield House, microfilmed them and returned them to the flat's locked filing cabinets. On the covert membership list, incidentally, were no fewer than 31 MPs.

Thus, although the CPGB started out in 1920 expecting to be the vanguard of a quick revolution, it settled into an increasingly minor role in British life and politics (*see Site 93*). I never believed in outlawing CPs, but I think it was crucial for democratic societies to have kept an eye and ear on these hostile organizations. Plainly this vigilance reduced the power of the CPGB to do real damage.

I admit, however, to having nothing but contempt for loyal CPGB members: for their willingness, even their eagerness, to betray their own country in order to further the aims of another, and for their slavish adherence to every change in Soviet foreign policy. Consider this example. The CPGB was fiercely opposed to fascism from at least 1935. Everything changed overnight when the Soviet Union and Nazi Germany signed their Non-Aggression Pact in August, 1939. CPGB members were universally stunned by the Pact, although the more sure-footed quickly came to terms with it. After all, the war was just an imperialist distraction; the real enemy of the communists was capitalism. Everything changed *again* overnight when Hitler invaded the Soviet Union in June, 1941. The CPGB now proclaimed itself fully behind Britain's war effort. But Party loyalty remained fully behind the USSR; only an accident of fate had made the USSR a temporary (and involuntary) co-belligerent of Britain.

Loyalty is undoubtedly a virtue, but loyalty to tyranny turns all morality on its head. Did loyal CPGB members not understand the full measure of Soviet tyranny? Did they really believe they were working strictly 'against fascism' and (after the war) 'for peace'? I must reject their claims of ignorance about the Soviet terror, the gulag, the state-induced famine, the brutal totalitarianism. Anyone who didn't know about those things didn't *want* to know.

A few doors to the E is

Site 101: **11 King Street.** Here was no dissembler, hiding behind a pretended patriotism. In this house, owned by the CPGB and within spitting distance of CPGB headquarters, lived the Party's national organizer, Douglas Frank Springhall.

Known as 'something of an extremist', Springhall went to prison for agitation during the General Strike of 1926. He was expelled by the Royal Navy for similar activities. But he was more than an agitator. A member of the CPGB's Central Committee since 1932, he was apparently used regularly, writes Andrew Boyle in *The Fourth Man*, as an intermediary between the talent-spotters at Cambridge and the resident director of Soviet Intelligence in London; Donald Maclean first met the Soviet *rezident* through Springhall, says Boyle. All the university communists knew of Springhall. At one large meeting during the 1932 Easter holiday at the home of James Klugmann's parents (*see Site 69*), Springhall's rhetoric inspired students from Cambridge, Oxford, the London School of Economics, and University College London.

Springhall went off to the first of the Comintern's wars in 1936, serving in Spain as political commissar of the British component of the International Brigades. There he met Allan Foote (*see Site 58*), whom he later recruited to the GRU. Foote regarded him, probably correctly, as 'the contact man for the Red Army in the British Communist Party.'

Site 101: **11 King Street.**

MI5 was obviously interested in this obviously disaffected Briton. Surveillance of him led in 1942 to an Air Ministry clerk, Mrs Olive Sheehan, who had given Springhall crucial reports on jet engine research. In exchange for a minimal jail term she promised to testify against him if he ever came to trial. In 1943 he did come to trial, charged with obtaining 'highly secret' information about British policy in Eastern Europe from a very young British Army officer in SOE, Captain Ormond Uren (*see Site 69*). The CPGB expelled Springhall immediately after his conviction — 'not because the Party disapproved of his activities as such,' the former editor of *The Daily*

Worker would later reveal, but 'because we had no desire, least of all at that moment of growing popularity, to get the public reputation for condoning spying by our members.'

It is no surprise that the CPGB piously denied any knowledge of Springhall's espionage activities. Overseas communist parties often danced the obligatory gavotte and denied any connection to Soviet intelligence work. Andrew Boyle writes that 'Springhall's disgrace had no deterrent effect whatever on the Party faithful' who, if anything, intensified their spying. The real surprise is that so very few of them were ever caught.

Retrace your steps to Bedford Street and continue across it to New Row. Turn L at St Martin's Lane; this will take you to Trafalgar Square. The National Gallery, especially with its splendid new addition, is worth a visit, as is the National Portrait Gallery where you can see Stephen Ward's portrait of Christine Keeler. Or you can rest inside St Martin-in-the-Fields, perhaps at a midday concert. On to Whitehall, with its long line of government buildings. To your L is

Site 102: **7 Whitehall Place.** This is where Scotland Yard, headquarters of the Metropolitan Police, was first located, we learn from a Blue Plaque on the building. Unannounced to the passing public, however, is that this is also where Colin Gubbins (*see Site 71*) began the Auxiliary Units of WWII. These civilian units were trained for intelligence and subversion work in Britain should Germany invade and conquer. Ultimately the units comprised 5,000 men – miners, gamekeepers, poachers, stalkers, farmers, parsons, innkeepers, blacksmiths – 'who had the ability to blend when necessary into the countryside around them, to keep a secret, to live rough and, if necessary, to go on fighting as they would be taught to fight until they triumphed or were killed,' as David Lampe writes in *The Last Ditch*.

Each unit of this underground army built its own hideout, *literally* underground: a thousand of them in the woods and fields and cliffs of Britain. With a Home Guard designation as cover, the men received the best training and the newest weapons and explosives. It is a measure of the patriotism of these men that Lampe's revealing

Site 102: **7 Whitehall Place.**

book, published in 1968, could refer to this resistance force as one of the best-kept secrets of WWII; one forgotten cache of weapons was turned in as late as 1964 by a recruit who had tended his munitions faithfully for 20 years after the Auxiliary Units were dissolved. Like the best of the SOE agents who followed them, the Auxiliary Units were prepared to die resisting the Germans − and were prepared to take the secrets of their organization with them.

Across Whitehall is

Site 103: **Horseguards.** From 1805 to 1815 the British Army's Depot of Military Knowledge occupied a room here, or perhaps only a portion of a room: not until well into the 20th century did the British begin seriously to acquire, assemble and analyse the information that could be considered 'military intelligence.' Until then, in the US Army and probably also in the British Army, intelligence postings

Site 103: **Horseguards.**

were traditionally reserved for the dimmer graduates of the military academies — for officers not bright enough to master the mathematics necessary for an artillery posting.

Cross the street into Horseguards Avenue and follow the Old War Office, on your L, into Whitehall Court. On your R is

Site 104: **2 Whitehall Court.** In 1909, rather late by European standards, Britain tackled the task of reorganizing its intelligence functions. Those charged with the job were appalled to discover not a single British agent in all of mainland Europe! By WWI two sections had been established: one for domestic intelligence (the forebear of MI5), the other for overseas intelligence (the forebear of MI6). This second section, along with a London flat for the man who founded it, was located in a confusion of passages and strangely-shaped rooms on the roof and uppermost floors here. On one side of the building was the National Liberal Club and on the other was the British & Foreign Bible Society, each of which (it is sobering to reflect) was then a fairly prominent institution on the national scene. In the building itself lived George Bernard Shaw, apparently unaware of the activity above him and of the identity of the building's commissionaires, who were Special Branch policemen.

Site 104: **2 Whitehall Court.**

An early agent of the new Special Intelligence Section describes their quarters: 'I had always associated rabbit warrens with subterranean abodes, but here in this building I discovered a maze of rabbit-burrow-like passages, corridors, nooks and alcoves, piled higgledy-piggledy on the roof. Leaving the lift, my guide led me up one flight of stairs so narrow that a corpulent man would have stuck tight, round unexpected corners, and again up a flight of steps which brought us out on to the roof. Crossing a short iron bridge we entered another maze until just as I was beginning to feel dizzy I was shown into a room ten feet square where sat an officer in the uniform of a British colonel.' (Who wouldn't feel dizzy? Atop every staircase along this journey a secretary would press a secret bell and, from within, the director would operate a system of levers and pedals to move a pile of bricks and reveal yet another staircase!)

I was recently escorted along these rooftop catwalks. Looking out over the parapet to all of London, and looking in finally to those tiny rooms, I imagined the pleasure which Mansfield Smith-Cumming must have given himself over each day to this dramatic arrival, this ritualized entry into the secret world. Anyone else might have struggled against the peculiarities of such a work-place. But the theatrical Smith-Cumming must have relished it as he relished the work itself, which he considered 'amusing' and 'capital sport.'

The office of the eccentric director was 'bathed in semi-obscurity,' an agent observed. A row of bottles hinted at chemical experiments and a table of mechanical devices added further to 'an already overpowering atmosphere of strangeness and mystery.' Another agent noted with bewilderment that Smith-Cumming's secretary 'kept coming up through a hole in the floor.' Such were the beginnings of Britain's modern intelligence service. But SIS dreamed big. In the early days of Soviet communism, Smith-Cumming's agent Sidney Reilly expected to manage nothing less than Lenin's overthrow. He had the plans to do so, and the funds, and the daring. But he also had the full counter-revolutionary apparatus of the Soviets against him.

Smith-Cumming went on various intelligence expeditions himself, carrying a swordstick, wearing an assortment of disguises, going even into Germany, although he spoke no German. Despite the eccentricities of the man and the legends about him (true or not), 'Smith-Cumming was an able and influential administrator,' writes Anthony Cave Brown in *Bodyguard of Lies*: 'It was he who established the worldwide system of "Passport Control Officers" behind which MI6 hid and worked for so long. It was he who played a major although undetected part in seeing that the government re-enacted (in 1911) the draconian Official Secrets Act of 1889, which effectively muzzled any public inquiry into the work of the service – and made it the grandest of crimes so to do. And it was Smith-Cumming who believed that the service was not only an instrument for gathering other people's secrets but also for making mischief among the King's enemies. Any act was permissible – even assassination. The only crime was to be caught.'

MI6 stayed here until its brief sojourn near Kensington High Street, followed by its move to Broadway in 1924 (*see Site 4*). Today the sole inhabitant of the building is the Royal Horseguards Hotel whose employees occasionally use these rooftop rooms. The hotel makes no public mention of former occupants, and that seems altogether proper for an agency whose very existence was unacknowledged through all its years here. The shade of Captain Sir Mansfield Smith-Cumming undoubtedly approves.

Leaving Whitehall Court you'll pass the elegant Liberal Club on the near-R corner (its premises somewhat larger than now required). Turn R at Whitehall Place and L at Northumberland Avenue. Charing Cross was a prime area for hotels in late Victorian times; on your L from here to Trafalgar Square are two massive former hotels, now annexes of the War Office. The near one is

Site 105: **the former Metropole Hotel, Northumberland Avenue.** The escape-and-evasion section of British intelligence occupied the 'vast barn-like office' of Room 424 from the start of the organization in December, 1939, until a German bomb damaged the building in 1940. Three weeks later MI9 took over Wilton Park, a country house 23 miles from London. Here at the Metropole the inventive Clayton

Hutton devised many of the objects for which MI9 was famous: compasses that fitted into a pipe or fountain pen; surgical saws that slipped into a bootlace; hacksaws that travelled in a trouser-leg.

Philip Aldridge, who also worked briefly in this building, was neither exemplary nor clever. A lance-corporal in the Intelligence Corps, he became in 1983 the youngest person ever prosecuted under the Official Secrets Act. Because of the sensitive nature of his job (destroying copies of documents no longer needed) and because of his age (19), he should have been carefully supervised. When he wasn't, he tried to sell 17 pages of top-secret material to the Soviets. Chapman Pincher considers Aldridge a 'textbook example of the axiom that what matters in the security world is not rank but access.'

Site 106: **the former Victoria Hotel, Northumberland Avenue.**

Closer to Trafalgar Square, just past Great Scotland Yard, is another of these impenetrable buildings used in both world wars by the War

Office. On your L, once a favourite trysting place of Edward VII and Lily Langtry, is

Site 106: **the former Victoria Hotel, Northumberland Avenue.** Here, during WWII, SOE's F Section recruited agents for the dangerous work in occupied France. Room 238 contained only two chairs, a table and an empty filing cabinet by one account; only two chairs by another. In this bare room the author Selwyn Jepson probed carefully into a candidate's motivation and character. 'Normal' views about the Nazis were enough, M. R. D. Foot relates; 'pathologically strong' views were suspect. Impulsiveness was also suspect. SOE wanted its agents to be prudent and reflective.

As to what else may have happened here − or may still be happening − we can only say with certainty that the Victorian splendours must have yielded throughout to the more modest decor supplied by the Ministry of Defence.

Ahead of you is Trafalgar Square again. Give an appreciative nod towards the valiant stone lions who guard this central spot from which all distances to London are measured. From here, you might want to browse among the bookstores in Charing Cross Road. Think on this: the world's largest bookstore began in 1904 when the brothers Foyle failed their civil-service exams and decided to sell their textbooks.

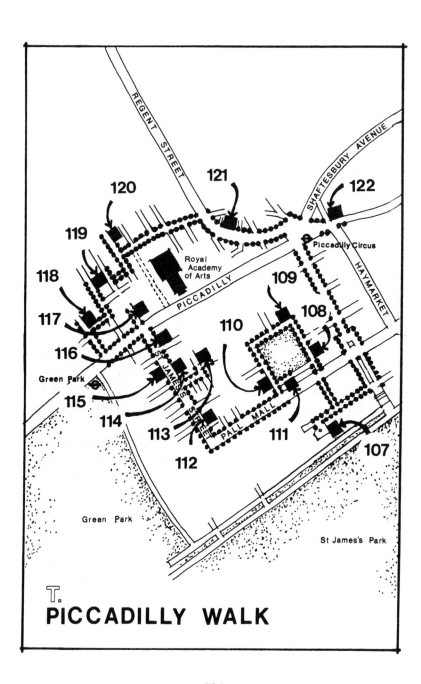

PICCADILLY WALK

T. PICCADILLY WALK

From Piccadilly Circus, walk S down Regent Street into Waterloo Place. Ahead is the Duke of York's Column; its great height, people joked, was to protect this son of George III from his creditors. Turn R into Carlton House Terrace and continue ahead into Carlton Gardens. In the small close at the end of the street is

Site 107: **3 Carlton Gardens.**

Site 107: **3 Carlton Gardens.** Section Y, located here after the war, was one of the 'most secret departments' of SIS, writes Nigel West. 'A tightly guarded secret even within SIS', Section Y intercepted Soviet military and diplomatic communications with the most sophisticated listening devices of the time.

George Blake worked here in Section Y processing raw intelligence for over a year – from September, 1953, after his release by the North Koreans, until January, 1955, when he left for SIS's Berlin Station. During this time he ensured that what was secret from much of SIS was not secret from the Soviets. He compromised any number of Section Y operations: the Berlin Tunnel (*see Sites 63 and 84*), the tapping of Soviet traffic from Vienna to Moscow, the bugging of Eastern bloc representatives at an international peace conference in Geneva, and more. How ironic that Blake should be brought back here to Carlton Gardens to be interrogated in 1961. The 'interviews' lasted three days before Blake's sudden confession (*see Site 84*). I'd have liked tapping into *those* discussions.

Exit from Carlton Gardens to the N and cross Pall Mall into St James's Square, which was laid out in the 1670s as the first of the West End's fashionable squares. The large edifice on your R, built in 1939 on the site of the townhouse of the Dukes of Norfolk, is

Site 108: **Norfolk House, 31 St James's Square.** This building housed the Anglo-American intelligence operations of Eisenhower's SHAEF. (The British carefully avoided mentioning that the site was the birthplace of George III.) M. R. D. Foot walked me past here one delightful lunch-hour and described the array of information once assembled inside – everything from the grandest strategic intelligence about the disposition of enemy forces to the smallest tactical details about enemy gun emplacements. So well-endowed an entity was naturally ripe for hostile penetration. The Germans didn't penetrate Norfolk House, but the Soviets did. (They were our allies at the time, of course, but don't forget that their alliance with the Western democracies was wholly involuntary. *They* never forgot.)

Site 108: **Norfolk House, 31 St James's Square.**

Headquartered here were those planning the cross-Channel invasion and those running the deception operation for the invasion.

Shortly before D-Day, Anthony Blunt got himself transferred to the deception operation. Astonishingly, as Chapman Pincher relates in

Site 108: **Norfolk House, 31 St James's Square.**

Too Secret Too Long, Blunt joined this most-secret unit 'after being rejected from an intelligence course on security grounds.' The chief of the unit, Colonel Noel Wild, later wondered ('with some justification but with no official answer,' says Pincher) who may have recommended Blunt. From deductions made after the fact (adds Pincher), Wild 'suspects that information about Allied moves in France may have been fed back to the Germans by the K.G.B. in order to delay the British-American advance while Soviet troops moved westwards.'

Ahead, in one of the original Georgian townhouses, is

Site 109: **the former Libyan People's Bureau, 5 St James's Square.** Anyone watching television anywhere in the free world in April, 1984, will recall what happened. Some 70 members of the dissident Libyan General Students Organization were demonstrating here, raising only their voices against Muammar Gaddafi. Without warning, someone in the embassy fired a submachine gun. This single burst of exemplary terrorism left 11 students injured and a British policewoman dying. Britain immediately severed relations with Libya and placed the embassy under siege — a siege that ended ten days later when some 60 Gaddafi supporters and officials were escorted to the airport still refusing to co-operate with the police. Britain had no choice but to stand by helplessly as the perpetrators flew off to Libya.

Site 109: **the former Libyan People's Bureau, 5 St James's Square.**

Host countries customarily give foreign diplomats immunity from prosecution for any violation of local law and custom. To arrest or harass foreign diplomats is to invite similar interference with one's own diplomats. All governments therefore turn a blind eye to a certain amount of abuse of diplomatic immunity, and most embassies conduct a certain amount of intelligence-gathering and even subversion.

But the Libyans, perhaps to show their contempt for the Eurocentric standards that govern international diplomacy, went beyond customary practice. They were blatant in their use of this embassy as a base for terrorism. Most dissident Libyans in London were under close surveillance, and the Gaddafi régime made no secret of its violent intentions towards them.

The idea of diplomatic immunity can only operate when governments share a consensus of civility. The world was shocked at what happened here, expecting Libya to be civilized and sane. But Gaddafi's regime was clearly barbaric and crazy. The Libyans took an insane delight in affronting civilized sensibilities and then depending on those civilized sensibilities to let them get away with it.

The policewoman murdered here was protecting the diplomatic sanctity of the embassy from any possible violence from the demonstrators. The mistake made by the British was in thinking that the Gaddafi régime was as civilized and sane as these demonstrators. This mistake cost WPC Yvonne Fletcher her life. And nothing could be done, for fear of jeopardizing everyone in the British Embassy in Tripoli and 7,000 other Britons working in Libya.

The day after the bloodshed, Gordievsky tells us, Moscow received 'reliable information' that Gaddafi had personally ordered the shooting. 'Thereafter,' writes Gordievsky, 'the Center tended to show some sympathy for President Reagan's description of Qaddafi as a "flaky barbarian" ' (but, of course, the Soviets continued to side with Libya in its brinkmanship with the US, giving the Libyans vital military equipment and spy-satellite data). By 1991 Gaddafi seemed to have 'genuinely mellowed with age', as *The Times* described his new image among some diplomats. He sent a cheque for £250,000 to a police charity in Britain (thereby accepting responsibility for Yvonne Fletcher's death) and he seemed ready to promise that Libya would stop supporting international terrorism. When London didn't respond, a not-very-mellow Gaddafi replied that Britain must now kneel before Libya and that Britain could also go to hell.

Continue round the square. At the SW corner is a building constructed in the 1930s to match the 18th-century Adam building next door at No. 20. This is

Site 110: **Winchester House, 21 St James's Square.** In the 19th century, reorganization of the military intelligence structure was frequent, as a Branch became a Division and then a full Department — or a Department was folded back into a Branch. In 1901 the new Mobilization and Military Intelligence Department moved its intelligence sections here from 16-18 Queen Anne's Gate,

Site 110: **Winchester House, 21 St James's Square.**

presumably to be near the commander-in-chief in Pall Mall.

Leave St James's Square at its SW corner. The large office building on your L (30-35 Pall Mall) replaced the former

Site 111: **Adair House, 20 St James's Square.** By 1855 the War Office had established a promising new Topographical and Statistical Department (*see Site 99*). But within 15 years this Department was viewed by its director, Captain Charles William Wilson, as deficient in every possible way. Wilson's critique was a two-page memo that Thomas G. Fergusson in *British Military Intelligence, 1870-1914* calls 'one of the most significant documents in the history of British military intelligence.'

Wilson's recommendations were enthusiastically received and in 1874 this house on the southern edge of St James's Square became headquarters of a new Intelligence Branch − at its core, a revitalized T & S Department. (Wilson is remembered less for his important role in the history of intelligence than for failing to rescue Gordon at Khartoum.)

Site 111: **Adair House, 20 St James's Square.**

In 1884 the entire Intelligence Branch moved to Queen Anne's Gate (*see Site 2*). Precious little needed to be relocated; despite the rapid growth of the Branch, only two officers and one clerk (for instance) covered all of Russia, China, Japan and India. But the Branch was involved even then in the *application* of intelligence — that is, in strategic planning — and Fergusson sees the Intelligence Branch as the start of a modern intelligence capability.

Turn R at Pall Mall and R again at St James's Street. In this area, young men-about-town once maintained their bachelor quarters and spent their time in coffee houses and clubs. On your R, at Overton's seafood restaurant, is

Site 112: **5 St James's Street.** For most of the war the escape-and-evasion organization known as MI9 (an offshoot of MI6) was notionally based in Room 900 of the War Office and actually headquartered at Wilton Park in the Chilterns. But MI9 used a flat in this building to brief agents who were going into enemy territory to build escape networks.

Site 112: **5 St James's Street.**

Early in the war MI9 developed many items to get the stranded aircrews and commandos to neutral Switzerland, Sweden, Spain or Portugal. There were hidden compasses, and maps printed on flight scarves, and flight boots that became civilian shoes and a fur-lined vest. (Unfortunately, as boots *or* shoes, these were so uncomfortable that the airmen rejected them.)

MI9 also developed equipment to be sent into POW camps: a screwdriver hidden in a cricket bat; a hacksaw blade hidden in a comb or toothbrush. Since Red Cross parcels couldn't be used (any discovery would have allowed the Germans to discontinue these life-giving food parcels), MI9 invented some three dozen likely-sounding groups. Parcels from such fictitious entities as the Licensed Victuallers Sports Association, the Prisoners' Leisure Hours Fund, the Welsh Provident Society, and others, all had authentic postmarks outside and proper newspaper wrapping inside.

The 12,000 civilians who aided the 5,000 escapers did so at great risk. An Allied serviceman, if caught, would be sent (or returned) to a POW camp. A civilian feeding and sheltering him, or passing him along to the next station in the network, would be executed outright or delivered to a death camp. Some civilians avoided capture by refusing to merge their networks with those of MI9. Maybe the same wariness that prevented these people from working with strangers also protected them from being fooled by *Gestapo*-controlled infiltrators.

MI9 bought this flat from Sir William Stephenson, a Canadian millionaire with long-standing ties to the Secret Service. I am told that the flat is described in a Graham Greene novel.

Walk N on St James's Street and turn into Ryder Street. At the NE corner of Ryder and Bury Streets is

Site 113: **14 Ryder Street.** This was the wartime workplace of many loyal British and American intelligence officers and of one British officer who was a traitor when he arrived here. The loyal officers

included Malcolm Muggeridge and Graham Greene of SIS's Section V (counter-espionage) and James Jesus Angleton of OSS; Angleton moved a cot into his office, the better to serve his country. Similarly burning the midnight oil here, as he did wherever he worked (telling his colleagues not to worry, he would personally lock up their desks), was Soviet mole Kim Philby.

Philby had entered Section V in September, 1941. By the time the section moved back to London in 1943 – to this building – he was running it during any absence of its chief, Felix Cowgill. Some time before D-Day the concept of a new anti-Soviet section took hold in SIS. The Soviets obviously wanted their man at its helm, and the clever Philby did his best to further his own chances and to damage Cowgill's. In September, 1944, after a contretemps precipitated by Philby, the anti-communist Cowgill left the service and the pro-communist Philby became head of the new Section IX. It was a remarkable double coup for the Soviets. Even those who don't fault SIS for accepting Philby into Section V (despite his prewar record as a communist) are aghast at the 'grotesque mistake' of giving him Section IX.

Before the end of 1944 Philby left Ryder Street for the Broadway Buildings (*see Site 4*). Within 18 months, Knightley tells us in *Philby, K.G.B. Masterspy*, 'Philby had transformed a one-man, one-room section into a major department, occupying a whole floor and employing a staff of more than thirty.' Under the broad charter he was allowed to draft he had 'the right to do just about anything,' writes Knightley, and it is likely that Philby himself moved Section IX into active espionage operations – well beyond the originally intended counter-espionage – thus giving the Soviets control of British intelligence ops directed against them. Naturally he told the Soviets everything. He mentions in his autobiography that SIS warned him 'on no account to have any dealings with any of the United States services' for fear the Americans might leak word to the Soviets. 'It was a piquant situation,' comments Philby.

The Americans had begun arriving at Ryder Street in 1943. At the urging of the British and with their substantial assistance, the OSS had set up a civilian counter-espionage section (X-2) in March of 1943, soon after the creation of OSS itself. The London office of X-2, located here at Ryder Street throughout the war, became the control point for all OSS counter-espionage operations in Europe, North Africa and the Middle East.

At the outset the Americans seemed a laughable lot. And who better to laugh at them than Malcolm Muggeridge? 'Ah, those first OSS arrivals in London! How well I remember them arriving like *jeunes filles en fleur* straight from a finishing school, all fresh and innocent, to start work in our frowsty old intelligence brothel. All too soon they were ravished and corrupted, becoming indistinguishable from seasoned pros who had been in the game for a quarter century or more.' (One of these pros 'turned out to be somewhat more of a seasoned whore than Muggeridge and his associates then knew,' George O'Toole comments in his encyclopedic *Honorable Treachery*.)

Philby was properly disdainful of the Americans. 'It was a notably bewildered group,' he writes in his autobiography, 'and they lost no opportunity of telling us that they had come to school.' The British fully shared with the Americans their extensive counter-espionage files and closely trained the Americans in the conduct of counter-espionage. The importance of this assistance 'cannot be overstated,' according to the official history of the OSS. Philby does not add that the Americans did well at school. Despite their late start, the X-2 group became experienced professionals, their training and work here an inseparable part of everything they would do later when some of these same people founded OSS's successor, the CIA.

It is a commonplace that WWII was the single most important experience for all who served in it, whether they returned to jobs they could talk about or whether they stayed in the secret world. One who stayed was James Angleton, a tall, thin poet from Yale, 26 years old when he arrived in London. Temperamentally more like his Mexican mother than his American father, he was introspective, sensitive, romantic, and enchanted by the world of intelligence. If it hadn't been for WWII he might have become the editor of an obscure poetry journal. Instead he became a founder of the CIA and ultimately its director of counter-intelligence. From his mother, he had learnt a certain fatalism and a great patience. From four years at British public schools, he had learnt much about the proper conduct of life. (He spent most of his adolescence in Europe; his father had bought the Italian operations of the National Cash

Register Company.) From his mentors in MI6, he had learnt much about the clandestine arts, although he soon impressed the British with his own ingenuity and subtlety. What may have most strongly affected Angleton's career, however, was his later realization that he had been completely snookered by Philby during their Ryder Street days. Many intelligence historians are persuaded, as I am, that Angleton's suspicious attitude during his CIA tenure was intensified by this betrayal almost to the point of paranoia – and some would exclude the word 'almost.'

After the war, when all of the Americans had gone back to the States and many of the Britons had gone back to 'civilian' life, Ryder Street was the site of the Special Liaison Centre that ran the ill-fated ops in the Baltics (*see Site 37*). Also after the war, Ryder Street was readied as a 'specialist centre' to handle Soviet defectors. Between 1948 and 1971, however, only one defector came over to the British – and he was almost certainly a plant. Nobody seems to have suspected that these postwar failures (to penetrate the Baltics and to attract defectors) were a sure sign that the Soviets had infiltrated the British services.

Back at St James's Street, turn R. In the block N of Ryder Street is London's second oldest club. Founded in 1763 (located here since 1783) is

Site 114: **Boodle's, 28 St James's Street.** While White's seems to have been the club for those who ran MI6, Boodle's seems to have been the club for its officers. So, while Menzies was a fixture at White's (*see Site 116*), his assistant Claude Dansey belonged to Boodle's. Dansey, unlike Menzies, was an intelligence officer with field experience.

Ian Fleming, when he was assistant to the director of naval intelligence, also belonged to Boodle's. In *The Gentlemen's Clubs of London*, Anthony Lejeune mentions that Fleming had left the livelier White's for the duller Boodle's. They 'gas too much' at White's, Fleming explained.

Boodle's will be familiar to readers of the Fleming *oeuvre*. The fictional Blade's, where 'M' spends his leisure hours, gradually

Site 114: **Boodle's, 28 St James's Street.**

comes to resemble Boodle's, observes Lejeune.

Cross St James's Street and reflect on fate: the man responsible for London's first private traffic island, on this street, thought he needed it to get safely to his club; he paused to admire his efforts one day and was struck by a passing cab. On the W side of the street is

Site 115: **Metro House, 57-58 St James's Street.** As WWII approached, MI5 moved out of central London and into Wormwood Scrubs Prison – unfortunately, not out of the path of German bombs. This venue was altogether unsuitable, as Nigel West writes in *MI5*: the staff worked in automatically locking cells and 'the stream of Mayfair types turning up each morning at the gates succeeded only in attracting attention.' A subsequent move to Blenheim Palace was not much better, with rooms either too small for comfort or too large for secrecy. Finally, in 1940, MI5's 'more vital departments' took over this large building in St James's Street and stayed throughout the war. (The name 'Metro House' came afterwards, when MI5 had gone and Metro-Goldwyn-Mayer moved in.)

Site 115: **Metro House, 57-58 St James's Street.**

Here, on 2 January, 1941, the first meeting of the Twenty Committee took place. Technically part of MI5 but including representatives from all of Britain's intelligence outfits (government and military), the Twenty Committee was cleverly named: the Roman numerals XX make a double cross. Throughout the war this committee decided which information to release to the German agents under Britain's control; a lot of minor truths had to be divulged in order to achieve some major deceptions. The job of the Twenty Committee was to assess the possible gain and risk from the release of every scrap of information, true or false, and to ensure that the scraps taken together would be consistent and therefore credible. Nigel West tells me that a secret wireless station was built on the roof of Metro House so that MI5's star double agent 'Garbo' could communicate with his German controllers in Madrid; much of the traffic connected with Operation 'Fortitude' (the enormously successful plan to confuse the *Abwehr* about D-Day) was transmitted in some 2,000 messages from this station.

Sir John Masterman, the Oxford don who headed the Twenty Committee, credited two factors with its success in controlling the entire German espionage system in Britain — yes, the *entire* system. First was the 'absolute personal integrity' of all British personnel, top to bottom. Second was Masterman's theory that espionage is easy in peacetime but 'usually unprofitable' in wartime, while counter-espionage is difficult in peacetime but 'comparatively easy' in wartime. Probably so. I have always wondered, though, whether the Germans were completely fooled by the double-cross system. Maybe Admiral Canaris of the *Abwehr* wasn't, and maybe the deception was quite OK with him. (Even if not working for or with the British, he was not altogether Hitler's man.) Counter-espionage in peacetime *or* wartime often depends on such lucky accidents.

Only a few dozen clubs remain in Pall Mall and St James's Street; before WWI there were 150. Above Jermyn Street is London's oldest club, founded in 1693 and known then and now as

Site 116: **White's, 37 St James's Street.** This most prestigious of London clubs was the favourite haunt of Sir Stewart Menzies, head of MI6 from 1939 to 1952.

According to Anthony Cave Brown's biography of Menzies, 'The fact that he was proposed, seconded and admitted immediately [to White's] was testament in itself to the power of the secret service and the influence and popularity of the man.' Brown cites a club historian's observation that many distinguished applicants waited through years of probation, 'and some waited forever.'

Despite the unwritten rules against discussing intelligence affairs in public, Menzies frequently met with colleagues over lunch here. He interviewed recruits in the billiards room and virtually 'held court' in the bar. He also had some of his most sensitive mail sent here, trusting the club's hall porter more than he trusted the mailroom clerks of MI6.

Menzies had a particularly interesting meeting at White's in 1947 with Sigismund Payne Best, one of his former officers (*see Site 96*). Best felt that Menzies had handled the Venlo Incident irresponsibly.

Actually, both men had reason to be unhappy about this 'incident.' Best was kidnapped by the Germans and, after telling them all he knew, spent the rest of the war in a concentration camp. Menzies, for his part, had not shared Best's misgivings about 'Captain Schaemmel' and Best was snatched when the good Kapitan turned out to be Walter Schellenberg of the *Sicherheitsdienst*. In the noisy billiards room of White's, Best essentially blackmailed his former

Site 116: **White's, 37 St James's Street.**

chief. Fearing yet another challenge to his competence (Read and Fisher tell us in *Colonel Z*), Menzies bought Best's silence for a handsome 'compensation' of between £4,000 and £6,000.

Cross Piccadilly into Albemarle Street. Third building on the R is

Site 117: **3 Albemarle Street.** In 1939, with the death of Admiral Sinclair imminent, chief of SIS, Claude Dansey rushed back to London from Switzerland to campaign for the post. As his

Site 117: **3 Albemarle Street.**

biographers write in *Colonel Z*, 'in many ways Dansey would have been an excellent choice.' His experience in intelligence went back 37 years: he had run spy networks in Somaliland and South Africa at the turn of the century; he had monitored Irish activities in the US early in the 20th century; he had controlled all points of entry to Britain for MO5 during WWI; he had helped the US create a military intelligence organization in 1917; he had been station chief in Rome; he had created the separate Z Organization in Europe during the 1930s (*see Sites 46 and 96*); he was essentially a one-man control in prewar Switzerland. Along the way, however, he had made a great many enemies – among Britain's defenders as well as her enemies – and he was, at 63, over age. The post went to Menzies, 14 years his junior, and Dansey became assistant chief. He lived in this building and often worked here. He worked, too, in the anonymous safe-house in St James's Street (*see Site 112*); Dansey kept outsiders away from SIS headquarters.

Menzies ran the service as a whole, but Dansey ran all *operations* of British intelligence world-wide. 'With the exception of Naval Intelligence, which the Admiralty kept jealously to itself,' write Read and Fisher in *Colonel Z*, 'Dansey was involved in just about every aspect of intelligence in the second world war.' He controlled most of the intelligence and espionage organizations of the governments-in-exile in London. He had effective control over MI9. He sought complete control over SOE and OSS. But did he have power over Menzies? Herein lies one of the many controversies about Claude Dansey.

Menzies had 'hero-worshipped' Dansey from their time together in Military Intelligence during WWI, say Read and Fisher. Menzies 'never found it easy to make decisions,' they continue. 'What Menzies needed was someone to make them for him. Partly out of gratitude, partly out of genuine admiration for the man, partly out of fear that news of his bungling might be leaked to his political masters, Menzies chose Dansey.' And so Dansey made a point of being at his chief's side at 6 pm every day, 'guiding the chief in any decisions that needed to be taken.' According to Dansey's biographers, his 'domination' of Menzies 'seemed total.'

But the biographer of Menzies presents a different case. Anthony Cave Brown in *'C'* finds it 'a peculiar characteristic of Stewart's life that there were lesser men always ready to claim credit for Menzies's work and, still more strange, given the sort of man he was, protagonists of Dansey who were ready to confer on him the laurels of omniscience and ubiquity.' Menzies saw Dansey not as a trusted mentor, writes Brown, but as an ambitious rival (although 'probably the best espionage man in the world').

Claude Dansey was the subject of wildly varying opinion. He was 'the outstanding officer in SIS... the best of them,' said William Cavendish-Bentinck, head of the Joint Intelligence Committee during WWII. And he was 'the only real professional in the SIS,' said Malcolm Muggeridge; all others at the top were 'second-rate men with second-rate minds.' But to Anthony Cave Brown he was a dangerous man 'capable of anything' and to Edward Crankshaw he was 'the sort of man who gives spying a bad name.' Did Dansey merit any of this? I don't know. He was ruthless, acerbic, charming − and elusive.

Site 118: **7-9 Berkeley Street.**

Return to Piccadilly and walk two blocks W into Berkeley Street. Just beyond Dover Yard, on the R, is

Site 118: **7-9 Berkeley Street.** At the start of WWII the government assembled an assortment of eccentric geniuses at Bletchley Park, outside London. Their mission: to break the codes of foreign governments. They constructed the world's first computer and performed feats of codebreaking no less impressive. Because of internal politics and morale problems, the head of the GC&CS operation at Bletchley (Commander Alastair Denniston) was exiled to London in 1942 to head a smaller operation. Bletchley thereafter decrypted only military traffic; the London section, here in Berkeley Street, handled only diplomatic decrypts.

These luxury flats became offices for the brilliant mathematicians and linguists who were the codebreakers and for the young aristocrats who were their support staff. On the ground floor was an upscale couturière. A guard was supposed to screen visitors, but he was often busy repairing watches (his lucrative sideline) and Madame Riché's customers occasionally wandered past him. Surprisingly, the operation above suffered no breach of security. Indeed, the Germans never knew it existed.

Berkeley Street decrypted diplomatic and commercial traffic in German, Japanese, Arabic, Hebrew, Portuguese, Spanish. (MI6 monitored allies and neutrals as well as enemies.) Churchill told Roosevelt that Britain had stopped trying to break America's codes after Pearl Harbor, but I'm not convinced − and FDR probably wasn't either.

Immediately S on Berkeley Street cut through Dover Yard to Dover Street. Turn L and walk half a block for the secondary entrance to

Site 119: **Brown's Hotel.** In the late 1960s here, in a room booked for the occasion, molehunter Peter Wright made 'one more try' at breaking Alister Watson, the defence scientist believed to have given secrets to the Soviets for decades. Also present was Anthony Blunt, who had confessed secretly to his own treachery and had agreed to inform on his colleagues in treachery. (I'm not aware that Blunt told MI5 about anyone who wasn't dead, retired, or otherwise beyond the reach of British law.)

At the time of the meeting here, Watson had just finished six weeks of daily interrogation by MI5 — and although, as Wright says in *Spycatcher*, 'no one who listened to the interrogation or studied the transcripts was in any doubt that Watson had been a spy, probably since 1938', there was no proof. And there were other questions. Who had recruited him? Was he one of the Ring of Five? (It was a Ring of Four, claimed Blunt.) And would Watson, like Blunt, accept an offer of immunity? At the end of Watson's lengthy interrogation, he was 'rambling incoherently', says Wright, and 'seemed unable even to understand the offer that was made to him.' Blunt would explain immunity, thought Wright.

Site 119: **Brown's Hotel.**

Watson and Blunt had been friends for 40 years. In 1927 they were elected together to the Apostles (the élite secret society of Cambridge students), and together they moved the Apostles from liberalism to Marxism. Blunt claimed to have learnt his Marxist theory 'at Alister's feet.'

Watson had done brilliant wartime work on radar and engineering design and in 1953 was appointed to the Admiralty's Submarine Detection Research Establishment. At the time of the MI5 investigation, in 1967, he was quietly removed as head of submarine detection research and sent to the National Institute of Oceanography until retirement.

Victor Rothschild, a fellow Apostle, had been the first to suggest an investigation of Watson, in 1951. Nothing happened. In 1965, Peter Wright recommended 'an urgent investigation' of Watson after suggestive comments by Blunt. Again MI5 took no action. The investigation and interrogation of Watson, when it finally occurred, showed Watson to have had contact with three known KGB officers. ('I wanted to find out more about Russia.') Microphones picked up his repeated muttering, 'They've got something, but I don't know what it is.' He admitted nothing. To Wright, though, one detail 'clinched the case.' Watson had spoken at length about KGB officer Sergei Kondrashev, saying that he (Watson) had found the man too bourgeois and hadn't continued their meetings. But a defector had mentioned a British asset who disliked Kondrashev's bourgeois ways; the defector knew this Briton only as Kondrashev's 'naval spy.'

The meeting here at Brown's provided no solid evidence of Watson's culpability. Blunt drank almost a complete bottle of gin; Watson, enough to launch 'a drunken attack' on Blunt's personal success. Watson still seemed unable to understand the offer of immunity. In the end, with both men upset and exhausted, Blunt said to Wright, 'I suppose you're right. I suppose he must be one of us.' Was it news to Blunt? Since he could tell MI5 only what he wished, he could have said anything.

My hunch is that when Blunt added, 'Sometimes I think it would have been easier to go to prison' (one imagines this line delivered with the back of the wrist applied to the forehead), there may have been some truth to his statement, self-dramatising though it was. He didn't like the role of informer. But I think he would *not* have preferred going to prison. He would only have preferred not getting caught, and he did his best to keep anyone else from getting caught. Difficult as this encounter at Brown's must have been for Blunt, it probably had its triumphant and even hilarious moments. I wonder what he made of it, in his remaining years: that the Soviets took their people to the basement of the Lubyanka, while the British took their people to Brown's.

Go through Brown's Hotel, perhaps stopping for the memorable tea.

Exit at Albemarle Street. Enter the Royal Arcade across the road and turn L when the arcade reaches Old Bond Street. This quiet path almost immediately becomes New Bond Street, place of attractive shops and shoppers. Bay windows look up and down the street at

Site 120: **Clifford Chambers, 10 New Bond Street.** Soviet mole Guy Burgess lived here from shortly after WWII until 1951. The bay-windowed flat on the first floor was his last residence before his alcohol-soaked exile in the USSR.

He had been hired by the Foreign Office press department in 1944 and accepted into the permanent staff in 1947. It has been widely assumed that he didn't do much spying at this point but merely circulated in that peculiar milieu of his — composed of Old Etonians, intelligence officers, homosexuals, Whitehall high-flyers, intellectuals, substance abusers, Oxbridge graduates, and working-class young men of the sort known to homosexuals as 'rough trade.' Not so, according to William J. West's *The Truth about Hollis* (1989). In the new postwar Labour Government, Burgess became what one might call the *'éminence rouge'* behind Hector McNeil, the new Minister of State to Ernest Bevin. As personal assistant to McNeil, Burgess saw almost everything going to the Foreign Minister — and when McNeil took over in Bevin's absence, Burgess saw literally everything. (The Soviets, naturally, saw whatever Burgess saw.) Burgess also influenced policy; arriving at the China desk in 1948, he 'contributed largely' (writes West) to Britain's decision to recognize Mao. But Burgess was disintegrating badly by now, drinking heavily and behaving outrageously even for Burgess. In 1949, he was reprimanded for security breaches.

In 1950, incredibly, the FO assigned him to the British Embassy in Washington as second secretary. I have never heard an acceptable explanation for this posting. Burgess's bizarre behaviour and habits were well known. He was filthy. He stank. A plate of shrimps he emptied into his suitcoat pocket at a party was still there a week later, to the dismay of his office-mates. He had taken to munching garlic the way other people chew candy mints. He was as vocal about his anti-Americanism as he was about his homosexuality. Altogether, no posting was less suitable than Washington in 1950. (When the FO Security Branch advised the Washington staff of Burgess's behaviour

Site 120: **Clifford Chambers, 10 New Bond Street.**

and warned that worse might be in store, someone remarked, 'Surely he can't mean *goats*?')

The week before sailing to America, Burgess hosted a farewell party here that was said to be 'by Burgess's standards at least, restrained and respectable' – and also a drunken brawl. (It was undoubtedly both.) But after less than a year in Washington he was recalled to London. By early 1951, MI5 knew of a Soviet mole in the FO and according to Philby's autobiography, he and Burgess expected the mole soon to be identified as Donald Maclean (recruited by Burgess himself). Therefore, still according to Philby, Burgess deliberately provoked the Washington embassy into firing him so that he could return to Britain and spirit Maclean away. If this were true, would Burgess have dallied in New York before travelling slowly home on the *Queen Mary*? And after arriving in London, would he and Maclean have pursued their normal lives (if Burgess's lifestyle could be so described) for another *three weeks* before leaving abruptly on 25 May for Moscow?

On that day, the Foreign Office finally authorized MI5's interrogation of Maclean – to begin on Monday, 28 May. (Not even a Soviet mole in the upper reaches of the FO could justify ruining the weekend.) Philby claimed, years later, that it was he who had warned Maclean, through Burgess, of the imminent interrogation. But as intelligence journalist Chapman Pincher points out, Philby in Washington was unlikely to have known of the plans in time to warn Burgess. Burgess was most probably alerted by an agent-in-place in MI5 or the FO; Philby was protecting that person by calling attention to himself. Recently, Soviet spymaster Yuri Modin has labelled it 'pure coincidence' that Maclean escaped just before the interrogation; the Soviets had been hurrying to get Maclean out, says Modin, and they finally managed it. This explanation, accurate or not, conveniently eases British concern over a mole in MI5 or the FO. Despite the new relationship between Russia and the West, the KGB's successors may well want to leave certain secrets to history.

I have long believed that when Burgess walked out of this building into New Bond Street on 25 May, he didn't know he was leaving for ever. He would have expected to escort Maclean to a Soviet or satellite embassy in Europe and then return to London to dine out on this latest and most outrageous escapade. His Soviet controller would have encouraged him in this belief. According to Modin, recently, that's exactly what happened. A reluctant Burgess was told he could return to London after seeing Maclean through the border. 'Of course, it was a lie,' says Modin. The Soviets realized that the unstable Burgess had to go; he was almost as likely as Maclean to name his recruits and associates.

The Cambridge spies were known to each other, contrary to usual procedure, and their friendship was widely known to others. The exposure of one would immediately jeopardize the others. The flight of Burgess and Maclean therefore placed Philby under suspicion. This couldn't be helped. Or could it? Here is Verne W. Newton in *The Cambridge Spies*: 'Moscow did not gamble with Philby's future. They did not even sacrifice it. They threw it away.' Why, asks Newton. 'Who can say?' According to Chapman Pincher, Hollis may have known why (*see Site 82*) but of course he couldn't say.

I am certain that Burgess had no idea of what was to happen; he left behind shoeboxes of letters and photographs implicating his associates. Incredibly, MI5 asked Anthony Blunt to search this flat after Burgess disappeared. (Blunt had maintained a close relationship with the Security Service after his resignation in 1945.) Blunt pocketed as much incriminating evidence as he could find, thus protecting himself and Kim Philby and uncounted others. But intentionally or not he overlooked material that soon focused suspicion upon John Cairncross (*see Site 25*).

Burgess was a weirdo − specifically, a British upper-class weirdo − who would have been miserable anywhere but London. Yet he was forced to spend his last 12 years in a backwater where his wit and upper-class accent counted for naught. He may have been useful to Moscow Centre, giving his take on personalities and events in Whitehall. But he was several things the KGB despised: a homosexual, a limousine Leninist, and a traitor to his own country, never fully to be trusted by the communists for whom he had put in half a lifetime of faithful service. Burgess must have returned the feelings fully. One can imagine his thoughts upon realizing that he, who had hoodwinked so many, for so long and with such arrogant delight, was now so devastatingly hoodwinked himself.

Walk into Burlington Gardens. Just past Burlington Arcade look L into Cork Street where for many years (Nigel West tells us) MI5's C Division had its 'anonymous offices above the art galleries' — dispensing security advice to businesses with government contracts, and receiving in return useful titbits gleaned by business travellers abroad. Continue on to Regent Street. Across the street is the handsome curve of

Site 121: **Imperial House, 80-86 Regent Street.** The American Refrigerator Company Limited, located here during the early and middle 1930s, was the business cover of the Soviet intelligence officer who originally ran the expanding Cambridge network. In those innocent days, 'William Goldin' was the last person MI5 would have suspected. The man was notionally an Austrian-born entrepreneur from America, a combination that would have explained his accented English, his frequent trips abroad, and any other odd behaviour. There is no evidence that MI5 even knew of the existence of this resourceful and accomplished officer in Stalin's secret army.

'Goldin' (a/k/a Alexander Orlov) was one of the legendary Comintern 'illegals' most of whom were later arrested and murdered by their mistrustful leader. In 1938, when Orlov realized that Stalin suspected him (incorrectly) of disloyalty, he fled from Spain where he was heading the NKVD takeover of the Spanish republic during that country's civil war. From America he got word to Stalin that if he or his family (some still in the USSR) were harmed, a lengthy memorandum revealing all of the Soviet agents he had worked with – and in many cases recruited, in Germany and Britain – would be made public.

The Soviets kept their part of the deal and Orlov protected his contacts and recruits even after he was obliged to debrief to American intelligence authorities. The Russians have only now rehabilitated his memory, releasing some (but only some) of the details of the epic story in which Orlov seemed to betray Stalin but actually remained true to the Soviet cause. John Costello and Oleg Tsarev are the conduit for this material, and in their book *Deadly Illusions* (1993) they note that Orlov could well have changed history if he had wanted to – that is, if he had wanted to betray Philby, Maclean, Burgess, Blunt, Cairncross, Rees, and all the others. How many others were there – in the Cambridge network, in the Oxford ring, in London, elsewhere? We do not yet know. Indeed, we may never know. But the Foreign Intelligence Service doesn't mind letting us think that there were moles burrowing everywhere. Inflated propaganda? Or incomplete history? We'll have to wait and see.

Several years after Orlov left Imperial House, the building sheltered another extraordinary spy – one who withheld his truths from the Germans and fabricated other 'truths' for his memoirs.

Dusko Popov has been called 'the winning but weaselly Yugoslav businessman' and 'the ablest double agent recruited by SIS.' Here on Regent Street he worked under the cover of a business created for him by MI5; he imported food and goods from Portugal and Spain, while he delivered British disinformation to the Nazis and Nazi secrets to the British.

Popov was the first British agent in direct contact with the *Abwehr*, having been approached by the Germans in the summer of 1940 and having himself then approached the British. For 40 months (until May, 1944) Popov participated in some of Britain's great disinformation ops: about the fake invasion of Norway and the real invasions of North Africa and Normandy. He steadily gave the

Germans disinformation about Britain's capability and morale, and he ran a series of sub-agents that the Germans thought were theirs but the British knew were *theirs*. He apparently supplied the British with information about Admiral Canaris and the possibility of an anti-Hitler coup, and along the way he constantly told the British what the *Abwehr* wanted most to discover. And thereby hangs an interesting tale.

In 1941 the *Abwehr* sent Popov to the US to build a new espionage organization (previous networks having been demolished by the FBI) and gave Popov a list of questions to research. More than a third of the questionnaire related to Hawaii, and half of this third related to Pearl Harbor. According to Popov, he knew immediately that the Japanese wanted the information for an attack on Pearl Harbor to take place before the end of 1941! He says he communicated this to the FBI in August, only to be angrily denounced for his sexual behaviour by J. Edgar Hoover. In *Spy Counterspy*, published in 1974, Popov suggests that Hoover 'pigeonholed' the information — somehow 'lost' it — and was therefore responsible for the US being caught by surprise at Pearl Harbor on 7 December, 1941.

Popov's charges against Hoover held sway for a decade. Hoover wasn't around to argue, having died in 1972. Perhaps the very colourfulness of Popov's book lent authenticity to his accusations. Or perhaps it was the glowing blurb by Graham Greene, or Popov's grandiose assertion that Ian Fleming had based the Bond character 'to some degree on me and my experiences.' Popov's book captured the imagination of the public — and the minds of historians — until the mid-eighties. Hoover was an easy target, and America too, in those years.

In another decade Popov too had died. He did not live to see his story demolished on both sides of the Atlantic. Nigel West was the first to label Popov's charges 'hindsight', in 1984, in *Unreliable Witness: Espionage Myths of the Second World War*. Two years later came a book by three American historians (*Pearl Harbor: The Verdict of History*), showing that Hoover *had* given Popov's questionnaire to US intelligence and suggesting that the information about Pearl Harbor would have been of obvious interest to the *Germans*.

The definitive counter-attack came in 1989 in a lengthy article by the American intelligence historian Thomas F. Troy in the *International Journal of Intelligence and Counterintelligence*. Troy finds major contradictions in Popov's claim that he deduced the Pearl Harbor attack before the event. Would the Japanese, Troy asks, have risked discovery of their plans by asking the Germans for information in this way? Would the Germans have failed to see anything of significance in Japan's several requests for information (not only about Hawaii but also about the port of Taranto, where the British had made a similar attack on the Italian fleet)? And would the British, if aware of Popov's warning in August, simply have forgotten it by the time they were surprised by the attack on Pearl Harbor in December? Popov's claim to have 'scored the analytical coup of the war,' says Troy, is just plain unbelievable, as is Popov's claim to have stressed the importance of his discovery to the FBI. Even Popov's defenders cannot be counted on for support. In what Troy calls a 'remarkable personal revisionism', Ewen Montagu (who had written the approving foreword to Popov's book) later suggested that the questionnaire could well have reflected a German interest in Pearl Harbor.

Popov undoubtedly did some of what he claimed (although he didn't, as claimed, use the first microdot). Possibly he did more than he imagined. As David Mure writes in *Master of Deception: Tangled Webs in London and the Middle East*, 'what has always astonished me was that there never seemed to be any consciousness in MI5 that important elements in the Abwehr were working against Hitler and, indeed, providing us with the opportunity to turn and use their own agents against them.' Could Popov have been used in this way by anti-Hitler forces? Phillip Knightley cites Popov, among others, as 'clear evidence of Abwehr complicity in the double-cross system.' Indeed, isn't it remarkable that after Popov's considerable failures (in German terms) – his failure to set up an American network for them, and his numerous failures to provide accurate information to them – he was kept on by the Germans and given ever more of their trust? The British seem to have been more cautious than the Germans about Popov; Nigel West tells us that Popov 'was always the subject of discreet surveillance': his flat wired, the flat above him 'permanently manned by MI5 personnel', and his office staff 'thoughtfully provided' by MI5.

Follow the curve of Regent Street into Piccadilly Circus, and exit on the far side at Coventry Street. Here at the head of Haymarket, just E of Windmill Street in the busy Trocadero, is

Site 122: **the former Scott's Restaurant, 18-20 Coventry Street.** Until 1966, Scott's was one of the more elegant spots in Piccadilly Circus, when one could still use the words 'elegant' and 'Piccadilly Circus' in the same sentence. In those days, Scott's was the favourite London restaurant of Ian Fleming. His customary place − the right-hand corner table for two on the first floor − became the favourite of Agent 007.

Fleming worked in intelligence himself, after a fashion, as 'go-fer' to Admiral John Godfrey, director of naval intelligence. Godfrey hatched some great ideas, among them asking the public for photographs of their holidays abroad; patriotic Britons sent in 80,000 'Aunt Minnie' snaps (beach scenes and the like) containing information useful in the Allied landings. Fleming had some less brilliant ideas, including one operation he attempted here at Scott's. He arranged a day of 'sightseeing' for two officers of a captured German U-boat and tried to get them drunk enough to reveal how they had avoided British mine fields in the Skaggerak. Nobody had done anything like this before and one can understand why. The waiters at Scott's, alarmed to hear Fleming and his guests conversing convivially in German, called Special Branch who promptly arrested the entire party. Many in the British intelligence community were amused by this incident; Admiral Godfrey was not among them.

You are at the end of this walk. If you haven't had lunch yet yourself, you might aim for Fortnum and Mason, grocery store to the royal family; it is on Piccadilly opposite the Royal Academy of Arts. On your way, you might stop in where John Hatchard became a bookseller in 1797 with a capital of £5.

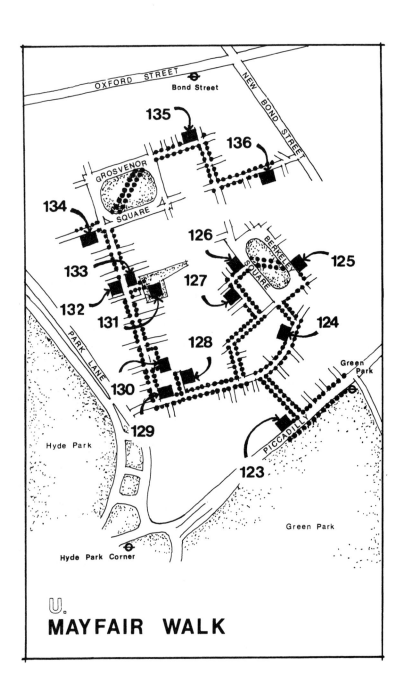

MAYFAIR WALK

U. MAYFAIR WALK

Walk W on Piccadilly from Green Park tube station. Just past Half Moon Street is the fine residence of Lord Palmerston, Prime Minister during the Crimean War. The building has been an officers' club for over a century. Officially the Naval and Military Club, it is known from its gateposts as

Site 123: **the In and Out, 94 Piccadilly.** Sir Vernon Kell, director-general of MI5 from its founding in 1909 until 1940, lunched here almost daily and often recruited from club membership. Many of his recruits had military backgrounds: not surprising, given his own career.

Kell, who was a year ahead of Churchill at Sandhurst, was abruptly sacked before the new prime minister had been in office a month.

Churchill had 'enjoyed a poor relationship with Kell,' writes Nigel West, and blamed MI5 (unjustifiably) for two painful incidents in 1939 and 1940: the sinking of the *Royal Oak* at Scapa Flow and explosions in a munitions factory in Churchill's own constituency. Kell, for his part, had long mistrusted Churchill; 'perhaps it went back to Churchill's attempts to merge MI5 and SIS in the Twenties,' writes West. The 67-year-old Kell departed from MI5 a broken man and died two years later.

Return to Half Moon Street and turn L. At Curzon Street turn R. On the L side of the street, the large building with no windows on the ground floor is

Site 124: **Curzon Street House, 1-4 Curzon Street.** When I first thought of doing this book, the secret world was rather more secret than it is today. I had decided, on principle, not to include any sites currently in use by HM Government. I had planned, with Curzon Street House, to take the walker past the building and mention its name only as an architectural checkpoint. Those who knew what went on inside would smile; those who didn't, wouldn't.

Now, however, *everyone* knows something of what has gone on inside Curzon Street House. In 1976, MI5 was 'in the process of moving to new offices at the top of Curzon Street,' according to Peter Wright's *Spycatcher*, and had already left Leconfield House for 'the dismal Gower Street offices' (*see Site 89*). Gower Street became the new headquarters; Curzon Street, the new location of administrative and technical offices. To learn exactly where in Curzon Street, one didn't need to be *inside*, as it were. A *Tatler* article in the mid-eighties showed a photograph. A more recent BBC 'Late Show' discussed the building at greater length.

'"Secret Architecture" in this country has traditionally been blind,' says the BBC commentator, pointing to 'bizarrely blind windows you can't see into or out of' and thick dirty net curtains 'allegedly to obviate the effects of bomb blasts.' He recites all the rumours. The peculiar canopy may be there for bombproofing. The basement may be linked to other buildings 'in an underground network that few people outside the secret state know about.' The royal family may have sheltered in the especially deep basement during the Blitz.

Site 124: **Curzon Street House, 1-4 Curzon Street.**

But (no rumour here) everyone seems to know about the Registry being here — with its files on individuals, on organizations, and on whatever 'could not easily be placed within either of the two previous categories,' as Peter Wright describes the system. The Registry had 'about two million' personal files when Wright joined the service in 1955. The number rose 'dramatically' in the next decades.

As to what may still be here after the move to Thames House (*see Site 10*), it's anyone's guess. But a certain mystery will always attach to Curzon Street House. From his wartime days at Berkeley Street (*see Site 118*), P. William Filby reported that the building opposite the Mirabelle restaurant 'housed hundreds of pigeons.' Filby (who is not to be confused with Philby, except aurally) never discovered 'if and how' the pigeons were used.

Immediately past the full block of Curzon Street House, you'll glimpse Berkeley Square. On the E side of the square is

Site 125: **Berkeley Square House.** By 1940 the *Wehrmacht* had occupied most of Western Europe; Britain was outgunned, outsmarted, and standing alone. Churchill came to power knowing that Britain couldn't counter-attack, couldn't even defeat an

invasion. But he was impressed by the unconventional warfare waged against the British by the Boers at the turn of the century (and by the Irish since the dawn of time) and he liked the idea of dishing out this kind of trouble instead of being on the receiving end.

Probably in response to the Left's occasionally accurate vision of intelligence work as the preserve of reactionary military types, Churchill established SOE within the new Ministry of Economic Warfare headed by Labourite Hugh Dalton. According to Patrick Howarth's *Undercover*, Dr Dalton was an impressive figure, 'a man of exceptionally combative nature. He had a large frame, a first-class mind, a booming voice, almost limitless energy and a virtual inability to conceive that in any circumstances he could be wrong.' Since Dalton's organization was housed here at Berkeley Square House, SOE began here. But it moved almost immediately to Caxton Street (*see Site 5*), far from Dalton − and from the War Office and MI6, both of which resented SOE's very existence.

Admire the 200-year-old plane trees as you cross Berkeley Square. N of Hill Street is

Site 126: **40 Berkeley Square.** Mussolini joked in 1940 that America must possess the world's best intelligence service because no one knew where it was. In fact it didn't exist, as he well knew. Before the formation of the Office of Strategic Services in 1942, America was the only world power lacking an intelligence service. By then the world's greatest industrial power, America had lacked a military service too at the start of the war, its army smaller than Yugoslavia's! When the OSS people began arriving in England, they were therefore newcomers not only to the conventional war that America's allies had been fighting for several years but also to the intelligence war that America's allies had been fighting for several centuries.

To this building − an early OSS headquarters in London − came some of America's brightest and bravest young men. They were altogether untried in overt or covert warfare but were altogether convinced that they were smarter and tougher than any of their enemies (or any of their allies). These high-spirited men were equally unimpressed by the well-connected political élite for whom the war was 'a splendid entertainment', as Major General John K. Singlaub

Site 126: **40 Berkeley Square.**

that visitors from both sides of the Atlantic received in the Maryland mountains (at the OSS training camp that subsequently became Camp David, the presidential retreat named for Eisenhower's grandson). One hapless visitor was Sir William Stephenson of SIS. As he spoke of the glorious destinies awaiting his listeners he heard a chant rising before him: '48,' called one man; '49,' called another. At the sound of '50' all shouted together, 'Some shit!' Singlaub apologizes to Stephenson, who would have commanded their utmost respect if he hadn't been part of these 'pep talks by sleek noncombatants.'

The OSS followed the British example in recruiting for intelligence and subversive activities heavily from the upper crust – mainly from the Ivy League colleges. This was unconventional warfare and these were unconventional warriors, essentially civilians: brash, self-confident (not to say arrogant), colourful, uninhibited, impatient with the traditional methods of the military. Thus one OSS agent committed 'what was possibly at once the most childish and the most magnificent *beau geste* in the history of the war,' write Stewart Alsop and Thomas Braden in *Sub Rosa: The O.S.S. and American*

Espionage. Long before D-Day, this legendary fighter hiked across the Yugoslav-Austrian border and sent a postcard to Hitler in Berlin: 'Dear Hitler: Fuck you. (Signed) An American Captain IN GERMANY.'

Like the Jeds who went into France despite Hitler's policy that, if captured, they would be shot immediately, OSS agents had no room for defeatist thinking. Many of them threw away their L-pills (the 'L' is for lethal), and a number of them died under torture.

Walk into Hill Street and then Hay's Mews; these coach houses once served the grand residences of Berkeley Square. On the far side of the road is

Site 127: **43 Hay's Mews.** Intelligence historian Robin Winks of Yale University tells me that various OSS people lived in this house, among them Yale faculty member Norman Holmes Pearson. In June, 1943, Pearson and six others became the 'founding core' of the counter-intelligence section of OSS − X-2, as it was named by Pearson.

By autumn, 1944, X-2 had grown to more than 500 members worldwide; Pearson ran its London branch. But perhaps his 'most significant wartime service,' writes Winks in *Cloak and Gown*, was as liaison between X-2 and Britain's very effective Twenty Committee (*see Site 115*). Also known as the XX Committee (a reference to the desired double cross), the Twenty Committee would ultimately work 120 doubled German agents, 39 of them on a long-term basis.

Pearson was intense, witty, gregarious. He was very good at what he did in London and what he went on to do in the academic world. (He became a leading Hawthorne scholar and a highly respected advocate of the new field of American studies.) At his death in 1975, it was rumoured that the North Koreans had poisoned him because of his supposed connection with the CIA. Pearson himself lent credibility to these stories: 'there was always something a trifle conspiratorial in Norman Pearson's manner,' says Winks.

Proceed down Hay's Mews to the pub called 'I Am the Only Running Footman.' Turn R into Charles Street, then L into Queen Street and R into Curzon Street. (To your L at No. 10 is Heywood Hill bookshop, which 'satisfied the reading requirements of the KGB agent Guy Burgess after he fled to Moscow,' according to The Times. *The bookshop calls this 'a complete fabrication' but you might want to have a look round anyway.) Walk W on Curzon Street to Chesterfield Gardens. Towards the back is*

Site 128: **6 Chesterfield Gardens.** Imagine this place as it was early in the war: the elegant home of the exuberant Tomás Harris, half-English and half-Spanish, a painter, a collector, and an art dealer specializing in Goya and El Greco. Hilda and Tomás Harris were generous hosts to 'a little drinking circle' of intelligence people. 'The regulars,' Kim Philby would recall, 'were me, Burgess, Blunt and perhaps Aneurin Bevan.' Often here too were MI5's Victor Rothschild, Guy Liddell (head of counter-espionage), and Dick White (later head of MI5 and then of MI6). The convivial evenings often ended at breakfast with coffee and pernod. Were these more than office friendships? I think so.

Harris's involvement with some of the 'Chesterfield Gardens Mafia' was crucial to their intelligence careers. Consider Guy Burgess. His 'most influential advocates' with Liddell were Blunt and

Harris (writes John Costello in *Mask of Treachery*); Liddell balked at having Burgess *in* MI5 but had no qualms about using Burgess as a free-lancer to pick up the odd bit of information on the homosexual circuit.

Site 128: **6 Chesterfield Gardens.**

Harris also helped manoeuvre Philby into MI6. They had become friends in 1940 when both were working at Colonel Grand's school for saboteurs (Harris as the caterer, a job he obtained through Burgess). In 1941, when Harris was working in MI5's counter-intelligence, he introduced Philby to his boss Dick Brooman-White (not to be confused with 'the other Dick White') and suggested that Brooman-White recommend Philby for a post in MI6. Philby got the job, and in rather little time moved from the Iberian sub-section of counter-espionage to the very centre of MI6's efforts against the Soviets (*see Site 113*).

Harris and Philby remained close. In 1946 Harris was a witness at Philby's wedding to Aileen, and in the 1950s, when Philby's livelihood was precarious, Harris provided half the £600 publisher's advance (a hefty sum in those days) for a book by Philby about his career. The idea for the book also came from Harris, and when

Philby abandoned the project it was Harris who repaid the publisher. In Moscow 30 years later, a handsome antique Spanish table adorned Philby's flat – a gift from Harris, we learn from Knightley. And in Knightley's extended interview with Philby just before Philby's death, the ever-charming Kim answers a question about his regrets by mentioning (at the top of a very short list) the loss of the relationship with friends 'like Tommy Harris.'

The Cambridge spies can have had very few friends 'like Tommy Harris.' In 1940, 'the person who suggested the appointment of Blunt' to MI5 was not Victor Rothschild, as often alleged, but Harris, writes Chapman Pincher in *Their Trade Is Treachery*. And Harris was with Blunt immediately after Maclean and Burgess fled, almost certainly implicating Harris in the attempt by Blunt to set up a false trail.

Harris was very busy in his own work too. As part of MI5's Iberian section (ultimately head of it), he ran a number of deception schemes against the Germans. He ran the double agent 'Garbo' ('best actor in the world') and a fictitious network of two dozen other notional *Abwehr* agents in the 'Fortitude' deception that camouflaged the Normandy invasion. This arduous effort was so successful that even after D-Day the Germans considered the Normandy invasion only a diversion for the anticipated landing in Pas-de-Calais. Harris ran other double agents, but at least one of his recruits was a triple agent – apparently working for the Germans, actually working for the British, but *really* working for the Soviets.

Was Tomás Harris working for the Soviets too? 'Effusive tributes' from Philby and Blunt suggest to John Costello that Harris was 'deeply involved in their web of conspiracy.' Blunt, of course, insisted that Harris was not, but this hardly gives Harris a clean bill of health. Flora Solomon, who denounced Philby to MI5 in 1962, named Harris as a Soviet agent. And it is 'curious to say the least', notes intelligence historian Richard Deacon, that Tomás Harris came into MI5 'largely through the influence of Guy Liddell' who was later suspected of treachery himself (*see Site 32*).

Many people were suspicious of Harris. The most specific charge, according to Costello, is from 'a former member of a Soviet network in Switzerland' to the effect that Harris was recruited by an Italian communist, an art dealer like Harris. 'Perhaps it was not coincidental,' adds Costello, that Harris was 'buying up Spanish art during the civil war at a time when the Soviet "advisers" to the Loyalists masterminded the systematic stripping of monasteries, churches and castles of their art treasures.'

Harris died in Mallorca in 1964 after a strange one-car accident: he was healthy and sober, his car was in excellent repair, the road was clear and dry. Yet the car suddenly veered off and struck a tree. Flora Solomon, among many others, was convinced that the Soviets had killed Harris. Is it merely coincidence that Harris died just as MI5 was about to question him in connection with Blunt?

Blunt, in fact, provides a curious footnote that may explain a good many things. Something happened in 1964, he said years later, that freed him from his loyalty to his friends. Was he referring to Michael Straight's having made a clean breast of his own Comintern involvement and having implicated Blunt (*see Site 95*)? Or, for Blunt, was the shattering and liberating event of 1964 the death of Tomás Harris? Did Blunt fear that the Soviets had killed Harris to silence him – and that he, Blunt, might be next? Blunt was supremely clever. From the end of the war he had foolproof protection against exposure by the British (*see Site 13*). From 1964, if not before, I believe that he had foolproof protection against assassination by the Soviets (*see Site 82*). Perhaps he only realized how much he needed this latter protection when his friend Tommy Harris died so suddenly.

Back at Curzon Street, bordering Chesterfield Gardens, is the full block of

Site 129: **Leconfield House, Curzon Street.** In this building in 1945 the British Security Service established its headquarters after the wartime sojourn at Blenheim. The organization would stay here, to an increasingly wide knowledge of its presence, until the 1970s.

Occupying the entire ground floor in the early seventies was the Registry. Some 300 women were needed to keep Registry files up to date and deliver them within the building, says Peter Wright, and it was a major headache to find the replacements necessitated by the frequent office marriages. (One couldn't really advertise.) This problem more than anything else, according to Wright, led to the Registry's belated computerization.

Site 129: **Leconfield House, Curzon Street.**

Occupying part of the top floor was the Pig and Eye Club; better to have officers drinking here than in some nearby pub where the eavesdropper at one's elbow might be a Soviet agent or − worse − a Fleet Street reporter.

Leconfield House was also, of course, the site of the intense molehunt of the 1960s and 1970s, during which at least one of the suspects had his office bugged and at least one of the molehunters had his safe rifled. This was also the site of the fruitless interrogations of Philby in November, 1951, and, it must be said, the fruitless attempts *for over 30 years* to uncover more than the single KGB 'illegal' who was exposed by MI5 during that entire time.

Before MI5 moved in, this building was the wartime command post for the local military authorities. Gun-ports were cut into the building's southwest corner, anticipating 'a street by street battle for Mayfair with Nazi parachutists,' writes Nigel West. (Hyde Park was a perfect drop-zone.) By the 1950s these guns were supposedly manned night and day against a mob of Britons who might storm MI5 from Speakers' Corner, but West tells us that the gun-ports 'had long since been blocked up' and the machine-guns replaced by teleprinters.

At South Audley Street, you and Leconfield House will turn the corner. Walk N on South Audley Street. At the near edge of the patch of concrete called Audley Square you'll see

Site 130: **the No. 8 lamp post, Audley Square.** An 'illegal' communicated with Moscow Centre either by sending an innocent-seeming letter to a cover address, or by using some system of prearranged signals to deliver a message to a 'dead letter box.' In one set of signals that we know about from Oleg Gordievsky, the agent would place a blue chalk-mark below the figure '8' on this lamp post. He would check the bench in St George's Gardens to make sure his signal had been seen (*see Site 131*). After placing the material at the DLB (*see Sites 47 and 48*) he would remove his chalk-mark from the lamp post. His KGB officer would collect the material and then remove *his* chalk-mark from the bench.

Better practice, well-known to the Soviets, would have involved a signal that was less noticeable in the doing and less noticeable when done − perhaps a horizontal chalk-mark at thigh level (made by someone walking casually past a wall), or a thumbtack affixed to the underside of a bench.

Site 130: **the No. 8 lamp post, Audley Square.**

Continue N on South Audley Street. You will pass the modest Grosvenor Chapel where American armed forces 'held Divine Service during the Great War of 1939 to 1945 and gave thanks to God for the Victory of the Allies.' Turn R into the landscaped area behind the church and sit for a while in

Site 131: **St George's Gardens.** The second bench to the right was

Site 131: **St George's Gardens.**

part of a signalling system between 'illegals' and their KGB support staff (*see Site 130*). The crucial chalk-mark was to be made 'in the middle on the upper part of the horizontal wooden (back) slat, on the rear side of the slat'.

In this peaceful garden, people often stop to rest on their errands, to read a book, sit quietly with a child, wait for friends. The conjunction of such simple and life-sustaining activities with the dark work of espionage and subversion seems altogether jarring and altogether natural. It has ever been thus.

Return to South Audley Street. On the W side of the street, N of Aldford Street, is another of those marvellous Victorian buildings that was once symmetrical (one imagines) down to the last brick. Second door from the corner is

Site 132: **the Counter Spy Shop, 62 South Audley Street.** Inside you'll find telephone scramblers, tape recorders, night-vision gear, bullet-resistant Kevlar vests, and other James Bondish toys of the burgeoning private security industry, all being sold just round the corner from what were (and still may be) the garages of MI5's Watchers.

Across the street, S of Mount Street, is

Site 133: **33 South Audley Street.** In an extraordinary investigation in the early 1960s, MI5's molehunters interrogated their own chief in this 'sparsely decorated' house that was bugged to the last room. Sir Roger Hollis, director-general of the entire security service, had come under suspicion because of the 'overwhelming proof,' as Nigel West states it in *Molehunt*, 'that MI5 had experienced high-level penetration.' Too many double-agent operations had failed; too many suspected agents had escaped interrogation; too few Soviet defectors had been attracted (only one, and he had been murdered); too few Soviet spies had been caught (none); and there were just too many instances where the Soviets seemed to know things that could only have come from MI5's innermost circle.

Site 133: **33 South Audley Street.**

The focus of the investigation had been narrowed by 1963 to Hollis and deputy director-general Graham Mitchell. Today the case against Hollis seems persuasive (*see Sites 52 and 54*), but opinion is still divided.

The case against Mitchell, as Nigel West tells it in *Molehunt*, is 'equally circumstantial, but rather more substantial' than that against Hollis. West points to the extraordinary White Paper written by Mitchell on the Burgess-Maclean defections – a document filled with errors, intentional or not, and a document allowing Harold Macmillan (then Prime Minister) to clear Philby publicly and to cast doubt upon the very existence of the person whom Macmillan labelled the 'so-called third man.' Other suspect behaviour by Mitchell included his rejection of the *bona fides* of Anatoli Golitsyn who defected in 1961; Golitsyn had brought word that the KGB's files contained top-secret documents 'from the British Security Service.' Positively 'damning' in West's view is Mitchell's deliberate falsification of the personal file of Bruno Pontecorvo, the atomic scientist who later defected to the USSR. And certainly disquieting is the fact that during Mitchell's three years as head of counter-espionage (from 1953 to 1956, just before his seven years as deputy director-general), MI5 caught no Soviet spies through its own efforts, nabbing a single spy only by lucky accident.

But what are we to make of Roger Hollis? He delayed requesting a tap on Mitchell's home telephone, and he delayed interrogating Mitchell until after Mitchell was out of the service. Had he, in fact, warned Mitchell of the investigation? Mitchell suddenly took early retirement in 1963, and his interrogation – when it finally came – was far less demanding than if he were still a serving officer. Perhaps predictably, the interrogation of Mitchell the private citizen produced nothing conclusive – thanks in large part to Hollis, whose own interrogation here was equally frustrating to the molehunters.

Keep walking up South Audley Street. As you approach Grosvenor Square, you'll see the modern US Embassy. Turn L into Upper Grosvenor Street. On the L is

Site 134: **46 Upper Grosvenor Street.** In an earlier building here, Stewart Graham Menzies was born in 1890. Chief of the War Office secret service before he was 30, he was soon deputy to the chief of SIS in everything but name. He was head of the military section of SIS in 1939 when 'Quex' Sinclair died, and he became 'C' himself after lobbying fiercely for the job (*see Site 117*). He won out over all rivals despite Churchill's considerable resistance. Churchill couldn't have known the details of the Venlo disaster earlier that month (*see Site 116*) but objected to Menzies because of his ties to Chamberlain.

Despite the Prime Minister's early opposition to him, Menzies became 'Churchill's most important adviser,' writes Anthony Cave Brown in '*C*', his detailed biography of Menzies. Brown considers Menzies to have been 'the greatest British spymaster, greater even than Walsingham, the man who stole the secrets of the Spanish armada.' To bolster this view Brown argues that Menzies inherited a badly damaged service, and during the war 'presided over *the* great technological revolution of his time – the penetration of Enigma.... Above all, in the end he won.' During his 13 years as 'C', Menzies may have lured Admiral Canaris of the *Abwehr* to the British side and may even have had some sort of connection with the KGB's

Site 134: **46 Upper Grosvenor Street.**

Beria. (This last is 'not unlikely,' writes Brown.)

For all his élite education, Menzies had few intellectual pretentions; he was, in the eyes of various colleagues, 'not quite literate' and depended instead on an 'almost feminine' instinct and on his powerful connections. He left the running of the service to subordinates. 'But Menzies had two essential qualifications for a British secret service chief,' writes Knightley; 'he ran his outfit on pennies and he inspired a feeling in his political masters that he was never likely to do anything really silly.'

How, then, to explain the matter of Kim Philby? Menzies gave Philby more and more responsibility within SIS, putting him in charge of the new anti-Soviet section, sending him to Washington as liaison between SIS and American Intelligence, and finally hoping to make him assistant chief (from which position he would have been in a direct line to be 'C' himself).

The conventional wisdom is that Philby outwitted Menzies. But Anthony Cave Brown suggests that 'C' manipulated Philby, using him as a 'high-grade unwitting double agent' and a 'sort of "human hotline" between officials of the secret service in London and the KGB in Moscow.' Brown has only the merest hints of this, from only a few people, but considers it 'sufficiently implausible to be plausible.' I find it *utterly* implausible. Surely Menzies could have used Philby against the Soviets without putting him in charge of anti-Soviet operations and in line to be head of the entire secret service! I doubt that Moscow has been fooled by this odd attempt to rehabilitate Menzies's reputation and simultaneously manipulate the Soviets. I doubt too that anyone in MI5 or MI6 has been fooled.

I am almost certain — as certain as these things will allow — that Philby was using Menzies, not vice versa. It 'did not suit' Menzies to suspect Philby (writes historian H. Montgomery Hyde), 'and he refused to do so'. That is almost certainly the way it was. With Menzies's background of wealth and privilege (he was rumoured to be the illegitimate son of Edward VII), with his belief in his class and his nation and his service and himself, I think he was simply incapable of imagining that he could be wrong about Philby. In Knightley's words in *Philby, K.G.B. Masterspy*, Stewart Menzies presided over 'a decrepit and incompetent service, riddled with nepotism and run by a chain of command remarkable for its feebleness. SIS was ripe for Philby's penetration. It deserved him, and he devastated it.' Harsh criticism of Menzies and SIS, but less fanciful, I think, than Anthony Cave Brown's assessment of the man who was 'C' from 1939 to 1952.

Enter Grosvenor Square and walk toward the memorial statue of Franklin Roosevelt, the money for which was raised in Britain in one day (five shillings the maximum allowable contribution). Leave the square diagonally opposite your entry point. This will be Brook Street. At the near-L corner of Davies and Brook Streets is

Site 135: **68 Brook Street.** 'It is no exaggeration,' writes William Casey, 'to say that Donovan created the OSS against the fiercest kind of opposition from everybody – the Army, Navy, and State Departments, the Joint Chiefs of Staff, regular army brass, the whole Pentagon bureaucracy, and, perhaps most devastatingly, the White House staff.' But Donovan had Roosevelt behind him. Donovan undertook fact-finding missions for FDR in 1940 and 1941, and came back urging the president to establish an intelligence capability that would be up to the difficult times ahead. The US then had perhaps 80 people in intelligence in Washington, another 30 overseas. The best of the lot were cryptographers; William F. Friedman had broken the Japanese diplomatic cypher. But even the best couldn't make up for a system where few people were seeing the raw intercepts (and these few were forced to return the material almost immediately) and

nobody was analysing the intercepts in a systematic way or using them to make judgments and predictions.

By mid-1941, FDR had created the Office of Coordinator of Information for Donovan; by year's end Donovan had assembled a staff of nearly 600 from academia, law, business, journalism, and anywhere else he could find creative talent for a job that was being defined as they went along. The 'established brass' (reports Casey in his memoir, *The Secret War Against Hitler*) were afraid of what they considered 'Donovan's private army' and 'did everything they could to kill it, including, paradoxically enough, trying to dismember it and pick up the pieces for their own use.'

By 1943, though, Donovan's outfit had evolved into the OSS, a single organization with authority to conduct espionage, counter-espionage, analysis, and propaganda; to support resistance groups; to operate guerrilla bands behind enemy lines. Two weeks after Pearl Harbor, it was Churchill who had urged that subversion be part of the Allied strategy; with both Churchill and Roosevelt behind him, Donovan had eventually won what Casey calls 'the battle of Washington'. (The battle of London would be another matter. Donovan had agreed not to send OSS agents into Europe from Britain without British approval, and Dansey, for one, was determined to hold him to the bargain.)

At the height of the war, OSS strength stood at 13,000 people, more than 2,000 of them here in London. And here at Brook Street, at one time or another, OSS personnel served in Morale Operations originating 'black propaganda', in Research & Analysis interpreting raw data, and − as M. R. D. Foot tells me − in Casey's Secret Intelligence branch collecting information of any and every kind useful to the conduct of the war. Also here, resembling a Salvation Army store and offering agents anything and everything made in Germany, was the OSS clothing depot.

Bill Casey, like many others early in the war, had 'pulled rank' to get into the 'Oh So Secret' organization emerging in Washington. Not an Ivy Leaguer himself, or what he called 'a white shoe boy', he had asked a friend in Donovan's New York law firm to arrange something (the friend had once parked cars with Casey at Jones Beach). Casey was in OSS by September, 1943, and with half a dozen other young lawyers was running Donovan's secretariat in

Washington. By November he was sent to London to set up and run a similar secretariat there. But the chief of OSS in Europe, David K. E. Bruce, wasn't interested in a secretariat. Casey became instead 'a sort of special assistant' in Bruce's office (according to Joseph E. Persico's biography of Casey), producing brilliant reports for Washington and hatching unusual ideas for the OSS brief in Europe. 'The fine-edged Casey pragmatism,' writes Persico, led him to suggest recruiting businessmen from neutral countries as agents; the businessmen would have nothing to lose, argued Casey, because the more damage done to German plants and ships, the more material the neutrals could sell to Germany.

Upon Donovan's arrival in London, just before D-Day, Casey became Donovan's 'troubleshooter in Europe', writes Persico, and in December, 1944, Casey became chief of OSS Secret Intelligence for the entire European Theatre of Operations. (The two main branches of OSS in London were Casey's SI and Special Operations.) As M. R. D. Foot writes in his Foreword to Casey's book, Casey had moved in a matter of months from being 'a senior clerk' to being 'a force that could help decide the fate of nations'. He was then only 31 years old.

It was Casey who organized the OSS penetration of Germany during the last year of the war; 58 of his teams were inside Germany by April, 1945, radioing vital information about plants still operating and about troops moving out to resist the Allies. Early on, Casey understood the communist threat and only reluctantly used communist refugees for this work. Early on, he experienced first-hand the lack of co-operation from the Soviets, who routinely withheld their help on matters of intelligence. ('These are allies?' Casey had asked.) Early on, he understood that the sins of Hitler did not make saints of Hitler's adversaries, the communists.

Early on, too, Casey saw the need for America to maintain a strategic intelligence organization after the war. He was secretary to the committee that studied this question for Donovan and Roosevelt before the war ended. 'I was there at the beginning,' he later said. 'Nobody saw me. But I was there.' This hard-charging son of Irish working-class immigrants worked easily with and for the powerful all his life. As Persico notes about Casey's OSS days, 'His comrades-in-arms had been the Brahmins − the Bruces, the

Morgans, the Armours, the Dulleses. And he had held his own with the best of them.' (But he knew that he was only *with* them, and not *of* them, Persico quotes an OSS man as saying.)

Casey resigned from the OSS immediately after the war – just before the OSS was disbanded – to make the fortune that would allow him to be *of* the powerful. He became a very wealthy tax lawyer (inventor of the 'tax shelter'), a venture capitalist, the head of the Securities and Exchange Commission, the undersecretary for economic affairs at the State Department, the president of the Export-Import Bank, the mastermind of Reagan's 1980 campaign for the presidency, and (his final job) the director of the CIA from 1981 to 1987. He had wanted to be head of the State Department. In the end, though, writes Persico, he elevated his 'staff job' as CIA director to the job of 'co-author of Reagan-era foreign policy.' Casey remains controversial. Was he simply doing in communist-controlled Nicaragua what he had been doing in Nazi-controlled Europe? Or was he exceeding his constitutional and legal role? Persico concludes his book, *Casey*, with this: 'He conducted virtually all his enterprises like law firms: you determine your client's best interests, and then you do whatever the law, stretched to the outermost, allows in pursuit of that objective.' So, for Persico, 'Even the CIA was another Casey law firm' – the US, another client.

Turn R into Davies Street, then L into Grosvenor Street. Down the block, on the R, is

Site 136: **70 Grosvenor Street/Bourdon Alley.** OSS needed nine London buildings for its offices by July, 1944. This building was the headquarters of OSS Europe and in it the patrician David K. E. Bruce, London branch chief, outfitted his command suite with Ming pottery and drawing-room furniture. Bill Casey, never the aristocrat, was pleased that the building had heavily-armed sentries just inside the door, and an elevator. (The rumpled Casey, by then head of Secret Intelligence for OSS Europe, was no athlete.)

The founder of OSS and its only chief was the remarkable American, William J. Donovan, grandson of Irish immigrants. Born in humble circumstances in Buffalo, New York, young Donovan made some important early decisions. At Columbia College and

Site 136: **70 Grosvenor Street/Bourdon Alley.**

Columbia law school he acquired polish and made contacts. Practising law in Buffalo, he joined the city's most exclusive club and the National Guard. During WWI, he secured a position of command with the US Army's famous 'Fighting 69th' (predominantly an Irish unit); by war's end he was its commanding officer and the war's most decorated American soldier. Between the wars he became rich as an international and Wall Street lawyer. He served with distinction in the Justice Department, heading the criminal division and then the anti-trust division. If he hadn't been a Roman Catholic, it was said, he could have been attorney general or even president. He ran for office only once, for governor of New York State, unfortunately against the hand-picked successor of the popular departing governor, Franklin Roosevelt. But as WWII began taking shape, another career beckoned. Donovan's distinguished military service, his connections with the power élite, his close attention to international affairs, and not least his identity as a prominent Republican (at a time when Roosevelt was attempting to forge a bipartisan wartime coalition) combined to make him FDR's choice to head America's first centralized agency for intelligence and subversive warfare.

'Wild Bill' Donovan was courageous, tough, perceptive, indefatigable, quick, free-wheeling. Of course he troubled the traditional military types. As one of his colleagues said, Donovan was pushing the subtle strategies of indirection at a time when the accepted style of warfare was still the frontal attack. And of course he threatened the military intelligence types who felt that they would be perfectly capable of doing Donovan's work if given Donovan's resources.

The OSS 'won its spurs' (Casey's words) in North Africa, paving the way brilliantly for the invasion and keeping casualties amazingly under 200. But in 'one of the minor mysteries of the war,' notes Casey, the Washington establishment still didn't accept OSS. The British too were slow to accord OSS real honour. Donovan rankled under SIS restraints, arguing bluntly that the British had developed their 'habit of control' through their dealings with refugee governments. 'We are not a refugee government,' he said.

The precise relationship between the British and the Americans may have been considerably more complicated. Anthony Cave Brown suggests in his biography of Donovan, *The Last Hero*, that Donovan may have worked for SIS in 1916 while on famine relief service in occupied Belgium. (In 1981, Brown tells us, the CIA revealed that during WWI Donovan had 'probably' received British 'military intelligence' training.) Unquestionably, Donovan was the British choice to head the new US intelligence agency. In fact, the OSS had developed from what Brown calls 'clubby conversations' between Donovan and Menzies and Gubbins. Perhaps it was only to be expected that Donovan would agree in 1942 to a very close co-ordination with the British (not to say a *de facto* control by them).

David Bruce, too, may have been closer to the British than admitted; clearly an Anglophile, he was also an alumnus of The Room (later called The Club), which was Vincent Astor's private intelligence organization during the interwar years and was closely tied to SIS. Undeniably, then, Donovan's OSS was structured by the British, it accommodated to the British, and its overall chief and its chief in London may well have been their men. The 'special relationship' between the intelligence services of the two countries can be said to date from the OSS days (*see Site 46*). Since then, however, Britain has become the junior partner, doing whatever is necessary to keep the Americans sharing their greater resources and capabilities with their one-time mentors.

OSS ended abruptly, dissolved unceremoniously by Truman, barely a month after the end of the war, much as Attlee had ended SOE (*see Site 71*). Attlee and Truman lacked the imagination of their more flamboyant predecessors concerning the secret world; each apparently feared 'a sort of Democratic International', as Anthony Cave Brown describes it in Truman's case. (The Soviets, of course, did not liquidate *their* instruments for intelligence gathering and subversion.) Perhaps, as the official CIA history tells us, Truman's action was a budgetary decision. Or perhaps, as Brown relates, an old grudge played a part. In 1918, Donovan's soldiers suffered heavy casualties when they were badly supported by Truman's artillery battery; Donovan made an official complaint and Truman never forgot it. (Donovan had many enemies. Douglas MacArthur distrusted the OSS mission in general and refused to have OSS in the Far East because he hated Donovan in particular: Donovan had won more medals than he had, in WWI. And J. Edgar Hoover, whose appointment Donovan had recommended while at the Justice Department, was another long-standing enemy, mostly later and mostly over turf.)

I have my own recollection of the end of OSS; Donovan and Company tried to save the organization by arranging much publicity about its wartime exploits. The radio series, *Now It Can Be Told*, made a powerful impresion on at least one ten-year-old boy. The organization was doomed, of course. But in its concept, formulated at the beginning by Donovan, lay the foundations of the CIA that would follow it two years later.

Behind these headquarters (in a mews house in the Grosvenor Hill alleyway, reached via the Bourdon Street alley), the OSS printshop produced documents needed by agents in enemy territory. Legitimate artists and engravers from the US were commandeered for the work — the OSS was not interested in convicted forgers (who were failures, after all). Newly counterfeited documents were aged by being worn under the armpit for a while or being strewn about the floor and walked on for several days. (During the high-tech Cold War, documents were typically aged by being tumbled in a clothes washer with a little dirt and a single tennis shoe but no water.)

Printshop workers always had cigarettes; they printed their own ration stamps. OSS was a resourceful bunch altogether ('those Wall Street bankers and corporation lawyers make wonderful second-storey men,' Donovan had joked) and some of them didn't mind who knew it, when the time for secrecy was over. One OSS veteran applied for a job at *Time-Life* after the war and was asked which civilian occupations his wartime service with OSS had prepared him for. Bemused, he listed forgery, blackmail, kidnapping, counterfeiting, arson and murder. Someone in the personnel department scrawled across his application, 'Hire him before *Newsweek* gets him.'

Here ends this walk. For a splendid tea you're near Claridge's (at the corner of Brook and Davies Streets); for an excellent lunch you're near one of my favourite pubs (the Coach and Horses, where Bruton Lane meets Bruton Street, E of Berkeley Square); for fine window-shopping you're near some of the most elegant shops in this cosmopolitan city. Here ends this book; you're on your own now.

GLOSSARY

Abwehr Nazi Germany's military intelligence organization.

active measures KGB term (*aktivniye meropriyatiya*) for a variety of political manipulation and propaganda operations – covert, overt, and semi-covert – with the single purpose of moving public opinion in the target country towards a pro-Soviet position.

agent A person who does the actual work of spying, passing information or material to a case-officer usually by means of a cut-out or a dead letter box. Agents are usually citizens of the target country.

agent-in-place A government employee who is influenced to co-operate with a foreign government. Instead of defecting geographically this agent stays in his or her job, now working for two employers instead of one. Penkovsky is a good example (*see Site 76*).

agent of influence Not an intelligence-*gathering* agent but a person who works within the government or media of the target country to influence national policy. The late American journalist I. F. Stone is a good example, as were the 31 Members of Parliament whose secret CPGB membership was discovered in the 1950s by MI5 (*see Site 100*).

agitprop Soviet (later world-wide communist) portmanteau word for 'agitation' and 'propaganda' usually involving the 'dramatisation' of some issue on the communist agenda. Anyone who remembers the 'peace' marches of the 1960s and 1970s has seen agitprop at work.

apparat German word (like much of pre-WWII Comintern vocabulary) describing the organization or structure of an intelligence entity. An *apparat* can be as large as the *Cheka* or as small as the Woolwich Arsenal ring (*see Site 51*).

asset A source of intelligence, usually human rather than electronic.

black propaganda Disinformation that is deniable by (and not traceable to) its source.

BND *Bundesnachrichtendienst*, West Germany's Federal Intelligence Service. Also known as the Gehlen organization after its founder General Reinhard Gehlen.

BUF British Union of Fascists.

case-officer See controller.

Cheka Nickname of the Soviet Union's first intelligence and counter-intelligence organization. While the Party's intelligence organization had many successive names (GPU, OGPU, NKVD, NKGB, MGB, MVD, KGB), it was always known as the *Cheka*; its officers, as *Chekisti*.

chickenfeed Accurate but unimportant information deliberately given to an adversary in order to legitimate a double agent or a playback operation.

CIA Central Intelligence Agency, America's foreign intelligence-gathering entity.

Comintern Communist International, founded by Lenin as headquarters of his planned world-wide communist revolution. Ostensibly a Congress of all CPs in the world (with the CPSU supposedly only one among equals), the Comintern was actually a branch of the Soviet Foreign Ministry. Stalin acknowledged the Comintern as 'a gyp joint' (his words) and, mistrusting many of its agents as being Trotskyists, he first purged its ranks and then dismantled it, giving its intelligence-gathering function to the *Cheka* and the GRU.

controller An officer of an intelligence agency who runs a string of sources or agents. Also known as a case-officer or handler.

counter-intelligence Spycatching. Sometimes called counter-espionage.

cover The ostensible occupation of an intelligence officer or agent. To be effective, a cover must be consistent with the subject's background and the subject's presence in the target area.

CPGB Communist Party of Great Britain.

CPSU Communist Party of the Soviet Union.

cut-out A courier or go-between who acts as an intermediary between a case-officer and an agent. Theoretically, if the agent is caught, the case-officer will be protected; if the case-officer is caught, the agent will still be available to the case-officer's successor. But it is possible to put a discovered agent under surveillance and thus get on to the cut-out and even follow the cut-out to the case-officer, as when MI5 used Gee and Houghton to find 'Lonsdale' and then followed 'Lonsdale' to the 'Krogers' (*see Sites 88 and 94*). Of course, if the cut-out defects or is caught, both the agent and the case-officer are burned, as when Whittaker Chambers burned both Alger Hiss and Colonel Bykov.

defector-in-place See agent-in-place.

discard An agent whom a service will permit to be detected and arrested so as to protect more valuable agents. The hope is that the target country's security service, thinking it has found all the enemy agents, will stop looking. 'Lonsdale' (*see Site 88*) may have been a classic example.

disinformation KGB term (*dezinformatsiya*) for its well-financed and multifarious programme to manipulate the West through lies. These lies have ranged from the elaborate forgeries of supposed government documents to the newspaper stories planted throughout the world claiming that the AIDS virus was invented by the US for Third World genocide.

double agent A spy who works for two employers, sometimes but not always including the country or agency that his first employer assigned him to spy on. Dusko Popov, for instance (*see Site 121*), was a double agent.

Dzerzhinsky Square Square in Moscow originally named for Feliks Dzerzhinsky (Polish founder of the *Cheka*; now renamed Lubyanka Square. The Lubyanka building that dominates the square was the *Cheka*'s headquarters under its various names and was also its prison and torture chamber until those functions went elsewhere during the last decade or so of Soviet rule.

Enigma An encyphering machine developed for commercial use and adopted by Germany during WWII. The Germans believed that the machine's ingenious system was too complex to be broken, and so it was until British cryptographers at Bletchley, building on the efforts of French and Polish cryptographers before them, cracked the Enigma system by building the world's first computer. The Germans never learnt that the British were reading their Enigma transmissions.

FBI Federal Bureau of Investigation; the US domestic counter-intelligence agency, analogous to MI5.

fingerprints Aspects of an operation that make evident (to the knowing observer) the identity of the perpetrators.

GC&CS Government Code and Cypher School, now part of GCHQ. During WWI and WWII, GC&CS was responsible for cracking new codes, decoding, and decyphering.

GCHQ Government Communications Headquarters, Britain's communications monitoring and eavesdropping organization. GCHQ was established in 1942 and is roughly equivalent to America's National Security Agency.

Gestapo *Geheime Staatspolizei*, Nazi Germany's secret police, which was controlled by the National Socialist German Workers Party as the *Cheka* was controlled by the CPSU. Hitler patterned much of the

Nazi state on the Soviet model: just as the *Gestapo* was analogous to the *Cheka*, the *Abwehr* was analogous to the GRU.

GPU *Gosudarstvennoye Politcheskoye Upravleniye*, or State Political Directorate; see *Cheka*.

GRU *Glavnoye Razvedovatel'noye Upravleniye*, or Chief Intelligence Directorate, the intelligence organ of the Soviet military. While the *Cheka* was answerable to the CPSU (and was known as the 'sword and shield of the Party'), the GRU was answerable to the Red Army's General Staff — but the *Cheka* oversaw GRU's internal security, thus ensuring Party control of every aspect of the Soviet armed forces.

handler See controller.

illegal KGB term for an intelligence officer operating in a foreign country under an assumed identity and without diplomatic immunity. The 'Krogers' were very competent illegals (*see Site 94*).

innocent postcard A means of verifying the continued security and well-being of an undercover operative. The operative periodically mails an ordinary picture postcard to an accommodation address, usually in a neutral country; the card carries an innocuous message and is signed with an agreed-upon phoney name.

Interpol International Criminal Police Commission, the transnational police organization based in Paris.

IRA Irish Republican Army. Operating outside the law both in the UK and in Ireland, the IRA is committed to unifying the six Northern Counties with the Irish Republic and using paramilitary means to achieve that end.

KGB *Komitet Gosudarstvennoy Bezopasnosti*, or Committee of State Security; see *Cheka*.

KPD *Kommunistische Partei Deutschlands*; Communist Party of Germany.

MI5 Britain's Security Service, conducting counter-intelligence operations on British territory.

MI6 Britain's Secret Service, gathering foreign intelligence; also known as SIS.

MI9 Britain's WWII escape and exfiltration organization.

mole A long-term penetration agent assigned to advance within the government or intelligence bureaucracy of his own country on behalf of a foreign power. The term became popular with John le Carré's use of it in fiction, but it is far older than that; Sir Maurice Oldfield found the word used in this context in something written by Sir Francis Bacon in 1622.

Moscow Centre Catch-all term for the headquarters of the Soviet Union's intelligence efforts.

NKVD *Narodnyy Komissariat Vnutrennikh Del*, or People's Commissariat for Internal Affairs; see *Cheka*.

Novosti The Soviet Union's overseas press agency, providing cover for a variety of intelligence and subversion ops.

OGPU *Obedinënnoye Gosudarstvennoye Politicheskoye Upravleniye*, or Unified State Political Directorate; see *Cheka*.

one-time pad A very secure cypher system based on two identical pads composed of sheets of randomly arranged numbers. One pad goes with the officer or naval vessel; the other stays at headquarters or base. Each sheet on the pads is used once and then destroyed.

OSS Office of Strategic Services, America's WWII organization for intelligence, sabotage, and subversion.

parol Russian term for recognition signals used by operatives who are meeting for the first time; the *parol* is usually a pair of unrelated sentences that must be recited precisely as written.

PNG Abbreviation of the Latin term *persona non grata*, frequently used as a transitive verb (to PNG) to describe the process of withdrawing diplomatic status from a foreign national, usually because of that person's intelligence-gathering or subversive activities.

positive vetting British term for the background check on a government employee. The term 'positive vetting' is of course a redundancy, having been coined to describe the normal loyalty check that goes beyond ringing up someone who was at public school with the subject or knew his father.

rezident The chief of the intelligence effort of a Soviet or Soviet-bloc embassy. As distinguished from an 'illegal' the *rezident* would have diplomatic immunity and would usually operate under the cover of a minor embassy job.

SHAEF Special Headquarters Allied Expeditionary Force, the WWII Allied High Command headed by General Eisenhower.

Sicherheitsdienst Literally 'Security Service' one of Nazi Germany's counter-intelligence agencies.

SIS Britain's Secret Intelligence Service, also known as MI6.

SOE Special Operations Executive, Britain's WWII sabotage and subversion organization.

Special Branch A subdivision of Scotland Yard (London's Metropolitan Police) frequently working with MI5 since Security Service officers do not have powers of arrest.

Ultra Code name given to the closely held secret that the British were deciphering and reading the radio traffic being sent on Enigma machines by the Germans; also, the designation for those decrypts.

vetting British term describing the security check on a government employee. Initially the British contented themselves with relatively perfunctory vetting, going only so far as to verify that there was 'nothing recorded against' the subject; after Burgess/Maclean/Philby, the process was upgraded to 'positive vetting.'

walk-by A method of verifying the continued freedom and well-being of an operative in hostile territory. The operative's case-officer (or some other superior) prearranges a distant encounter with the operative, usually on a busy street. The two walk in opposite directions, usually on opposite sides of the street. The operative may have a security check known only to him and his case-officer − an innocent gesture by which he can signal that all is well, or that all is not well.

Wehrmacht Nazi Germany's army.

INDEX

Note: Numbers refer to sites. The occasional italicized numbers refer to the italicized walking directions after a site.

Abel, Col Rudolf, 88, 94
Abwehr, 42, 72, 75, 115, 121, 128, 134
Admiralty, Naval Intelligence, 12, 36, 117; Submarine Detection Research Establishment, 119
Agca, Mehmet Ali, 97
Air Ministry, 36
Aldrich, Richard, 58
Aldridge, L Cpl Philip, 105
Alsop, Stewart, 126
Andrew, Christopher, 25, 35, 47, 57, 97
Angleton, James Jesus, 76, 97, 113
Apostles, 55, 119
Arcos, 26, 32, 92, 100
Astor, Lord, 86
Astor, Vincent, 136
Atkins, Vera, 40, 72, 87
Attlee, Clement, 71, 136
Auxiliary Units, *48*, 71, 102

Baden-Powell, Lord, 2
Baldwin, Stanley, 92
BCRA, 60, 73, 80
Bearse, Ray, 81
Beevor, J. G., 69
Beria, Lavrenti, 134
Best, Maj Sigismund Payne, 96, 116
Bethell, Lord, 57
Bettaney, Michael, 53, 57
Beurton, Len, 95
Bevan, Aneurin, 128
Bevin, Ernest, 120
Blake, George, 7, 76, 77, 84, 90, 107

Blunt, Anthony F., 12, 13, 22, 23, 25, 31, 32, 35, 36, 54, 55, 77, 82, 83, 95, 108, 119, 120, 128
BND, 97
Bond, Cdr James, 4, 29, 33, 122
Bossard, Frank, 76
Bourke, Sean, 84
Bower, Tom, 76
Boyle, Andrew, 43, 77, 101
Braden, Thomas, 126
BRAL, 73
Brandes, Mary, 79
Brandes, Willy, 32, 79
Brandt, Willi, 54
Brooke, Gerald, 94
Brooman-White, Dick, 128
Brown, Anthony Cave, 1, 69, 96, 104, 116, 117, 134, 136
Bruce, David K. E., 73, 135, 136
Bryce, Ivar, 15
Buckmaster, Col Maurice, 69, 70, 72
BUF, 8, 13, 39
Bulloch, John, 44, 79
Burgess, Guy Francis de Moncy, 19, 22, 23, 25, *27*, 31, 32, 35, 42, 55, 78, 82, 83, 90, 95, 120, *127*, 128, 133
Bystrolyotov, Dmitri, 50

Cabinet, 1
Cairncross, John, 25, 32, 54, 120
Canaris, Rear Adm Wilhelm, 42, 115, 121, 134
Casey, William J., 36, 135, 136

Cavendish, Anthony, 35
Cavendish-Bentinck, Victor Frederick
    William, 36, 58, 117
Central Intelligence Group, 62
Centrale Inlichtingen Dienst, 20
Chamberlain, Neville, 39, 71, 81, 96, 134
Chambers, Whittaker, 82
Cheka, 50
Chisholm, Janet, 76
Chisholm, Rauri, 76
Chochlov, Nikolai, 97
Churchill, Sir Winston Spencer, 1, 13, 14,
    36, 39, 41, 45, 46, 52, 58, 60, 69, 71,
    74, 78, 81, 86, 118, 123, 125, 134, 135
CIA, 34, 36, 37, 42, 46, 58, 62, 63, 76,
    81, 88, 97, 113, 127, 135, 136
Cohen, Lona, 94
Cohen, Morris, 94
Cohen, Paul, 8
Comintern, 22, 23, 26, 51, 92, 94, 95,
    100, 101
Connery, Sean, 29
Connolly, Cyril, 15
Conseil National de la Résistance, 73
Conservative Party, 8, 77, 86, 91
Cookridge, E. H., 71
Coote, Sir Colin, 86
Corson, William R., 50, 91, 92
Costello, John, 13, 23, 25, 32, 35, 44, 50,
    51, 54, 77, 78, 79, 90, 92, 121, 128
Cowgill, Felix, 113
Coward, Noel, 6
CPGB, 8, 12, 25, 26, 51, 69, 77, 92, 93,
    100, 101
CPSU, 93, 100
Crankshaw, Edward, 117
Crowley, Robert T., 50, 91, 92
Cruickshank, Charles, 65
Curiel, Henri, 84

Dalton, Dr Hugh, 71, 125
Danischewsky, Irene, 81
Dansey, Sir Claude Edward
    Marjoribanks, 46, 58, 96, 114, 117
Deacon, Richard, 12, 32, 50, 56, 58, 69,
    99, 128

de Blommaert, Baron Jean, 38
de Borchgrave, Arnaud, 21
de Borchgrave d'Altena, Count
    Baudouin, 21
de Gaulle, Gen Charles, 60, 72, 73, 80, 87
Deighton, Len, 45
Denning, Lord, 86
Denniston, Cdr Alastair, 118
Depot of Military Knowledge, 99, 103
Deriabin, Peter S., 34, 76
Déricourt, Henri, 46
Deuxième Section, 21
Directorate of Military Intelligence, 44
Donovan, Gen William J., 1, 135, 136
Dorril, Stephen, 12, 86
d'Oultremont, Georges, 38
Dourlein, Peter, 75
Driberg, Tom, 77
Dübendorfer, Rachel, 58
Duchess of Windsor, 13, 41
Duke of Windsor, 13
Dunlap, Jack, 76
Durzhavna Sigurnost, 97

Edward VII, 134
Eisenhower, Gen Dwight D., 80, 108,
    126
Eitner, Horst, 84
Eliot, T. S., 33
Elizabeth I, 99
Elizabeth II, 13
'Elli', 32, 54
Elliott, Nicholas, 42, 52
Ellsberg, Daniel, 81
EMFFI, 80

Fairbairn, William, 70
FBI, 42, 78, 81, 82, 88, 90, 94, 95, 121
Fergusson, Thomas G., 99, 111
Field Intelligence Department, 46
Filby, P. William, 124
Fisher, David, 46, 58, 96, 116
Fleming, Anne, 15, 33
Fleming, Caspar, 15, 33
Fleming, Lt Cdr Ian, 15, 17, 29, 30, 33,
    49, 114, 121, 122

Fletcher, WPC Yvonne, 109
Fluency Committee, 52
Foot, Prof M. R. D., *4*, 6, 38, 60, 64, 67,
    68, 70, 71, 72, 73, 80, 87, 106, 108, 135
Foote, Alexander Allan, 32, 58, 95, 101
Foreign Intelligence Service, 11, 25, 121
Foreign Office, 25, 30, *31*, 32, 50, 57, 78,
    91, 92, 99, 120
Forster, E. M., 23
Franco, Francisco, 8, 42
Fraser-Smith, Charles, *4*
Freeman, Simon, 23, 82, 83
Friedman, Litzi, 35
Friedman, William F., 135
Fuchs, Klaus, 32, 35, 54, 78, 90, 94, 95,
    100
Furnival Jones, Sir Martin, 52

Gaddafi, Muammar, 109
Gaitskell, Hugh, 97
Galleni, Hans, 50
'Garbo', 115, 128
GC&CS, 25, 98, 118
GCHQ, *6*, 54
Gee, Ethel, 88, 94
George VI, 4, 13
Gestapo, 75
GHQ, 27
Giskes, Lt Col Hermann, 75
Glading, Percy, 51, 100
Glees, Anthony, 54, 55, 77
Godfrey, Adm John, 33, 122
Goebbels, Josef, 96
Gold, Harry, 90
'Goldin, William', 121
Goleniewski, Michal, 84, 88, 94
Golitsyn, Anatoli, 52, 54, 76, 97, 133
Gorbachev, Mikhail, 93, 100
Gordievsky, Oleg, 25, 32, 47, 48, 53, 54,
    57, 88, *93*, 97, 100, 109, 130
Gouk, Arkady, 53
Gouzenko, Igor, 32, 52, 54
GPU, 35, 79, 92
Grand, Col Laurence Douglas, 18, 19,
    128
Gray, Olga, 51

Greene, Benjamin, 49
Greene, Graham, 112, 113, 121
Greenglass, David, 90
GRU, 11, 34, 53, 57, 58, 76, 81, 86, 88,
    92, 95, 97, 101
Gubbins, Maj Gen Sir Colin, 71, 102, 136
Guinness, Alec, 30

Hall, Virginia, 72
Hampshire, Stuart, 22
Hankey, Lord, 25
Hanley, Sir Michael, 52
Harris, Tomás, 32, 83, 128
Hess, Rudolf, 41
Heydrich, Reinhard, 3
Higham, Charles, 13
Himmler, Heinrich, 42
Hinsley, Prof F. H., 58
Hiss, Alger, 42, 78, 82, 91
Hitler, Adolf, 1, 13, 14, 19, 41, 42, 58,
    60, 65, 68, 69, 71, 76, 77, 81, 95, 96,
    100, 115, 121, 126
Hochhuth, Rolf, 14
Hollis, Sir Roger, 12, 32, 52, 54, 76, 82,
    86, 90, 95, 120, 133
'Homer', 32, 78. See also Maclean,
    Donald
'Homintern', 55
Hoover, J. Edgar, 78, 121, 136
Houghton, Harry, 54, 88, 94
Howarth, Patrick, 36, 125
Hutton, Clayton, 105
Hyde, Douglas, 100
Hyde, H. Montgomery, 134

Intelligence Branch, 2, 99, 111
Intelligence Corps, 105
Interpol, 94
'Inter-Services Research Bureau', 69
Ivanov, Yevgeny, 12, 86
Iveson-Watt, Bob, 61, 62

Jepson, Selwyn, 106
Jervis, Maj Thomas Best, 99
Johns, Cdr Philip, 21, 28
Johnson, Robert Lee, 76

Joint Broadcasting Committee, 19, 83
Joint Intelligence Committee, 36, 58, 117

Katz, Rudolph (Rolf), 22
Keegan, John, 35, 71
Keeler, Christine, 12, 86, *101*
Kell, Sir Vernon, 7, 10, 12, 44, 89, 123
Kelso, Nicholas, 43, 75
Kennedy, Caroline, 86
Kennedy, John F., 15, 34, 76, 82, 86
Kennedy, Joseph P., 1, 81
Kent, Tyler, 8, 39, 41, 45, 49, 81
Kerr, Sheila, 54
KGB, 11, 12, 15, 23, 25, 35, 42, 47, 48,
    53, 54, 57, 76, 78, 84, 88, 91, 93, *93*,
    97, 108, 119, 120, *127*, 129, 130, 131,
    133, 134
Khrushchev, Nikita, 76, 90
King, Capt John Herbert, 32, 50
King, Stella, 70
Klugmann, James, 25, 69, 78, 101
Knight, Maxwell, 12, 30, 39, 45, 49, 51,
    81
Knightley, Phillip, 7, 35, 58, 78, 86, 95,
    96, 98, 113, 121, 128, 134
Koenig, Gen Joseph-Pierre, 80
Kondrashev, Sergei, 119
Korda, Alexander, 96
Kostov, Vladimir, 97
KPD, 95
Krivitsky, Walter, 50, 79, 92
'Kroger', Helen, 88, 94
'Kroger', Peter, 88, 94
Kuczynski, Jürgen, 32, 95
Kuczynski, Robert, 95
Kuczynski, Ursula Ruth, 95

Labour Party, 8, 22, 42, 77, 91, 92, 97,
    120
Lampe, David, 102
Lamphere, Robert J., 94
Last, Anne, 54
Lauwers, Huburtus, 75
LCS, 1, 65
le Carré, John, 14, 30
Lees, Michael, 69

Lehmann, Rosamond, 23
Leitch, David, 25, 78
Lejeune, Anthony, 114
Lenin, Vladimir Ilyich, 57, *90*, *93*, 95, 104
Liberal Party, 22
Liddell, Guy Maynard, 12, 23, 32, 50, 54,
    78, 83, 92, 128
Lockhart, Robin Bruce, 43
'Lonsdale, Gordon', 52, 94. See also
    Molody, K. T.
Lownie, Andrew, 81
Lucy ring, 35, 46, 58
Luxemburg, Rosa, 95

'M', 33, 49, 114
MacArthur, Gen Douglas, 136
Macartney, Wilfred, 92
Maclean, Donald, 22, 23, 25, 31, *31*, 32,
    35, 42, 54, 78, 82, 100, 101, 120, 128,
    133
Maclean, Melinda, 78
Macmillan, Harold, *31*, 42, 86, 133
Major, John, 10, 11
Maly, Teodor, 32, 51, 79
Mao Tse-tung, 120
Markov, Georgi, 97
Marks, Leo, 75
Marshall, Robert, 46
Martin, Arthur, 52, 54
Martin, David, 69
Marx, Karl, *90*, *93*
Masaryk, Jan, 91, 97
Masterman, Sir John, 115
Masters, Anthony, 49, 51
Maugham, W. Somerset, 29, 46
McCarthy, Sen Joseph, 95
McNeil, Hector, 120
Menzies, Sir Stewart Graham, 4, 46, 96,
    113, 114, 116, 117, 134, 136
MI5, 7, 8, *9*, 10, 12, 18, 23, 25, 30, *31*,
    32, 34, 39, 41, 42, 43, 44, 45, 49, 51,
    52, 53, 54, 55, 57, 58, 63, 69, 76, 77,
    78, 79, 81, 82, 83, 86, 88, 89, *89*, 90,
    92, 93, 94, 95, 97, 100, 104, 115, 119,
    120, 121, 123, 124, 128, 129, 133, 134;
    C Division, 54, *120*; F Division, 54;

Iberian Section, 128; K7 Branch 52; Registry, 124, 129; Watchers, 57, 63, 77, 79, 132
MI6, 3, 4, *4*, 5, 6, 9, *9*, *10*, 11, 13, 14, 15, 16, 20, 21, 25, 27, 28, 30, *31*, 32, 34, 35, 36, 37, 42, 46, 47, 48, 52, *52*, 55, 56, 57, 58, 63, 65, 69, 70, 73, 75, 76, 84, 96, 98, 104, 107, 112, 114, 116, 117, 118, 121, 123, 125, 126, 128, 134, 136; anti-Soviet operations (Section IX), 113, 134; counter-espionage operations (Section V), 113; Baltics, 37, 113; Production Research Department, 7; Section D, 5, 6, 19, 42, 65, 69; Section Y, 107
MI9, *4*, 24, 38, 59, 105, 112, 117
Midland Bank, 91
Mikhailović, Gen Draža, 69
Mikhailsky, Sigmund, 12
Mikoyan, Anastas, 77
Military Intelligence Service, 46
Miller, Joan, 39, 45, 49, 81
'Minimax Fire Extinguisher Company', 4
Ministry of Economic Warfare, 125
Mitchell, Graham, *31*, 32, 52, 54, 133
MO5, 44, 117
Mobilization and Military Intelligence Department, 110
Modin, Yuri, 25, *27*, 31, 82, 90, 120
Molody, Konon T., 34, 88
Monaghan, David, 30
Monckland, George, 92
Moneypenny, Miss, 33
Montagu, Ewen, 121
Moscow Centre, *31*, 35, 42, 47, 48, 50, 51, 53, 57, 78, 82, 94, 95, 109, 120, 130
Moseley, Roy, 13
Mosley, Sir Oswald, 8, 13, 17, 39
Moss, Norman, 90
Muggeridge, Malcolm, 4, 6, 15, 35, 39, 81, 83, 98, 113, 117
Mure, David, 121
Mussolini, Benito, 8, 13, 126

NATO, 78
Neave, Lt Col Airey, 24, 38, 59

Newman, Edwin, 42
Newton, Verne W., 78, 120
Nixon, Richard M., 95
NKVD, 14, 25, 37, 51, 57, 78, 81
Novosti, 43, 76
Nunn May, Alan, *90*

Occleshaw, Michael, 27
Office of the Coordinator of Information, 135
OGPU, 44, 50
Oldfield, Sir Maurice, 30, 32
Oldham, Ernest Holloway, 50
Oldham, Mrs Ernest Holloway, 50
Olivier, Sir Laurence, 14
Oppenheim, Phillips, 29
Orlov, Alexander, 82, 121
OSS, 1, 36, 46, 61, 62, 72, 73, 80, *83*, 95, 113, 117, 135, 136; Morale Operations, 135; Research & Analysis, 135; Secret Intelligence, 36, 135, 136; Special Operations, 135; X-2, 16, 113, 127
Oswald, Lee Harvey, 97
O'Toole, George J. A., 113

Page, Bruce, 78
Parker, John, 13
Pearson, John, 17, 29, 33
Pearson, Norman Holmes, 127
Penkovsky, Col Oleg, 34, 57, 76, 86, 90
Penrose, Barrie, 23, 25, 82, 83
'Percy', 94
Persico, Joseph E., 135
Pétain, Marshal Philippe, 39
Pettigrew, Miss, 33
Philby, Aileen, 35, 42, 128
Philby, Dora, 42
Philby, Harold Adrian Russell ('Kim'), 4, 6, 9, 14, 22, 25, 31, *31*, 32, 35, 36, 37, 42, 43, 52, 53, 54, 58, 78, 82, 84, 88, 94, 113, 120, 128, 129, 133, 134
Philby, Harry St John Bridger, 9
Pincher, Chapman, 25, 52, 53, 54, 58, 82, 84, 86, 88, 90, 95, 105, 108, 120, 128
Political Warfare Executive, 69, 96

Pontecorvo, Bruno, 133
Portland ring, 54, 88, 94
Popov, Dusko, 121
Pottle, Pat, 84
Poyntz, Juliet Stewart, 79
Prime, Geoffrey, 54
Profumo, John, 12, 86
Profumo, Mrs John, 86
Prosper/Physician network, 18, 46

Radó, Sándor, 58
Radosh, Ronald, 78
RAF, 69
Ramsay, Capt Archibald Henry Maule,
39, 45, 81
Randle, Michael, 84
Read, Anthony, 46, 58, 81, 96, 116
Reagan, Ronald, 109, 135
Rees, Goronwy, 22, 23, 32
Reilly, Sidney, 104
Reiss, Ignace, 79, 97
Right Club, 39, 41, 45, 81
Rimington, Stella Whitehouse, 10, 89
Roosevelt, Franklin D., 1, 39, 41, 45, 74,
81, 118, *134*, 135, 136
Rosenberg, Ethel, 90, 94
Rosenberg, Julius, 88, 90, 94
Rositzke, Harry, 88
Rostovsky, Semyon, 43
Rothschild, Victor, 22, 36, 83, 119, 128
Ruby, Marcel, 71, 72
Rudellat, Yvonne, 17, 18, 70, 72

SAS, 68
Schecter, Jerrold L., 34, 76
Schellenberg, Walter, 116
Schick, Joseph S., 74
Scotland, Lt Col Alexander, 56
'Scott', Mr, 32, 50. See also Oldham,
Ernest Holloway
SHAEF, 36, 72, 80, 108
Sheehan, Olive, 101
Shaw, George Bernard, 104
Sicherheitsdienst, 3, 4, 42, 72, 75, 96, 116
Sikorski, Gen Wladislaw, 14
Sillitoe, Sir Percy, 12

Simpson, Wallis, 13
Sinclair, Adm Sir Hugh ('Quex'), 96,
117, 134
Singlaub, Maj Gen John K., 126
SIS, See MI6
Skinner, Dennis, 91
Smiley, George, 30
Smith-Cumming, Capt Sir Mansfield, 3,
98, 104
SOE, *4*, 5, 18, 19, 21, 28, 36, 37, 40, 42,
46, *46*, 60, 66, 67, 68, 69, 70, 71, 80,
85, 96, 102, 117, 125, 136; Balkans
Section, 5; Belgian Section, 21, 28;
clothing section, 64; Dutch Section,
20, 28, 75; F Section, 40, 60, 69, 72,
75, 80, 87, 106; Jedburgh teams, 60,
68, 87, 126; Operations Section
(SO2), 6; RF Section, 60, 72;
Scandinavian sections, 65; technical
sections, 64; Yugoslav Section, 69
Solomon, Flora, 128
Solzhenitsyn, Aleksandr, 97
'Sonya', 32, 54, 58, 95. See also
Kuczynski, Ursula Ruth
Sorge, Richard, 95
Special Branch, 8, 32, 81, 92, 104, 122
Special Forces HQ, 80
Springhall, Douglas Frank, 100, 101
Stafford, David, 21
Stalin, Josef, 13, 14, 50, 58, 69, 78, 79,
84, 95, 96, 121
Stephenson, Sir William, 112, 126
Stevens, Maj Richard, 96
'Stevens, Mr and Mrs', 51, 79. See also
Brandes, Mary and Willy
Stoyanov, Gen Dimitar, 97
Straight, Michael Whitney, 25, 82, 95,
128
Summers, Anthony, 12, 86
Sûreté de l'Etat, 21
Sweet-Escott, Bickham, 5, 60, 69
Sykes, Eric, 70
Szabo, Violette, 72

Tennant, Sir Peter, 65
Thatcher, Margaret, 54, 77

Theatre Intelligence Organization, *83*
Thompson, Carlos, 14
Tito (Josip Broz), 69
Topham, Diana and Romer, 18
Topographical & Statistical Department, 99, 111
Trades Union Council, 100
Treasury, 25
Trend, Lord, 52
Trevor-Roper, Hugh, 46
Trotsky, Leon, 60, 97
Troy, Thomas F., 121
Truman, Harry S., 78, 136
Tsarev, Oleg, 25, 50, 121
Turner, John Frayn, 94
Twenty Committee, 16, 115, 127

Ubbink, Johan, 75
UN, 78
Uren, Capt Ormond, 69, 101
US Signal Intelligence, 74
Ustinov, Klop, 57

Vassall, John, 12, 52, 76, 90
Vermehren, Dr Erich, 42
Vivian, Col Valentine, 35
Volkov, Anna, 39, 41, 45, 81
Volkov, Konstantin, 32, 35, 52, 53
Volkov Adm Nikolai, 45
von Ribbentrop, Joachim, 13
Voynovich, Vladimir, 50

Wallace, Henry A., 95
Wallinger, Maj Edmund A., 27
Walsingham, Sir Francis, 134
Ward, Stephen, 12, 86
War Office, 36, 44, 45, 99, *104*, *105*, 125
Watson, Alister, 54, 119
Wehrmacht, 42, 125
West, Nigei, 12, 23, 28, 34, 35, 42, 46, 63, 67, 68, 69, 73, 75, 79, 84, 86, 88, 90, 96, 107, 115, *120*, 121, 123, 129, 133
West, Dame Rebecca, 12, 88
West, William J., 120
Whalen, William, 76

White, Sir Dick Goldsmith, 12, 32, 35, 52, 128
Whitemore, Hugh, 94
Wild, Col Noel, 108
William the Conqueror, 99
Williams, Robert Chadwell, 90
Wilson, Capt Charles William, 111
Winks, Prof Robin W., 16, 127
Winterborn, Hugh, 100
Winterbotham, Wg Cdr Frederick W., 58
WL Bureau, 27
Woolwich Arsenal ring, 12, 32, 49, 51, 79
Wright, Peter, 13, 25, 32, 35, 52, 54, 57, 63, 88, 89, 100, 119, 124, 129
Wynne, Greville, 7, 34, 76, 88

Yeltsin, Boris, 84

Z Organization, 46, 56, 58, 96, 117
Zieger, Henry A., 15, 33
Zhivkov, Todor, 97